Run Away Somebody's Coming

ROBERT HOUGHTON

Copyright © Robert L Houghton 2004

ISBN 0-9547505-0-0

First published in the UK in 2004 by
R L Houghton and J M Houghton

Authors e-mail: robert@milford24.freeserve.co.uk

The right of Robert Houghton to be identified as the author
of this work has been asserted by him in accordance with
the Copyright, Design and Patents act 1988

All rights reserved.
No part of this publication may be reproduced, stored
in a retrieval system or transmitted in any form or by any means,
electronic or otherwise, without prior permission from the publishers

Typeset and illustrated by J M Houghton

new e-mail address
roberthoughton24@o2.co.uk

Run Away Somebody's Coming

CONTENTS

PROLOGUE		4
CHAPTER 1	1939 - 43 CIVVY STREET TO DAD'S ARMY	7
	LET BATTLE COMMENCE	9
	BATTLE COMMENCES	17
	PART TIME KHAKI	24
CHAPTER 2	1943 - 44 THE PROPER ARMY	31
	INFANTRY TRAINING	33
	DRIVER TRAINING	42
	WORKING COMPANY	47
CHAPTER 3	1944 - 45 MONTY'S LIBERATION ARMY	61
	ON THE ROAD	63
	WIMEREUX - FRANCE	92
	TOURING HOLLAND	97
CHAPTER 4	1945 - 47 OCCUPATION ARMY - GERMANY	107
	NO FIXED ABODE	109
	KLEVE	113
	IN LIMBO	123
	LUDENSCHEID AND IBURG	129
	DETMOLD	135
	OSNABRUCK	145
EPILOGUE		155
ACKNOWLEDGEMENTS		161
BIOGRAPHY		162
APPENDICES	(A TO K)	163

FOREWORD

Many stories have been written about events that happened during the Second World War. Most of these are about the heroic adventures of commandos, fighter pilots, or tank commanders etc., which are very exciting.

This book is different only in that it is an honest, down to earth account about one soldier's (my dad) everyday life as a driver in the Royal Army Service Corps (RASC), one of the war's unsung heroes, who played an equally vital role for the war effort, transporting much needed troops, munitions and various other supplies without which the front line and the army in general would have quickly ground to a halt.

Surprisingly, very little has been documented about the RASC, as we found out when doing extensive research into the subject, making this book all the more special for historians and future generations to read.

John M. Houghton

PROLOGUE

My original intention in writing this book was to respond to repeated requests from my son to write about the five years I spent in the armed forces from April 1943 onwards. Prior to this I had spent two years as a member of the Home Guard and it seemed only right to record, at least, some comment relating to that time. Having made this decision, my thoughts went back to those days and reminded me of the reasons leading up to my enrolment in 1941 in 'Dad's Army', as it later became known. I felt that I may as well go the whole way and start at the beginning and record my memories of the time between the outbreak of war in September 1939 and April 1943. It was not my intention to write a detailed account of that period but merely to record the more memorable facets of my life during the first half of the war.

I became a member of the armed forces in April 1943 and served for a total of five years. I actually enrolled on February 16th. Except for an initial training period of six weeks, the whole of this service was with the Royal Army Service Corps, which was primarily responsible for transporting men and materials to support the fighting units of the army.

As the majority of my memoirs are concerned with my army life in the RASC, I decided that the title of the book should recognise this. Why the title 'Run Away Somebody's Coming'? I don't know where this alternative interpretation of the letters RASC originated from, but it was in common use by units other than ours. It was, of course, taken with the proverbial pinch of salt in the Corps as we knew we didn't have to run, we had vehicles at our disposal. Thus adoption of this particular witticism in the title is done in the interests of humour rather than disrespect to the Corps.

My story is not one of action in the heat of battle. It is well documented that probably upwards of seventy five percent of army personnel were employed in giving support to the remainder who were in contact with the enemy. It is merely the remembered experiences of an ordinary soldier doing as he was told, (most of the time), in what today might be considered a fairly mundane occupation, namely, driving a truck. The fact that behind you there may be stacked tons of high explosive or fuel never seemed to be worth discussing, this was your job and you just got on with it.

Although we were forbidden to keep diaries, some of the events I have recorded owe much to the surreptitious keeping of notes. As we were also not allowed to use cameras until after hostilities had ceased, it must be obvious that some of the photographs were shot by individuals who were prepared to risk disciplinary action being taken against them. I owe much to my possession of an excellent memory aided considerably by the retention of letters written at the time.

My early days in Aldershot were complemented by lots of spit and polish and going about smartly as the army prefers you to do. Overseas, until the middle of 1947, we were probably somewhat less than smart. Our 'walking out dress' hardly saw the light of day, we lived, ate and a lot of the time, slept in our 'denims', particularly in the early days, when our bed was in the back of our trucks. From September 1944 to Easter 1946 we went about in a more or less permanent fug of diesel fumes. Some of the photographs picture groups of men whose casual demeanour, and dress, lend no credence whatever to the description 'soldier'. Our job, in common with other RASC units, was to transport vast quantities of munitions and other supplies to where it was needed, and this is what we did, and did it well.

Extract from the book 'The story of the Royal Army Service Corps 1939-1945'

On Monday, November 26th, 1945, the Commander-in-Chief, Field-Marshal Sir Bernard Montgomery, visited the Headquarters of the RASC Training Brigade, BAOR, at Lippstadt, Westphalia, (Germany), to inspect 1500 men and 50 vehicles, representing a cross section of RASC units which had maintained the the armies in the field during the North-West Europe campaign. After he had taken the parade and decorated those who had won awards for gallantry in the campaign, Field-Marshal addressed all those present, and he paid tribute to the Corps in the following words:

> "I consider the work done by the RASC has been quite magnificent. I know well that without your exertions behind - and often in front - we should never have been able to advance as we did. No corps in the army has a higher sense of duty than you. You have delivered supplies in all weathers and over all roads; you have driven your vehicles in mud, rain, snow and ice, and you never once let us down. Without your supplies, our battles could never have been won. It is a fine record, and I am glad to be able to be here publicly to pay the RASC the tribute it deserves".

Raised in 1794 as the Royal Waggoners the Corps became the Land Transport Corps in 1855, the Army Service Corps in 1869, the Royal Army Service Corps in 1918, and the Royal Corps of Transport in 1965. Headquartered in Buller Barracks, Aldershot, the R.C.T. was later amalgamated into the Royal Logistics Corps signalling a sad day for those who were proud to have been a part of a great and honoured Corps.

> *Please note that there is a comprehensive appendix at the back of this book which provides useful information such as maps, technical info, glossary, pictures and lots more. Please take the time to see what this section has to offer before reading any further as it is designed to assist both the reader and to complement the four main chapters.*

CHAPTER 1
1939 - 43
CIVVY STREET TO DAD'S ARMY

The declaration of war against Germany on 3rd September 1939 ended all the speculation which had pervaded since the occupation of Czechoslovakia by Germany in 1938. Great Britain and France had subsequently given a guarantee to Poland, promising their support in the event of German aggression against it. The German invasion of Poland on the 1st of September invoked this Treaty, and as a result we found ourselves, along with France, again at war with Germany. Following a period of eight months, the so called 'Phoney War' came to an abrupt end with the invasion by Germany of Denmark and Norway, followed by the Blitzkrieg through Holland, Belgium and into northern France. The fall of France and the evacuation of the British Expeditionary Force from Dunkirk, was followed by the Battle of Britain, which resulted in the defeat of German day time air attacks as a prelude to the intended invasion of Britain.

The possibility of such an invasion saw the formation in 1940 of the 'Local Defence Volunteers' (LDV), a volunteer force, initially, which Churchill later renamed the 'Home Guard'. A large portion of the LDV were 'old sweats' from WW1 who had no small knowledge of the Germans and infantry fighting. The LDV had vital tasks to perform including observation and reporting of enemy movements and general harassing operations. Their most important job however was to relieve the hard-pressed British Army of guard duties - on railways, at road blocks, on river bridges, by crashed aircraft and at a multitude of other points.

LET BATTLE COMMENCE

The weather during the last week of August 1939 was what we imagine summer should always be like, the sun shining out of a cloudless sky on a shimmering sea and a soft sandy beach. Well, memory can play some funny tricks and I like to think that it was just as I have described. We were as near to being abroad as we were ever going to be that year, or for any number of years ahead as far as that goes. ('We' consisted of mother and father, brother Kenneth aged twelve and a half, and myself, three months short of my fifteenth birthday, sister Joan, just six and a half years old, had been left at home with relatives.) We had taken the train from Goole to Hull and then across the city to board our holiday ship. Aboard that ship from Hull and out of sight of land (nearly) we could have been journeying to anywhere our imagination could conjure up, but it wasn't long before that faraway shore came in sight and in no time at all we were disembarking at New Holland on the Lincolnshire side of the Humber Estuary. Our destination was Cleethorpes, a short train ride away, our arrival there preceded by the unmistakable aroma of the fishing port of Grimsby.

However, before this momentous event occurred there was the engine room to be visited. Two vessels operated the Humber ferry service from Hull to New Holland, both were shallow draft paddle steamers owned and operated by the London and North Eastern Railway Company. The

p.s. Lincoln Castle of the Humber Ferry Service

engines were reciprocating steam engines with the cylinders and related cranks horizontally mounted and were fully visible from each side of the engine room and the sight, sound and smell proved a magnet for every child, and indeed, many adults during the journey. The building of the Humber Bridge brought to an end this historic service. Later I found one of the two vessels moored at The Embankment in London serving as a lunch bar. It was still there when I revisited in late 1998.

So, back to New Holland which was quite basic, two wooden platforms, and although I don't remember ever having seen it, I presume a ticket office of sorts, and on to the waiting train for Cleethorpes. In those far off days not many people in our walk of life spent their holidays in a hotel, static caravan parks were yet to make their appearance, so our abode for the week was to be in what were known as 'digs' or lodgings in private guest houses. Guests paid for the use of one or more bedrooms, depending upon the size of their family, meals were prepared for them by the house owner usually from guest's own provisions purchased locally. Rooms had to be vacated each day after breakfast and occupants were not allowed back in before five in the afternoon.

Cleethorpes provided all that people looked for in those days, a beach and a pier, indoor amusements for children and a plentiful supply of novelty emporiums. The beach was not tide washed in its entirety, leaving the opportunity for semi permanent structures to be located above high tide mark, with air space underneath just in case some quirk of nature caused the tide to reach this point. The only one that I can remember with any clarity was the one selling sheet music, complete with an array of singers and a piano in support. The disadvantage of this area of the beach not being washed by the incoming tide became immediately obvious if you had the courage to venture under the structure.

The holiday pursued its usual familiar format, beach during most days with one or two visits to the amusements (Wonderland, as it was optimistically entitled), so far as parents' funds allowed. Good behaviour brought its reward in the form of a trip in one of the two amphibious boats which carried twenty odd passengers along the beach and into the sea for a short, choppy sail. These vessels had the appearance of a liner's motorised lifeboats fitted with four wheels and painted white and garish green, adventure indeed! Little did we realise that this would be the last time we would visit Wonderland, Cleethorpes or indeed any other holiday venue for many years. The threat of war hung over us although my brother Ken and I were not yet of an age to fully comprehend what this implied and the sight of elements of the Home Fleet in the Humber Estuary was hardly earth shattering so far as we were concerned.

However, by the time it was Friday we became aware that all was not as it should be, our beloved Wonderland was about to be taken over by the Military and had, therefore, to be vacated by its present occupants by the end of the week. Hoopla stalls and the like were in the business of virtually giving prizes away for a minimum investment and I remember we collected a large velvet doll for sister Joan and Ken procured a pair of ornaments for mother and father. (Replica Dutch boy and girl, he has them still.) The aforementioned music emporium singers were bravely assuring us, by way of a current popular song, that there would always be an England.

Our arrival on Saturday the 2nd of September, at New Holland for the return journey, was marked by the sight of hundreds of children in the process of being evacuated from the city of Hull into Lincolnshire. I can only presume that mum and dad must have faced the immediate future with some trepidation while to Ken and I it was still an adventure to come.

Evacuees leaving for the countryside

Sunday morning dawned sunny and warm but whatever we did before 11.15am has long been forgotten as it pales into insignificance when one considers what we did after that fateful hour. The voice of Prime Minister Neville Chamberlain (left), (in the context of the German invasion of Poland) "...I have to tell you now that no such undertaking has been received, and that consequently this country is at war with Germany."

Our holiday was already part of the dim past, as though it had never been which was a pity because we would have need of pleasant memories during the arduous times to come.

Our parents major fear was that we were about to become the recipients of hundreds, if not thousands, of tons of high explosive delivered by the German Air Force. Such thoughts were not exactly uppermost in the minds of most teenagers. Suddenly the world was a place of strange and novel events. The first of these came during the Sunday evening, possibly about 9pm, in the form of wailing air raid warning sirens. We were rapidly bundled next door into their garden shed, with mother complaining loudly that she didn't want to be buried under tons of bricks. An understandable sentiment, but I did have some reservation concerning the nature of the shed's resistance to high explosives. Our neighbours did not have any children of their own but had compensated for this by breeding budgerigars. So there we were, waiting for Goering's bombers to do their worst, standing in a small shed full of birds complaining that their sleep had been interrupted.

I think our vigil only lasted for half an hour or so before we heard the welcome sound of the 'all clear'. We never graced the shed with our presence again

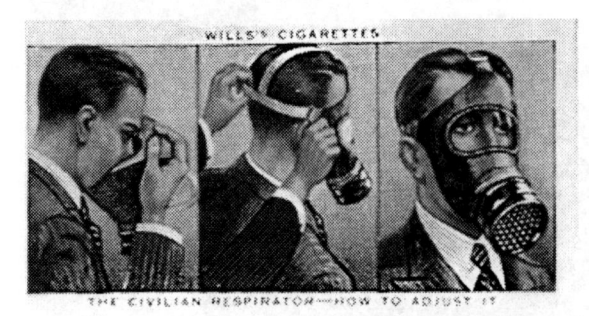

We had all been issued with gas masks during the previous year and now we were told that they had to be carried at all times. Wherever you went your gas mask had to be with you, neatly packaged in its cardboard carton which would be well on the way to total disintegration during the first few minutes of a shower of rain. Within a week or two opportunists were selling water proof covers for your flimsy cardboard box, complete with a carrying strap to replace the original length of string. Gas mask trials were entered into with enthusiasm by us youngsters eager to see who could produce the most revolting noise, created by exhaling heartily thus causing the rubber face mask to vibrate noisily.

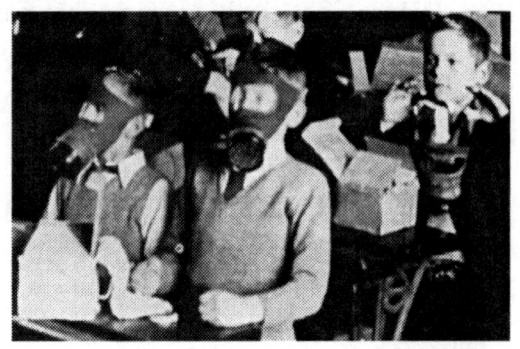

Gas masks with their flimsy cardboard boxes

All street lighting, shop window illumination, external neon signs and so forth had been extinguished on the first of September, and internal lighting was not permitted to be visible from outside. This was the 'blackout' and was to continue for virtually the whole war. Lamp posts and other impedimenta were painted with white rings as were pavement edges at corners. Motor vehicles had to have white painted edges on their wings, (used to be called mud guards), and headlamps were fitted with masks with a slot measuring four inches by half an inch cut in them. (See picture right). Hand torches were a necessity

An ARP sets blackout time

but had to be carried with the beam pointed downwards. Pedestrian deaths doubled almost overnight as people stumbled about in a world which they would not be equipped to deal with for some while. The cry of: "Put that light out", was heard incessantly as Air Raid Wardens patrolled their patches looking for chinks of light.

BLACKOUT

Left: Trying to beat the black-out!

Right: Even striking a match was not allowed!

The black-out started on 1 September 1939. The purpose was to make cities difficult to see and bomb from the air. All street illumination was turned out and houses had to cover their windows with thick dark curtains. You could buy special black-out material at 2s. (10p) a yard. Larger factories and offices etc. painted their windows black. This darkness obviously made it very difficult to see and people constantly fell off pavements, bumped into lamp posts and knocked each other over. Even cars were not allowed to have headlights (or very little) making it very difficult to drive anywhere. Accidents increased, including people drowning. One man after seeing his girlfriend home took a short cut home along the canal: "It was pitch black and after groping along by the bushes for ten minutes, I decided to crawl on my hands and knees all the way home. I met two other people crawling the other way! I was frankly terrified."

Girls of the Worthing 'Blackout Corps' paint over the windows of a local hospital.

To help traffic and pedestrians to see - white rings were painted around lamp posts...
...and white stripes on the edge of the pavement.
Even some cattle had white lines painted on them!

RASC Page 13 Chapter 1 1939 - 1943

A SHELTERED LIFE

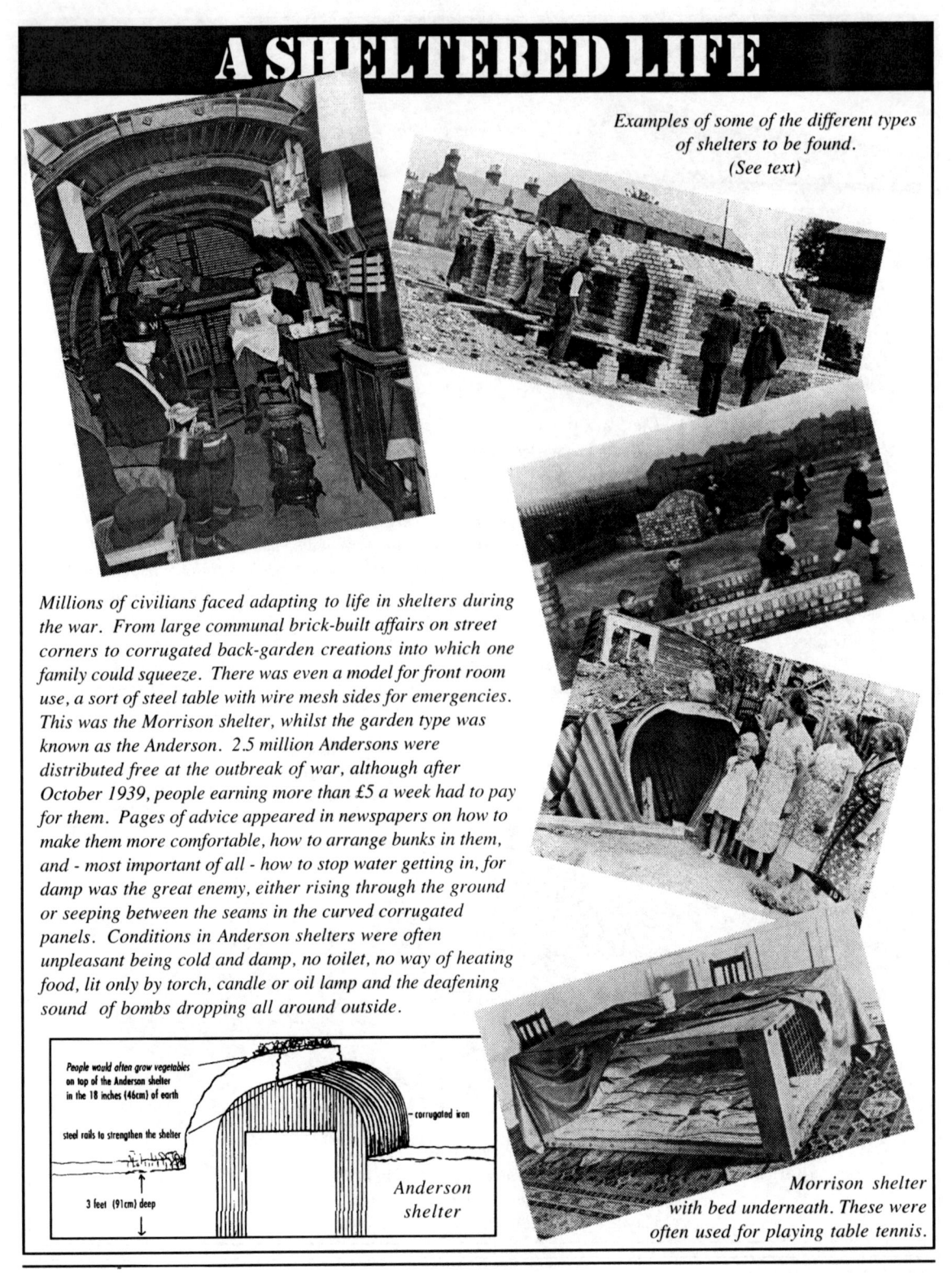

Examples of some of the different types of shelters to be found. (See text)

Millions of civilians faced adapting to life in shelters during the war. From large communal brick-built affairs on street corners to corrugated back-garden creations into which one family could squeeze. There was even a model for front room use, a sort of steel table with wire mesh sides for emergencies. This was the Morrison shelter, whilst the garden type was known as the Anderson. 2.5 million Andersons were distributed free at the outbreak of war, although after October 1939, people earning more than £5 a week had to pay for them. Pages of advice appeared in newspapers on how to make them more comfortable, how to arrange bunks in them, and - most important of all - how to stop water getting in, for damp was the great enemy, either rising through the ground or seeping between the seams in the curved corrugated panels. Conditions in Anderson shelters were often unpleasant being cold and damp, no toilet, no way of heating food, lit only by torch, candle or oil lamp and the deafening sound of bombs dropping all around outside.

Anderson shelter

Morrison shelter with bed underneath. These were often used for playing table tennis.

RASC   Page 14   Chapter 1   1939 - 1943

In these early days there was little or no entertainment available to us. All cinemas and theatres were closed, football matches were banned and the BBC had evacuated large numbers of its staff out into the country. We were treated to what seemed like a continuous performance by Sandy McPherson at the BBC theatre organ. (It was too large to be moved to the country, or was that Sandy?)

The art of blacking out house windows became a national pastime and brought to the fore the innate British skill for invention. Our dad was good at making things, and in no time at all he had constructed external shutters of roofing felt fixed to wooden frames, for our downstairs windows. As far as I can recall the plan for upstairs windows was based on fairly thick curtains or no lights at all, most probably the latter.

All of this provided an inexhaustible source of conversation at school, all of it suitably embellished for effect as we all waited for the war to start. But it didn't! This situation of war but no war became known as the 'Phoney War', which would last until the following spring. Meanwhile although the familiar street lamps, around which we kids used to congregate after dark, remained unlit, we still ventured out into the night equipped with torches, or able to find our way about by the reflection from searchlights shining on the clouds. (There always seemed to be several searchlights shining, pointing upwards and for most of the time, stationary.) Consider how times have changed. Here we were, groups of children, some not even teenagers, wandering unlit streets totally without fear, either our own, or our parents'.

Shortly after the affair of the 'budgie shed', dad, assisted by neighbours, had constructed an air raid shelter at the bottom of our garden. This consisted of a 3 feet deep trench with walls made up of planks of wood to a height of about 5 feet. The whole was then roofed over with timber and the excavated soil heaped on top. It possessed a central entrance and could accommodate some two dozen people, and at the time, the trials associated with getting people in and out were great fun. It didn't last. The nature of the land meant that a sump had been dug in the middle to collect seeping ground water. This had to be emptied two or three times a week and it seemed that our dad was the

Anderson shelter - See feature left

only one willing to do it, so in the end the shelter flooded. In the event the council moved with the times and built us a brick surface shelter the following spring, which to be truthful we never occupied other than as somewhere for Ken and I to mess about in.

I was now in my last year at Goole Grammar school and had before me the prospect of examinations in June of 1940 to obtain the School Certificate, which I suppose can best be described as a combined 'O' and 'A' level qualification. Christmas came and went and left no indelible memories with me. Food rationing began in January, butter and bacon, 4 ounces of each, and 12 ounces of sugar a person per week. More rationing would follow and would continue in some form or other until 1953! Identity Cards had been issued some time earlier and you were obliged to carry them at all times.

The 'it'll all be over by Christmas' experts had long ceased to sing this particular song and no one was coming forward to suggest what was going to happen. It appeared that the British and French troops in France were just as reconciled to this lack of activity as were the Germans on their side of the frontier.

Our 'Phoney War' was due to come to an end in the very near future.

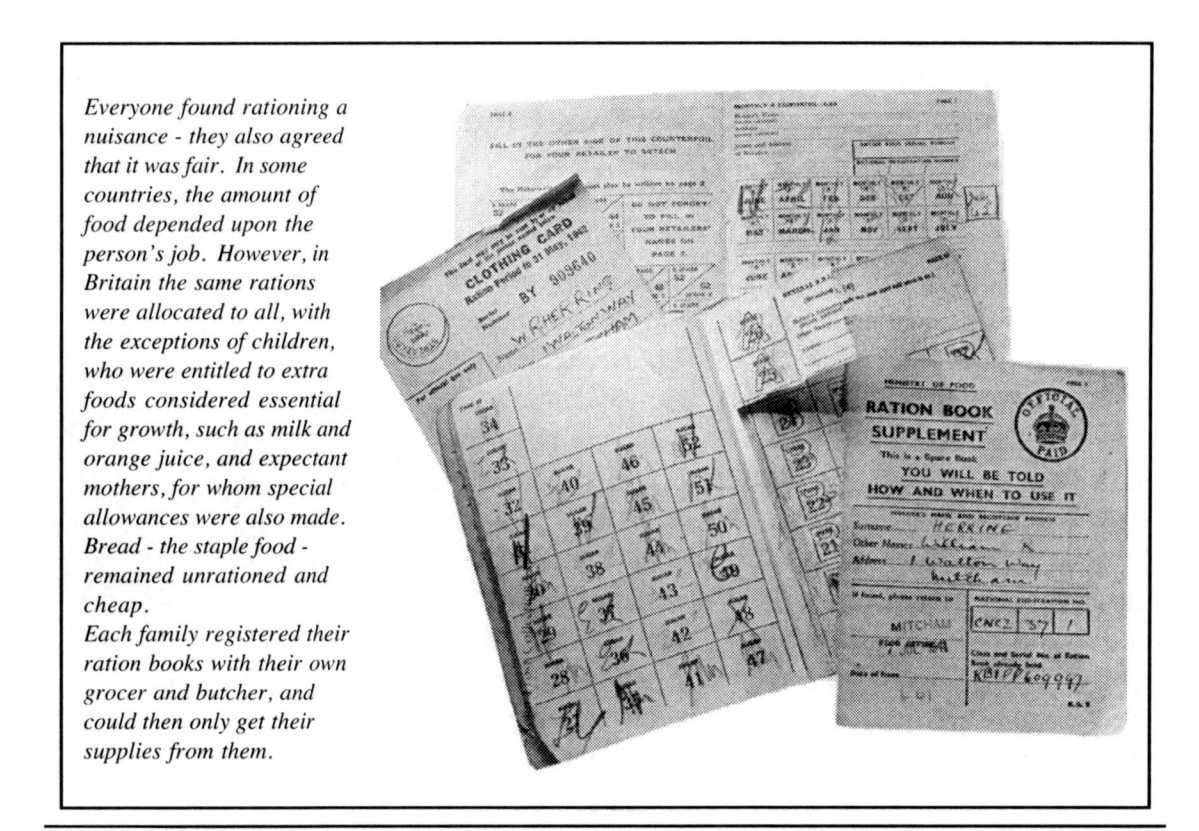

Everyone found rationing a nuisance - they also agreed that it was fair. In some countries, the amount of food depended upon the person's job. However, in Britain the same rations were allocated to all, with the exceptions of children, who were entitled to extra foods considered essential for growth, such as milk and orange juice, and expectant mothers, for whom special allowances were also made. Bread - the staple food - remained unrationed and cheap.
Each family registered their ration books with their own grocer and butcher, and could then only get their supplies from them.

BATTLE COMMENCES

The months of April and May 1940 brought more news than we could handle, the successive invasions, by Germany, of Denmark and Norway, followed by the 'Blitzkrieg' through Holland, Belgium and Luxembourg and on into France left us reeling. Before we had time to come to terms with these events we were holding our breath as the major part of the British Expeditionary Force in France was evacuated from the beaches of Dunkirk.

Winston Churchill, (pictured right with his famous 'V for Victory' sign) and now Prime Minister, spoke over the wireless, (radios came later), to tell us that the Battle of France was over and that the Battle of Britain was about to begin. He told us that we were to fight on the beaches and in the streets and any and every where else, and that we would never surrender! I'm sure this pleased a lot of people who had, up until now, been wondering what the hell were we going to do?

Large numbers of soldiers, back from Dunkirk, appeared in our neighbourhood billeted in empty houses. They paraded in the streets and marched about and drilled a lot, but looking back I think that the major objective was the restoration of confidence. For us youngsters their presence was an attraction not to be missed and we hung around, after school, avidly observing the various comings and goings.

The formation of the Local Defence Volunteers was announced by Anthony Eden, the Minister of War. A total of 250,000 men came forward during the first twenty-four hours following his broadcast. This figure had increased to nearly 1,500,000 by the end of June 1940. In July, following Churchill's suggestion, the force was renamed the Home Guard.

Dad was a railway man with the London Midland and Scottish Railway, employed as a Coal Foreman, responsible, in better times, for organising the movement of coal from coal mines to the docks to be loaded into ships, mostly for delivery to southern power stations or export to Europe. The current situation with the German army securely installed in France, Belgium and Holland, left little scope for exporting coal to the

Mr R. W. Houghton.

RASC   Page 17   Chapter 1   1939 - 1943

continent, although there were still coastal shipments to manage. Along with large numbers of others, dad joined the Home Guard and became a member of the LMS Railway Home Guard Company. He had been in the army towards the end of the 1914 war, a cavalry man in fact, and along with his brother-in-law Alfred Beverley who was married to dad's sister Anne, had served in the Middle East. During his service with the Home Guard, until December 1945, he was promoted successively to Sergeant, Company Sergeant Major and finally to Lieutenant.

The LMS office in Goole was the control centre for a number of local railway stations as well as a large part of the docks at Goole, and possessed a large telephone switch board providing direct communication with these places. This had to be manned continuously on a three x 8 hours shift basis, as it was the centre's responsibility to relay air raid warnings to the various outposts. I gather that it could be more than a little boring particularly at night, although three or four people would be on duty and, especially in winter, there was always a roaring coal fire to sit in front of.

Whilst all this was going on I was struggling to equip myself with enough knowledge to enable me to succeed in the June examinations. Four large surface air raid shelters had been constructed on the playing field using steel panels and then covered with earth. Each shelter was capable of accommodating a quarter of the student population of about 800 with the teaching staff more or less equally distributed between the four. When the shelters were first built we had practised the orderly evacuation of pupils from class rooms to shelters. The school was co-educational, so I'm sure you can imagine the St. Trinian's like rush to get into your nominated shelter and end up sitting next to your current object of admiration. There was, initially, in each shelter a supply of bottled soda water, ostensibly to settle upset stomachs, the incidence of which must have been of epidemic proportions as, unpalatable as soda water was by itself, the stock of full bottles became rapidly depleted. Lessons were sometimes interrupted as a result of air raid warnings with the resulting dash to the shelters to await the sound of the 'all clear'.

The learning process had, however, to carry on, including mind boggling amounts of home work. It all came to fruition in July when I learned that I had scraped through the exam and was now the proud possessor of a School Certificate, including a credit (an 'A') in art. There followed six weeks glorious holiday much of which was spent with my good friend John Montgomery from Howden, and our respective lady friends. Back to school in September for my last term which would end in December.

Hampden Bomber

Token forces of our own bombers were starting to bomb Germany and it was very sad for me, still a pupil, walking to school one morning and seeing the remains of a Hampden, that had crashed during the early morning, near to Dunhill Road school.

However, in late November I was offered a position with a local shipping agent, as a result of which I joined Mr Tom Sherburn in his offices in Church Street in Goole. I became his entire staff as the rest had gone off to the war! I was the proud possessor of my own large office equipped with six desks, four typewriters, a large coal fire and a kettle and teapot. The fire making was the responsibility of the cleaning lady and all I had to do was to keep it replenished with huge amounts of coal. The level of business was, to put it simply, abysmally low, but we still had the odd coastal shipment to deal with. Part of my job was to complete the necessary forms and formalities connected with movement of cargo, (coal to power stations around the Thames Estuary usually), and visit the ship in dock taking money to the Captain, on behalf of the owners. I enjoyed moving around dock land in Goole and I absorbed a lot of interesting knowledge by observing how things were being done in relation to loading and unloading vessels.

Other shipping agents in the town were similarly short of work and staff, but all of them had someone of my age working for them. Once a week my boss would go to Hull to meet with ship owners and I was left in charge. This gave me the opportunity to invite some other junior to call in at my office for tea. This was a reciprocal arrangement and in this way I met a lot of people in the shipping world. Our office was on the second floor and it was late one December afternoon, when I looked through the window to see a German Heinkel bomber roaring past at little more than roof top height! It was gone before I could draw breath! Where it had come from or where it was going remained a mystery.

My stay with Tom Sherburn did not last long as I heeded dad's wish for me to obtain employment with the LMS Railway Company. A career within the LMS was seen as being secure and long lasting, and as the company operated a Pension Scheme, (or superannuation as it was then called), eventual retirement would be a little more comfortable than most would enjoy. This was the philosophy of the times, security in tandem with loyalty and a job for life. I suppose today's world would regard this as being short sighted and bereft of ambition, but that's the way it was!

I was made aware that the position of Staff Messenger was open at the LMS offices so I duly applied. I was offered the job and after a fairly sad parting with Tom Sherburn, joined the LMS Railway. The job of Staff Messenger was just as the title implies, I ran messages, collected and distributed internal mail and learned how to operate the main switchboard, but my feet were, theoretically, on the promotion ladder. To use a present day expression it all went 'pear shaped' when I failed the obligatory medical examination due to poor sight in my left eye. This after having been with the company for a number of months, but I was given notice to quit! Considering that I was intending to pursue a purely clerical career the company's policy did seem to be somewhat short sighted. (Oops!)

Within a week or so I obtained a job as a shorthand typist, (which was part of my skills), with a company called Yorkshire Hennebique, involved in constructing a runway extension at the bomber airfield near Holme-on-Spalding-Moor. This necessitated riding on a special workman's bus leaving at 6.30am, walking across acres of mud to a wooden cabin on the field perimeter. I took dictation and typed a few letters for two weeks and then called it a day, 6.30am indeed!

I had no problem in finding new employment and within a matter of days I joined the Goole Co-operative Society as a clerk at their Red Lion Street head office. Excepting for one other male, Wallace Utting, the remaining five or six staff were female. The manager, Mr Handley had his own office and I don't remember seeing a lot of him, except on Saturdays when cash from the shops was brought into the office.

So I settled down to a fairly mundane life which was brightened up to some extent by my learning to drive. I obtained a Provisional Driving Licence in May of 1941, and having become friendly with one of the Co-op Dairy van drivers I started accompanying him on Thursday afternoons, my free half day, when we travelled out into the countryside collecting milk, in churns, for the dairy. He taught me to drive, in his van, a Morris Commercial box on wheels complete with fuel mixture and spark advance and retard controls on the steering wheel, but on the whole a fairly easy vehicle to drive. In those days traffic was so sparse that when you met another vehicle you waved at each other!

The following 2 pages show buildings of interest in the author's home town of Goole.

GOOLE 1

*Goole Co-operative Society at their Red Lion Street head office.
The office I worked in was on the first floor of the centre building.*

Goole Grammar School.

GOOLE 2

Goole Bank Chambers.
Tom Sherburn's office was on the top floor, far left.

Goole LMS Office. (To the mid left of picture)
Part of the first floor, fronting the road on the right, was the Home Guard Headquarters.

Leisure pursuits in war time Goole were somewhat limited. The town market hall boasted a Saturday night dance but I was not a regular supporter. There were three cinemas, Tower, Cinema and Carlton, reopened after initial closure, with programme changes twice a week. Saturday evening was an absolute must in the company of one's best friend and at the time mine was Dennis Dunford (see photo) who lived a few doors away from me. We not only did the Saturday film night together but managed Fridays as well, where we tried to emulate men of the world by acquiring the smoking habit. This involved purchasing a packet of five Wills' Woodbines, along with a book of matches for the princely sum of two old pennies, (less than 1p), providing us two and a half cigarettes each. As with most early experiments it failed and we discontinued the habit there and then. Madame Addy's dancing school in Burlington Crescent was honoured by our presence for a few weeks as was the Railway Tavern (now gone) where we drank our slow, under age, way through a half pint of lukewarm mild beer.

Dennis Dunford

Life in Goole during 1941/2 was, for many people, very dreary. We were aware that ships were being sunk and the country was being bombed, but our information was only what the censorship in force permitted. The loss of Singapore and Burma in the Far East added to the depression. We had to wait until November 1942 when news of victory at El Alemein in North Africa did lift our spirits, it being our first land victory since the beginning of the war.

The sound of planes during the night was always with us, provoking the comment - 'sounds like one of ours'. The truth was that it hardly ever could have been one of ours. Air raid warnings became commonplace but progressively disregarded in terms of rushing out to sit in a cold, damp and unlit shelter. This was Goole (Sleepy Hollow as it was to some). This torpor was dramatically disturbed in the early afternoon of Bank Holiday Monday, August 3rd 1942, by the dropping of four bombs resulting in the destruction of some houses, loss of life, and a large crater in Boothferry Road, the main road into town.

My enrolment into the Home Guard, resulting in Sunday morning parades and two or more evenings a week of other activities, did relieve the boredom for me and we did achieve some satisfaction, particularly during summer months, watching our own bombers on their way to bomb Germany. We had by this time become adept at aircraft recognition and knew beyond any doubt that these were quite definitely, 'ours'.

PART TIME KHAKI

During February of 1941 I had enlisted in the LMS Home Guard, to be accurate the unit was E company of the 47th West Riding Battalion. The Home Guard had been formed, initially, as a 'citizen's army', ostensibly to act as local militia helping the regular army repel the anticipated 1940 invasion. To what degree they would have been able to acquit themselves in this context was never tested, as during those early days of the Home Guard's existence, in the summer of 1940, the supply of arms was virtually non existent. The picture of men drilling and practising offensive action armed with broomsticks having carving knives lashed to them, was not too far removed from the truth. During the intervening time between then and my enlistment, the arms had been forthcoming along with uniforms, steel helmets, army gas masks and associated straps and pouches etc.

Most of the personnel of our unit were either too old for military service or in reserved occupations, where the job they were doing was considered to be of prime importance to the overall war effort. They were therefore, debarred from leaving that occupation in order to join the armed forces. There was, of course, a number of youngsters, such as myself, who were 'marking time' until we were called into the forces when we reached the age of conscription which at that time was set at eighteen.

Fix bayonets! A platoon of the Home Guard gets to grips with the intricacies of drill.

Shown right is the original Certificate Of Enrolment issued to the author on 20th February 1941

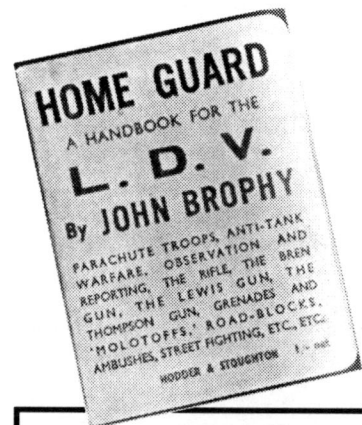

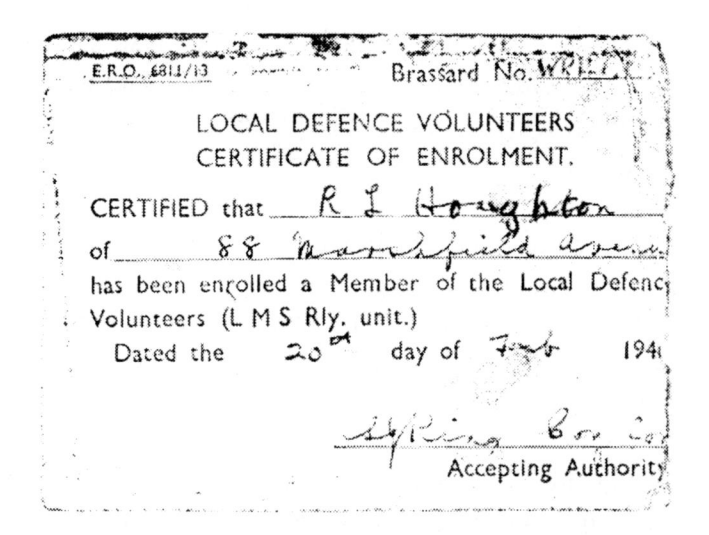

> E.R.O. 6811/13   Brassard No. WR...
>
> LOCAL DEFENCE VOLUNTEERS
> CERTIFICATE OF ENROLMENT.
>
> CERTIFIED that R I Houghton
> of 88 Marshfield Avenue
> has been enrolled a Member of the Local Defence
> Volunteers (L M S Rly. unit.)
> Dated the 20th day of Feb 1941
>
> Accepting Authority

HOME GUARD
A HANDBOOK FOR THE
L. D. V.
By JOHN BROPHY
PARACHUTE TROOPS, ANTI-TANK WARFARE, OBSERVATION AND REPORTING, THE RIFLE, THE BREN GUN, THE LEWIS GUN, THE THOMPSON GUN, GRENADES AND 'MOLOTOFFS,' ROAD-BLOCKS, AMBUSHES, STREET FIGHTING, ETC., ETC.
HODDER & STOUGHTON   1/- net

Below is a reproduction from a typical L.D.V. handbook (left) on sale in 1940 where it is made quite clear what this army was intended to do. The book, by Hodder & Stoughton, cost one shilling.

THE LAST WORD

It is suggested that the substance of this brief postscript be got by heart.

The main duties of the Home Guard are :
1. Guarding important points.
2. Observing and reporting - prompt and precise.
3. Immediate attack against small, lightly armed parties of the enemy.
4. The defence of roads, villages, factories and vital points in towns to block enemy movements.

Every L.D.V. should know :
1. The whole of the ground in his own district.
2. The personnel of his own detachment.
3. The Headquarters of the detachment and where he is to report for duty in the event of an alarm.
4. What the alarm signal is.
5. The form of reports concerning enemy landings or approaches, what the reports should contain, and to whom they should be sent.
6. The personnel of the civil defence services, police, wardens, A.F.S., etc., in his own district.
7. The uniforms and badges of any units of the regular army stationed near at hand, in order to be able to spot enemy agents in disguise.

In the event of an alarm, the L.D.V. might use the check list before he leaves his home or his work. He should take with him :
1. Full uniform, including steel helmet and warm underclothing.
2. His arms and ammunition.
3. His gas-mask.
4. Rations for twenty-four hours.
5. A filled water-bottle.
6. Identity cards.
7. (If a smoker) pipe and tobacco or cigarettes and matches.
8. Two handkerchiefs.
9. A supply of money.
10. Bicycle (or other means of transport as ordered) in good working order, including front and rear lamps.

All these should habitually be kept handy, ready for an emergency.

There were certain similarities to the Dad's Army of television fame in that I remember we did have a 'Pike like' character, and we had more than one Private Godfrey in our ranks. Our Commanding Officer, a Major, was a demon for exercises and was obsessed with the tactic of 'pincer movements' which involved the act, in theory, of surrounding enemy forces in the manner of a pair of pincers closing. In fact I think that there were more than certain similarities between us and the fictitious Dad's Army. I recall one particular evening exercise, when two of our number fell asleep under a bush and didn't wake up until some time during the night, and finding that no one else was around, naturally, went home. No one knew of this as there had been no roll call at the end of the exercise! We only found out a day or so later.

The threatened invasion never came, and progressively the Home Guard went on to man anti aircraft defences, assist the Civil Defence organisations, and also to relieve the regular army of mundane guard duties, for example, of strategically important installations.

During the next two years I was to become competent in the handling of a lot of weaponry. Progressively the company received enough rifles for every man to be armed. These were North American Ross .300 inch weapons which arrived covered in protective grease, still in the cases they had been packed in after the 1914-18 war. This did not detract from the fact that they were a good rifle with a magazine capacity of five rounds and were reasonably accurate over several hundred yards range.

We also came into possession of a number of machine guns, one each of a Browning and a Lewis, belt fed, tripod mounted weapons and really intended for more static siting rather than mobility. They required a three man crew to handle them! Our remaining automatic armoury consisted of a Thompson sub machine gun, (Tommy gun - see picture below), a Browning Automatic Rifle (BAR), and a Hotchkiss light machine gun. In addition we were equipped with a Blacker Bombard, which was a spigot mortar for use against armoured vehicles. This was also a heavy lump of metal to lug around and needed a crew of three to handle it, weighing as it did, some 360 pounds. It could project either a 14 or 20 pound missile over a distance of maybe 200 yards.

TheTommy Gun.
For more information on weapons,
see feature in Chapter 2.

We were also the wary owners of the much derided Northover Projector, which was an extremely cheap weapon to produce, (and it showed it), consisting of a four feet length of three inch diameter steel tube mounted on a pair of legs. A simple breech and trigger mechanism allowed the loading of a glass bottle containing liquid phosphorous, an explosive charge and percussion cap. The theory was that the bottle would be hurled a distance of some 150 yards and shatter upon hitting a solid object, thus causing the contents to be exposed to the air and there to burst into flame. (This is what phosphorous did when exposed to air.) The shortcomings of this apparatus were such that we never really considered using it. At the end of the tube was mounted a rudimentary sight and if this was badly fitted it could cause the bottle to fracture as it left the barrel with disastrous results. Also during practice shoots we had occasions when the bottles did not shatter and they had to be retrieved very carefully.

Progressively we amassed considerable quantities of rifle and automatic weapon ammunition and also Mills hand grenades. Another deadly weapon, in more ways than one, was the Sticky bomb. This consisted of a nitro glycerine filled glass sphere, about six inches or so in diameter, covered with a sock which was impregnated with a strong adhesive, mounted on a seven or eight inch long handle. The whole was enclosed in a two part metal cover which was discarded by releasing a catch on the handle when it was intended to use the bomb. Now this was the interesting bit!

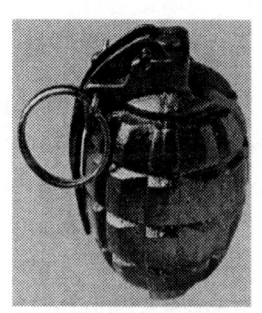

Mills hand grenade

It could be thrown, but don't let it brush against your clothing otherwise it would stick, quite firmly, and demolish the thrower rather than the enemy objective! Apparently the correct way to utilise this weapon to the best advantage was to casually saunter up to an enemy tank, plant the bomb on it and then retire hastily before it exploded!

This total armoury was comfortably installed in our headquarters within the LMS office building on the corner of Mariners Street and Stanhope Street in Goole. I understand that most of it was still there up until, and maybe after, the standing down of the Home Guard at the end of December 1944. I wonder how many citizens of Goole passed this building totally unaware of its explosive contents.

I became quite expert in the handling of automatic weapons and one of our favourite activities involved stripping guns down, and reassembling them, whilst blindfolded, and due to my interest and skill was promoted to Corporal, responsible for light machine guns, at some time during the year. We were given ample opportunity, particularly in

Taking advantage of natural cover, defence procedures and target shooting were put into practise

1942 as ammunition became more plentiful, to target shoot with all our weaponry. Our 'range' was behind Fison's factory on the outskirts of the town and the majority of our shooting was done there on Sunday mornings. During the week we managed some fun shooting with a couple of Remington .22 inch rifles at 25 yards range alongside of Goole's West Dock sheds.

Our Company being formed of mostly LMS personnel was, naturally, designated as being responsible for mounting guard at the Company's office which, as I have indicated earlier, acted as a major communications centre. This involved night sentry duty from 8pm to 8am and the guard consisted of twelve men, each one of whom stood guard outside for one hour during the twelve hour period. I remember that at that time I did not own a watch so I had no mechanical means of knowing what time it was. I knew that records of most popular tunes played for about three minutes, so I used to go through tune after tune in my mind, to try and calculate what time it was. No matter what I did it always seemed like a very long hour. Don't forget that there were no lights other than the diffused light from the odd searchlight, or, if the sky was clear, moon and stars. The monotony was some times alleviated by the passing of an army convoy and at such times I used to ponder over what the future held for me.

Our guard room, (where all our munitions were stored), was quite cosy, a huge coal fire, lots of tea and, during the early part of the night, a chance to play cards, usually a kind of five card whist called 'nap'. This was where I learned to lose money as well as win it! There was a number of beds, where those not actually on duty could obtain some rest. In addition to the man on sentry duty someone else had to remain awake otherwise the poor devil outside would never get relieved!

We undertook numerous exercises usually on a location called Glew's Hollow which was situated between the rail tracks to Wakefield and those to Doncaster. (This semi wilderness, as it was, is now part of the Goole Industrial Estate.) We took part in mock battle tactics, one of which necessitated our walking across Skelton railway bridge, in half light, one Sunday morning, to establish defensive positions on the Hull side of the bridge.

One weekend we marched the four miles or so to Rawcliffe and spent the weekend under canvas. Unlike television's Dad's Army we did manage to get up for breakfast and there wasn't a steam road roller in sight! Weather permitting, Sunday mornings were reserved for full parades and a few hours on the rifle range or an exercise of some kind. I have very clear memories of dad and myself marching in step with rifles slung on our shoulders, (we were allowed to keep them at home), on our way to these Sunday morning assemblies.

It would be remiss of me not to mention that whilst father and me were 'doing our bit' in the Home Guard, mother had taken on the job of forewoman at the flax works located in nearby Howden. Flax was used in the manufacture of ropes and mother had been involved in this process during the 1914-18 war.

Members of the Home Guard marching. There was to be much marching later on...

There is no doubt in my mind that my time with the Home Guard went some way in preparing me for life in the army, in terms of both weapon handling and foot and rifle drill. Meanwhile life and the ever increasing burden of rationing, dragged on through the remainder of 1942 and I began thinking more and more about what the year ahead would bring for me.

Home Guards learn to operate a machine gun

A Home Guard dressed in denim uniform gets his gun

Hitler will send no warning – *so always carry your gas mask*

CHAPTER 2
1943 - 44
THE PROPER ARMY

The British nation was probably the most mobilised of all the warring nations, in that all able bodied men and women above the age of eighteen, could be conscripted (directed), to either become members of the armed forces, or perform work of national importance in agriculture, coal mining, (men only), or munitions production. Having reached the age of eighteen in December 1942, I anticipated being conscripted by volunteering for the army, and as a result found myself, after initial training, a driver in the Royal Army Service Corps. It is a record of fact that the RASC, responsible for transporting men, tanks and ammunition, and delivering to the troops their food, fuel, clothing, and everything else required to keep the army in action, constituted one eighth of the strength of the whole army at this time.

I was to spend fifteen months at the home of the British Army, Aldershot, until my departure for mainland Europe late in September 1944 for a tour of duty lasting until November 1947.

INFANTRY TRAINING

I have no clear memory of New Year's Eve 1942. The absence of church bells or factory hooters to herald the new year coupled with the continuing night time blackout didn't exactly promote enthusiasm for wild celebration. Since the outbreak of war the sounding of factory hooters had been suspended to avoid confusion with air raid warnings. After the fall of France in June 1940 with the threat of invasion hanging over us, it had been decreed that church bells would only be rung if invasion actually took place. New Year's Day also passed without incident (as far as I can remember). The last three years had not produced a lot in the way of victories - other than in North Africa - to give rise to wild celebration and the road ahead seemed endless. We were, however, absolutely sure that we would win the war - but don't ask when.

My mind was made up that I would have to go off and help. My eighteenth birthday was now three weeks in the past and this meant that I would be conscripted into the Armed Forces (called up was the term used). I didn't fancy the Navy and I was sure that my eyesight would not be good enough for the Air Force other than in some out of the way clerical job. I wanted something a little more exciting! I was also aware that I may be sent into the coal mining industry as a Bevin Boy. No thank you!

Bevin boys

I waited January out and then decided that I would volunteer for the Army which would give me the opportunity to express a preference for a particular unit. Early in February I took myself off to the Recruiting Office in Doncaster and opted for the Tank Corps but I was told that no new recruits for tank training were being accepted so I had to agree to a second option which was the Royal Army Service Corps (transport). I went home to await a date for medical examination and a day or two later I had a letter instructing me to attend for the medical at the United Reform Church Hall in Hallgate in Doncaster on the 16th February 1943.

Picture of the actual letter sent.

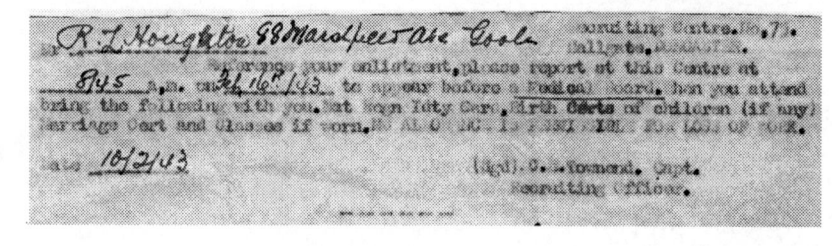

RASC   Page 33   Chapter 2   1943 - 1944

Presence of a pulse and a modicum of body heat ensured that I was passed fit! I was duly sworn in and received one shilling (5p) this being known as the King's Shilling due to some old established rite. My official enrolment into His Majesty's Forces was accomplished on this date.

A week or so later I received my 'Call up papers' instructing me to report to the 19th Infantry Training Centre at Formby, on the coast between Liverpool and Southport, on the 1st of April next. I was to be identified as Private Houghton R L, - army number 14422360.

Thus it was that on the first day of April my life changed. I suppose that looking back it was all a bit exciting, and although the war was, obviously, a deadly business, it did provide excitement for a lot of teenagers. I might not have been quite so enthusiastic had I known just how much life was to change.

Since the Autumn of 1941 I had been employed in the Head Office of Goole Cooperative Society on the first floor of their office building in Red Lion Street, Goole. Part of the ground floor of this building was taken up by the Co-operative butcher's shop and talking with one of the junior employees - a guy called George Coult - I found out that he was going into the army on the same day as me. Not only this but he was going to the same place!

George and I took the train to Liverpool where we arrived too early to go to the Training Camp and spent a few hours wandering around Liverpool. The city seemed to be full of eighteen year olds waiting for the time to report and for the first time in my life I met up with people who spoke a different form of English than I did - Liverpudlians who spoke the local dialect or 'scouse'! They were almost impossible to understand.

About two o'clock we took the train to Formby, to the 19th Infantry Training Centre, at Harington Barracks, and wended our way to the camp. (I didn't know at the time but this would be the last time that I ever 'wended'! From now on I would 'march'). The camp was huge - a seemingly never ending succession of barrack huts and roads plus a great number of very serious looking military persons. Whenever you were ordered to identify yourself by anyone in authority (and there was a lot of them), your response would be your name followed by the last three digits of your number, thus - Houghton 360 sir - loudly! My army number became such a part of my life that I have never forgotten it. In the course of the next day or so we were issued with two Identity Discs, on which we had to stamp our name, number and religion. These had to be worn round your neck at all times.

We were conducted to huts - I think each one held 40/50 men - where we found ourselves a bed. These were what today are called bunk beds, the bottom bed was twelve inches off the floor and the top bed was about four feet higher than the bottom one. We were then marched (roughly) to the Mess Hall for a tea meal - I can't remember what but I am sure it must have been wholesome - during which I fell off the wooden bench on which I was sat (at the end) and got a nosebleed.

Back to the hut and then to the Quartermaster's Stores to get blankets - four of them - all good prickly ones brown or grey - back to the hut - back to the stores to be issued with full kit and uniform - back to the hut to pack up our civilian clothes and sort out clothing for the following day, then to sleep. The beds were of wooden construction and each bed had three small mattresses which the army called biscuits laid over a metal mesh. Pillows were not deemed to be necessary. During the exercise of climbing up and making my bed I snagged my best gabardine trousers on the mesh and tore them - it didn't seem to matter a great deal. They were packed up with the rest of my civilian clothes to be sent home.

Full kit and uniform in simple terms meant clothing and footwear plus the clutter of straps and assorted packs and pouches to carry it all in, not to forget respirator (gas mask) and steel helmet. Also included were oddments such as a button stick to help in cleaning brass buttons and a hold-all of sewing equipment which the army chose to call a housewife! The uniform itself (in glorious khaki colour) consisted of two sets one of which was made out a denim material, this was your working uniform the other one being the dress uniform for parades and 'walking out'. Two forage caps were provided plus one greatcoat, anti gas cape and rubber ground sheet. Shirts and underwear were issued two of each as were socks and boots. (See appendix for full inventory).

Wake up time or reveille as the army chose to call it arrived some time in the middle of the night, or so it seemed, actually it was 06.00 hours. We were made aware that it was time to rise by some person as yet unknown crashing in through the hut door, hitting beds and floor with some blunt instrument whilst screaming loudly about the need to let go of our extremities and grab our socks. Somewhere in the distance some fool was blowing a bugle. Washing and shaving etc (ablutions in army talk) were conducted in the ablutions hut - where else? This was equipped with the usual amenities to meet the needs of bodily functions plus a series of metal troughs at waist height complemented by taps above to provide water. Cold of course!

Back to the hut to complete dressing then outside in some form of order to march to the mess hall for breakfast - porridge, followed by bacon and egg and lots of tea. Don't forget to wash your knife, fork, spoon and mug as these were part of your personal kit and were not provided in the mess.

It's as though I'm back in that time reliving the whole experience. We have now been sorted into platoons thirty strong and moved into our platoon hut - same bunk beds but the top bed not so high this time. In charge of us are a sergeant and two corporals who are on the permanent staff of the camp, they have their own separate rooms at the end of the hut. We have received instruction and demonstration of bed and kit layout where the blankets have to be folded in a precise manner on the bed and elements of kit laid out on the bed, this being inspected each day. The hut has to be kept clean which includes dry scrubbing the white wood floor with a long handled stiff bristled brush, the occupants of each bunk bed being responsible for the area under and around their bed.

Having absorbed all this excitement we are formed up and marched to the Medical Room for smallpox immunisation and various other inoculations for tetanus etc. Within fifteen minutes the floor is littered with soldiers (?) who have passed out at the sight of the needle. Funny, but it seems that it's always the apparently tough guys who flake out.

More marching! To the arms store where we are to be entrusted with weapons. We receive, and sign for of course, one rifle - Lee Enfield Mark IV - weight about nine pounds and naturally it needs cleaning. It also has a serial number which has to be memorised which I eventually forgot when we were later issued with Sten sub-machine guns. We were not, however, entrusted with ammunition. On the subject of cleaning, it has been explained to us that our belts, gaiters, back packs, ammunition pouches and associated straps (webbing) are to be 'blancoed' every two or three days. This involved mixing a coloured powder, khaki green No. 3, with water and applying it with a brush. All this gear is liberally equipped with shiny brass buckles which are to be kept in a highly

Similar to that used to blanco webbing

polished state. This 'highly polished state' also applies to two pairs of boots which each carry about two dozen studs deeply embedded in the soles. Sometime during all these comings and goings the army had found time for us to have our hair cut. There's not a lot I wish to add about this!

At this point I suppose that I was grateful for the time that I had spent in the Home Guard. At least I was familiar with the feel of rough khaki uniform and I knew which end of the rifle should be pointed at the enemy. However the thought of what I was doing a week ago was still fresh in my mind, my bedroom at home which I shared with brother Ken and the warm Co-op office with its full complement of female staff seems a million miles away, and no mum and dad around.

We do get to eat of course and to be fair the food is plentiful - three good meals a day. Naturally we are marched to the Mess Hall. We do a lot of 'marching' and we are now introduced to what is known as 'square bashing'. This starts, of course, with a lot more marching and being taught how to tell left from right, stopping and starting and keeping in step. All this is done whilst carrying your rifle, not any old how but in a proper military manner - on your left shoulder with your left hand holding the butt end - at the slope as it is called.

I am particularly impressed with the ability of NCOs (non commissioned officers, specifically - corporals, sergeants and sergeant majors), to string separate commands together in such an effortless and repetitive manner when, for example, the order to 'halt' is given it is immediately followed by 'and stand still'! Even more astute is their comprehension of the laws governing movement of the human body. The order to 'forward march' is more often than not issued in a more complicated form - thus:- "Platooooooon - by the left - forwaaaaaard - wait for it - march." The point in time when the operative command 'march' is given is very precise, in that the platoon, upon hearing the command 'forward' and anticipating being ordered to 'march', have started to move! They are therefore, left teetering slightly off balance and the command 'march' comes at exactly the right time to save them from falling over!

One thing I have done is to learn a lot of unprintable new words! These can be used throughout conversations and/or instructions to place emphasis on what is being said and, more often, shouted. There is a lot of shouting. A very rude awakening for us all.

The six weeks spent at the 19th Infantry Training Centre was a succession of days filled with drilling, cleaning equipment, cleaning the hut and, of course, marching. We also had to endure testing our respirators (gas masks) by being exposed to tear gas. Physical training at 06.15 hours became the norm followed by hot showers and then breakfast. We undertook obstacle courses - swinging on ropes and so forth - runs in full kit along the beach for three to four miles plus route marches wearing what was known as battle kit, which included rifle and steel helmet, outside of the camp across rough terrain for a number of miles. As each week passed these route marches became longer so that by the end of the course we were marching ten to twelve miles.

During my two years with the Home Guard I had done some rifle drill but not to the extent which we were now experiencing. Rifle drill, for those who have never done it, can be very tiring handling a nine pound rifle and moving it from ground to shoulder and all positions in between, to precise time intervals and most importantly doing it in unison with the other members of the squad. Foot drill sought to achieve the same unity when marching, turning and halting: "You 'orrible man" became one of the more repeatable phrases we became accustomed to. The fact that the army had only six short weeks to teach us the basics of soldiering and the understanding that, most importantly, orders were to be obeyed and were not open for discussion, meant that whatever the weather outside activities were not suspended. After all we did have ground sheets which converted to a form of rain cape.

If there was one activity that I detested it was the dreaded blancoing of webbing equipment and polishing of brass buckles and buttons (brass buttons were only fitted to the greatcoat and forage cap). This needed to be done every two to three days to keep your gear in that condition necessary to meet the regular inspections. Rifles also need regular attention, cleaning and oiling the mechanism and the barrel. It was guaranteed that any time rifles were inspected at least one instance of spiders dwelling in the barrel was brought to the attention of the unfortunate owner of the weapon.

We had hours of weapon training both theory and practice - rifle - Bren light machine gun - anti tank mortar - hand grenades. Shooting live ammunition and grenade throwing was done at Altcar Ranges near the beach. As a result of the all the shooting I had done with the Home Guard this was no problem for me and I did OK.

(See feature opposite)

WEAPONS 1

Blacker Bombard

Mills hand grenades

The Blacker Bombard was a spigot mortar for use against armoured vehicles. This was a heavy lump of metal to lug around and needed a crew of three to handle it, weighing as it did, some 360 pounds. It could project either a 14 or 20 pound missile over a distance of maybe 200 yards.

Vickers .303 medium machine gun

Weapons the author used whilst serving in the Home Guard.

The British Vickers .303 medium machine gun with steam condenser to recycle cool water during sustained fire. It was designed in 1912, was an improved Maxim water-cooled, recoil-operated, belt-fed weapon. With a rate of fire of about 600 rounds per minute, it was extremely reliable and capable of continuous fire for extremely long periods.

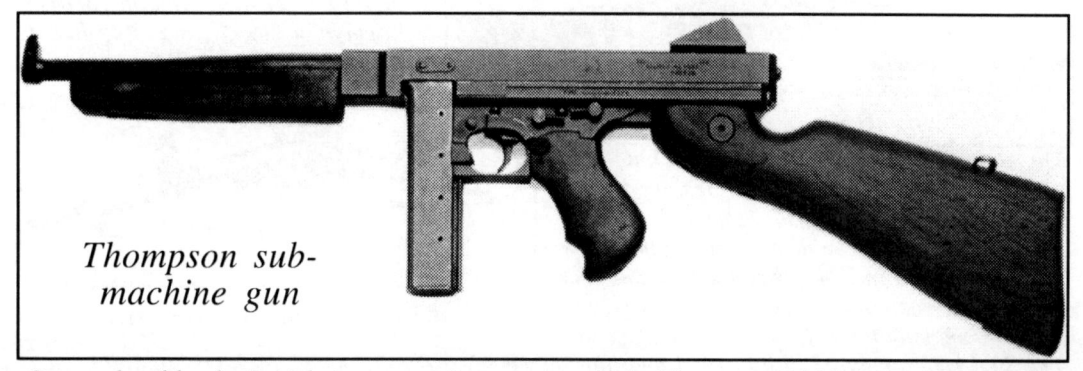

Thompson sub-machine gun

Once refused by the British Army as a 'gangster gun', the Thompson M1A1 SMG (Tommy Gun) served the Allies well and was especially favoured by Commandos and other Special Forces for the stopping power of its .45in rounds.

WEAPONS 2

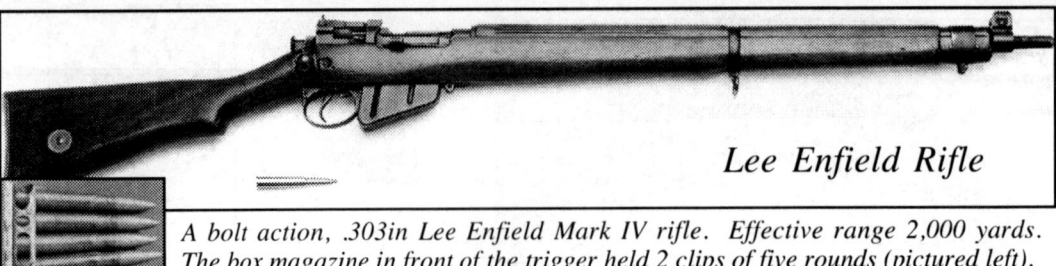

Lee Enfield Rifle

A bolt action, .303in Lee Enfield Mark IV rifle. Effective range 2,000 yards. The box magazine in front of the trigger held 2 clips of five rounds (pictured left).

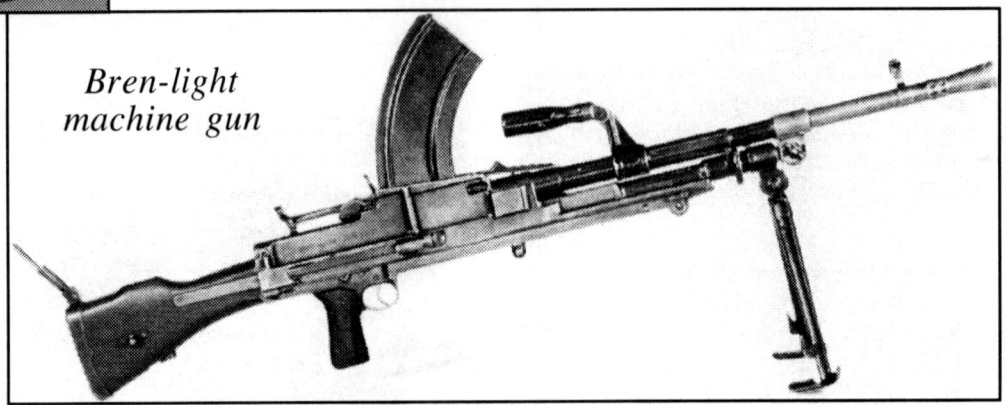

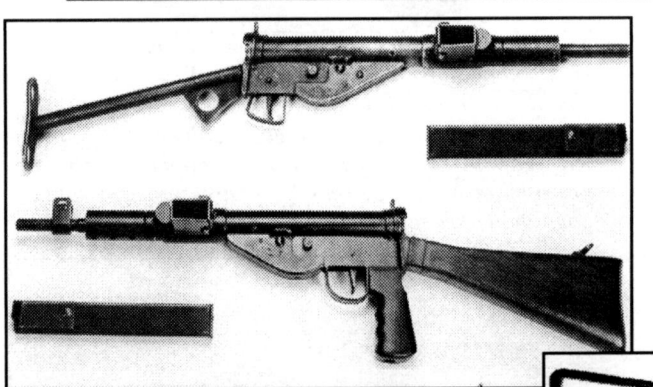

Bren-light machine gun

The original production version of the world's finest light machine-gun: the Bren (pictured above). The name come from Brno, the Czech armaments works which produced the original gun and Enfield, where British designers modified it. The Bren Mk 1 entered service with the British army in 1937 and its direct descendants are still in service.

The British 9mm Sten Mk2 sub-machine gun (above and bottom right) was designed after Dunkirk as a cheap and easily produced weapon with a 32-round box magazine. The Mk2, introduced in 1941, was a crude and ugly weapon and sometimes unreliable, but was easy to clean and maintain.

Sten sub-machine gun

The Sten Mk5 appeared in late 1943 and introduced several refinements to the original design. It carried the foresight of the No. 4 rifle and first saw extensive action in the hands of the paratroopers in 1944. It became the standard British SMG after the war.

Weapon handling also included a session in a special building where moving film of aircraft was projected on to the ceiling whilst you attempted to shoot the planes down using a mounted machine gun which projected a light beam when you pulled the trigger.

After the first week we were allowed to go out of camp either into Liverpool or Southport but had to be back into camp by 22.30 hours. The local railway station was on the line between these two places and it was only a short run either way. The trains were electric - much like the London Underground in design. I still remain amazed that we had the energy to go any where other than bed when the day's training came to an end. But go out we did and enjoyed it, particularly Southport which I found a most attractive town, being most impressed with Lord Street.

At some point late in the course we were taken by train to Liverpool to take part in a Wings for Victory parade, marching through the streets of the city in company with other troops and assorted service men and women. Wings for Victory was a national campaign to coax people to lend money to the Government to fund production of aeroplanes. Every town had its Spitfire Fund, or equivalent, £5,000 reputedly paid for a Spit.

The six weeks ended with a 'Passing out Parade' which involved marching, in proper military formation of course, round the parade ground with the Commanding Officer of the Centre taking the salute.

I was now a (partially) trained soldier for which I was paid three shillings a day (15p). Out of this I arranged for seven shillings to be sent home to my parents each week.

We were now ready to be posted to our various units and the news, good or bad, came on the last day of our stay. Sighs of relief, both George Coult and myself were to go to Hadrian's Camp near Carlisle for eight weeks driver training.

Our last night here and it is lights out (10.30pm or 22.30 hours in army speak) and some damn fool is playing the bugle again! He is, like us, some poor soldier, only carrying out his orders to sound 'lights out' as he does every night.

DRIVER TRAINING

The journey north to Carlisle on the 13th of May was by special train from Liverpool, and then by truck to Hadrian's Camp which was east of Carlisle near to the village of Brampton. This was a very large camp where the accommodation was in what were known as 'spiders', where six wooden huts were set out in two groups of three around a central core which contained the ablutions and accommodation for NCOs. Usual bunk beds but plenty of room between them. We were to be here for eight weeks at the end of which we would be competent drivers - hopefully! Those that passed were issued with a drivers permit like mine pictured right.

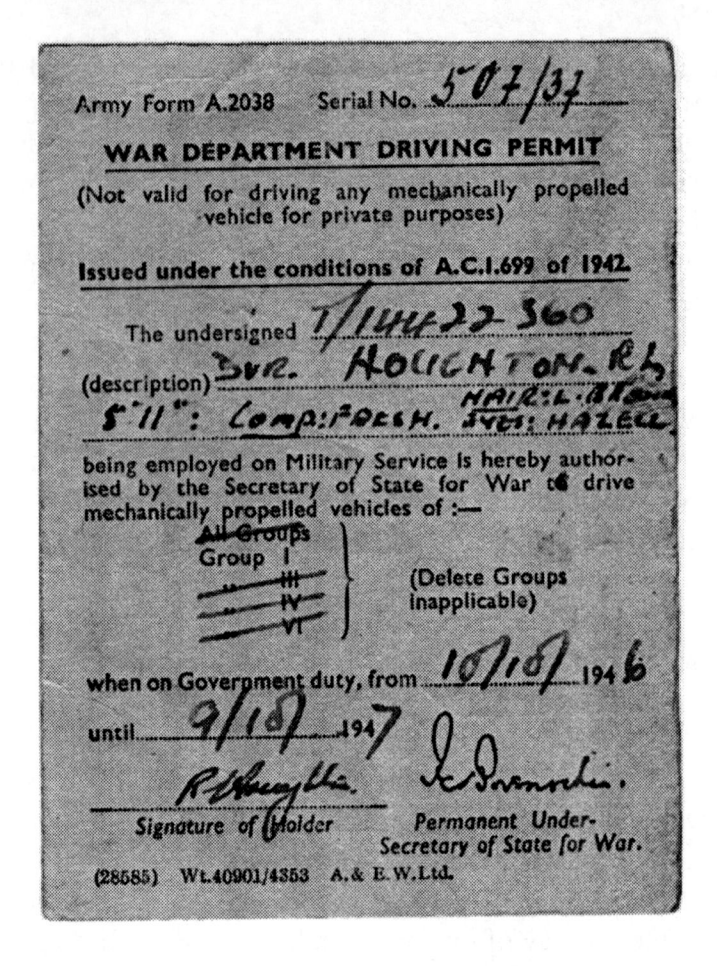

The routine was that one week would consist of theory during the morning and driving in the afternoon, the following week this procedure was reversed. Theory covered vehicle systems - electrics - brakes - steering - engine etc., both in a classroom or garage area where stripped down trucks were available to assist in understanding how things worked. In addition we were introduced to the army system of vehicle maintenance which was the 'task system' in that on each day of the month a specified element of maintenance would be carried out, for example day one might be fuel system, day two chassis U bolts and so on. The system consisted of 28 tasks plus one day free for platoon vehicle inspection - carried out by a platoon NCO and one day for Company Workshop inspection.

Most of the vehicles for driving instruction were three tonners, Bedford, Austin, Fordson and Leyland Lynx. (See Appendix G). During the actual instruction periods six or seven would be drivers climbed into the back of the truck while a sergeant or corporal instructor, with one learner in the cab with him, drove out to special roads reserved for the purpose of instruction. The instructor would then explain the controls to the first trainee, sit him in the driving seat and off we went - stop - stall - restart - lurch and so on! In those days ignition keys as such were unknown, ignition was turned on by a simple switch. Eminently sensible - can you imagine being on active service and having to start your vehicle in a hurry and trying to remember where you put the keys!

Bedford OYD 3 ton, 4 x 2

Leyland Lynx 3 ton, 4 x 2

Each man would have about a half hour instruction day after day until, eventually, he became reasonably able to get the thing moving, point it in the right direction and more importantly, bring it to a halt.

To ensure that clutch control was quickly learned, the Sergeant in charge of the truck I was in asked you to put your cigarettes (or his if you didn't smoke), behind the rear wheel when the truck was on an ascending slope. He then instructed you to move off without squashing the cigarettes! I was not aware of any instance of the sergeant's cigarettes being even marked, let alone anything worse.

Ford WOT2 15 cwt

Bedford MWR 15 cwt

I was fortunate in that I had held a Provisional Licence since May 1941 and had learnt to drive with one of the Co-op Dairy drivers. I therefore managed to pass my driving test within the first two days and after that, in company with others who could drive, spent the rest of the eight weeks driving periods just driving around in a truck shared between two of us.

We were in a superb area to practise driving. On our doorstep was the Lake District - narrow roads combined with tough gradients necessitated competent gear changing - double de-clutching of course as gear boxes didn't include synchro-mesh arrangements. The roads were virtually free of traffic as petrol for civilian use was very restricted.

Compared to Infantry Training Centre, Hadrian's Camp was the other end of the spectrum in that parades were unheard of, other than the assembly each morning and afternoon to proceed to either class or driving. Rifle drill was non existent and the dreaded blancoing was restricted to belt and gaiters. The objective of the unit was to turn out reasonably competent drivers at the end of the eight week's course.

This does not mean that there was a total absence of discipline - we were still in the army and we were reminded of this when we went off camp and had to pass inspection at the Guard House situated at the main gate. Herein dwelt a Provost Sergeant, a one Sergeant Frost who would pose such questions as: "Have you polished your boots today lad?" To which you answered that you had, whereupon he suggested - loudly - that you should double march (run) back to your hut and put on the pair that you had polished as those you were wearing certainly had not been attended to! When, or if, you returned he would then carry out a minute inspection of you and your uniform and only when he was satisfied that you looked like a proper soldier would you be allowed to go out.

The weather was on the whole good. The Lake District would not be itself without the odd few days of rain, but mid May to mid July has to be a good time of year to be there and not to forget the blessing of double summer time being in force. During the war from February 1940 onwards, what we know as 'summer time' became normal time, being Greenwich plus one hour. In summer the clocks were put forward an extra hour, ergo - double summer time.

I remember one particular weekend when we went out for the two days and parked the trucks in an idyllic spot not far from a crystal clear, but icy cold river. We had taken haversack rations with us and slept in the trucks on the Saturday night. We trekked a little, did some rock climbing and generally had a very enjoyable week end. If only I could remember exactly where that was! I have a feeling that it may have been somewhere not too far from Keswick.

Towards the end of the course we attended a few 'current affairs' sessions where we could enjoy open discussion on any number of topics. I remember one occasion when we were asked if anyone had civilian experience in the motor trade or associated business. One guy volunteered that he had worked for Dunlop Rubber Company before he had been called up and agreed to give us a short dissertation on the nature of his job. He's going to talk about tyre manufacture isn't he? No he's not! He had been employed in that part of the business which manufactured condoms, as they are called today. Or so he said and went on to give expert comment on testing procedures and so forth. To this day I still don't know if we were conned, but it was entertaining!

During the last week of the course in mid July, we were told where we would be posted to when we returned from the seven days home leave due to us on completion of the course. There were some disappointments as some of the guys just hadn't made the grade. George Coult and I were to go our separate ways, where he was going to I cannot recall but I was to join 270 Company RASC (Royal Army Service Corps) at Clayton Barracks in Aldershot, Hampshire. I now ceased to be a private, I was now a driver. My serial number was now T/14422360. (T = transport).

It is worth noting that in 1943 very few people, other than those whose job it was, could actually drive.

Goodbye to Hadrian's Camp and Carlisle - it wouldn't be long before I came to appreciate how laid back it had been there, but now it was south to Goole for seven days leave and some home comforts.

This being my first Privilege Leave - the correct army term - I looked forward to seeing family and friends now that I could swagger about in my uniform. Actually I would have no choice as it was not permissible to put on civilian garb in public. In the event, friends of my own age were few and far between, they were all doing what I was doing, helping the war effort. I soon realised that in some respects my standard of living was much better than the civilian population. I was better fed, I didn't have to juggle with Ration Books and I was clothed and housed, all free and my pay, meagre as seems in retrospect, was adequate to meet my needs as I didn't smoke and was not in the habit of consuming large amounts of beer.

One of the things that was a continual source of amusement was that when ever you met anyone when you were on leave, they would say hello and then: "When are you going back?" Every soldier I knew said the same thing happened to them!

It was nice to be at home with my family and having so much to relate to them. The army had provided me with the necessary Ration Card(s) so that I was able to contribute my share of food during my leave period. After I had done the rounds of visiting grandparents, aunts and uncles and ex employers I found that I was becoming out of touch with civilian life. I was now part of a different culture and had grown used to the company of men in my own age group, who were all in the same situation, out of which a comradeship had developed even though I knew that this would to some extent be dismembered when I returned from leave. In the years to come I would learn and appreciate that this comradeship would be generated wherever I was moved to as long as I remained in the army, and that it was not the kind of relationship that could be duplicated in 'civvy street'.

So, after seven days leave, although I was sad to leave my family, mum, dad, brother Ken and sister Joan, I left Goole, of necessity, en route for Aldershot.

"I am now identified as a member of a famous Corps"

Brass cap badge worn on either forage cap or beret of 'best' battle dress, but not on denim work uniform. Forage caps were worn until we went overseas, when berets were adopted.
Photograph in Appendix K shows everyone, including platoon the officer, wearing forage caps.

Cloth shoulder flash (yellow letters on deep blue background), sewn to top each sleeve on best battle dress.
Divisional Insignia sewn under RASC flash. The yellow and blue colour bar was mounted under the Divisionsal Insignia with the yellow facing forwards.

For further examples of RASC insignia see Appendix C.

WORKING COMPANY

Travelling as a member of the Armed Forces in 1943 was not a problem. You had no need to purchase train tickets as you were issued with a Travel Warrant and transit across London from King's Cross to Waterloo was by army truck. The only problem you had was all the gear the army insisted you carry with you. Usual webbing with ammunition pouches attached, small pack, respirator, steel helmet, large pack and kit bag and don't forget your rifle! Also bear in mind that the trains are full of forces personnel most of them similarly burdened. Compartments full - corridors full - but all in a spirit of togetherness which may never be repeated.

My travels prior to joining the army had been limited to the north of the country and not so much of that! Blackpool was probably the furthest I had been in addition to Hull and the Yorkshire seaside resorts, and of course Cleethorpes! So it was with some surprise that, even in wartime, the country south of London looked so clean and tidy. Outside of London itself the absence of factory buildings did not go unnoticed and the cleanliness of the railway stations impressed, though this was obviously due to the rail system being electric rather than steam powered.

Aldershot is a small town in Hampshire having a population of about 35,000 in 1943. Civilian population that is! The military have had a presence in the town since God was a lad and I cannot guess at the military populace during the time I was there, but there was a lot of us about. If you can imagine a barracks that may hold maybe one thousand troops then multiply this by the number of different barracks that were spread around. Probably fifty could be a good guess. I don't know but the area covered was extremely extensive. Not walking country!

Transport at Aldershot station took me to Clayton Barracks about one and a half miles away, one of the nearer barracks! This was to be my home for as long as the army thought necessary as a member of B Platoon, 270 Company RASC (Command (Mixed) Transport), see photograph in Appendix K.

Our barracks comprised a number of two storey blocks each having a central door and stairway leading to two barrack rooms on each floor. Our platoon occupied the two rooms on the first floor each accommodating about twenty four men. The usual bunk beds in line ahead down each side of the room with a central chimney with a coal fire on each of two sides. The central core held the usual ablutions with gallons of unrationed hot water available. Each bed space had two wall mounted cupboards along with coat hooks under plus a proper rack for rifles. Each room was also provided with two tables and bench seats and all in all this was a comfortable billet.

Behind the blocks was a tarmac parade ground but more of that later. Across the public road in front of the barracks, (the road was only used for servicing the various barracks), was the Mess Hall and next to it the NAAFI Canteen. (Navy, Army and Air Force Institute). The Mess Hall could easily absorb one thousand men at one sitting and the canteen was just as large.

Whether I was an early or late comer I can't remember but I finished up with a top bunk on the left. The guy under me was called Corbett, his first name escapes me but he did become a good mate. A number of those who had been at Carlisle with me were here so I was among friends. Gear stowed and over for tea - walking in a smart and orderly manner. Later in the evening into the canteen for tea and buns.

The Company was organised in a manner common to all similar Companies in the RASC. It consisted of four platoons A B C and D plus a Workshops platoon which undertook monthly inspections of all vehicles plus repairs and repainting. Somewhere in territory totally unfamiliar to us peasants, there must have existed a Headquarters Platoon and a Company Commander and his minions but we saw little of these people with the exception of the Company Sergeant Major (can't remember his name even if I wished to) and a Captain Fuller who we shall meet later.

My platoon - B - was equipped with three ton Bedford General Purpose trucks - thirty three of them. The platoon also had a number of other vehicles - platoon officer's pick-up, fifteen hundredweight water tanker, fifteen hundredweight truck and

Bedford OYD 3 ton, 4 x 2

a three ton Bedford which on active service would serve as the cook's vehicle. The personnel of the platoon consisted of one lieutenant, two sergeants, three corporals, five lance corporals and forty drivers. We also possessed two motor cycles for NCO's use.

During my entire army service in the RASC I found that my horizons were limited to the platoon that I was in. I had very little knowledge of, or indeed interest in, the other platoons in the Company. This became particularly true when we eventually went overseas and operated more often than not as independent platoons. At Aldershot we knew that we were a platoon of young soldiers, both in terms of age and service, whilst the rest of the Company consisted of anything but youngsters. One of the platoons was equipped for troop carrying, with ex civilian buses suitably camouflage painted. (In 1943 specialised troop carrying vehicles had not yet arrived in our neck of the woods).

The best was yet to come! Certainly one platoon was operating horse drawn transport. Real horses and wagons. The troops involved seemed to be long serving men who had been in the army before war broke out. They also seemed to be excused a lot of things such as boots and gaiters and generally those elements of uniform which contributed to making them look like soldiers. (Men who had been medically regraded were excused some duties and the wearing of certain items of kit).

Some of the foregoing we were not to become aware of until later. Our immediate interest was what were we going to do?

Reveille was 06.00 hours and loud banging on the door was sufficient to rouse us. Wash, shave and so forth, dress and over for breakfast then back to barrack room and make up bed in usual manner with prescribed kit laid out on top of it.

Aldershot had one thing in common with the Infantry Training Centre, if you went anywhere as a group you marched, but at least for normal daily duties denims were the order of the day, no webbing or packs. March to MT (motor transport) Yard about a quarter of a mile away. This yard along with our barracks was situated on a high enough point for us to be able to look down on the rail line Aldershot to Waterloo. In times to come we would gaze down at trains which we knew would be taking some lucky blokes on leave or up to London on a week end pass, but for the present our interest lay in other directions.

We were each allocated a truck, a three ton Bedford. My vehicle was numbered B4 in addition to its normal army number. The yard had its complement of open fronted garages each complete with an inspection pit. Your truck had to be reversed into its allocated space without dismantling the cab door on the steel upright holding up the roof of the garage. The cab door was usually held open to assist reversing.

Enthusiasm was the order of the day, this was your truck and yours alone - no one else would get to drive it as long you stayed in this unit and you behaved yourself and looked after your vehicle. This meant that the army system of daily maintenance tasks had to be slavishly followed. The truck had to be kept clean and there was a shortage of car washes. Actually there were none! Hose pipes there were, I seem to recall, but there was a need to perform a lot of crawling over and under but it was worth it. We were to some degree still being trained. Lubrication by hand held grease guns had to be done, wheels had to be disassembled and re-tubed - the Bedford had split wheels in that after you had taken the wheel off the truck and deflated it, a further set of bolts was undone which released the wheel into halves enabling removal of the tyre and tube. Failure to deflate the tyre before undoing these wheel bolts resulted in the half wheel decapitating the stupid clown with the spanner in his hand! It had happened we were told, so don't forget!

Once a month your truck had to undergo two inspections, at two weekly intervals, one by your section NCO and the other by Company Workshops. If you had not been carrying out your daily maintenance practice then you laid yourself open to discipline in the form or a reprimand or more seriously being put on a charge. This latter meant that you had to appear before your platoon officer and if found guilty then punishment in the form of a number of days confined to barracks or 'jankers' as it was known, doing cook house duties, could be forthcoming. Our enthusiasm at this time was such that there appeared to be little danger that such events would be precipitated. We were all very keen to retain our status as competent drivers.

After a few days spent in the MT yard we were allocated duties which varied from picking up bread from the RASC bakery and delivering to various barracks in the area or parking at the railway station and, as troops came off trains, taking them to their various units. We very rapidly began to find our way around Aldershot and the surrounding district. Time was allowed during each week to perform vehicle maintenance and we soon settled down to an ordered existence.

The countryside around Aldershot was somewhat different to that surrounding Goole in that we were on the northern edge of the North Downs. It presented (and still does) a very pleasant landscape, a noticeable lack of heavy industry with large areas of heath land not given over to agriculture. As I remember, roads were good and the Guildford Bypass astounded me as it was the first dual carriageway road I had ever seen - miles of concrete.

We also indulged in other activities. As I have recorded we were a young platoon in a Company of older troops and our platoon officer Lieutenant Skellam, a super guy, liked to show us off and would have us do rifle drill and a bit of proper military marching. We were also not allowed to forget that we were still soldiers and it was essential that we stayed fit and towards this end we undertook route marches - mostly on Saturday mornings over a distance of perhaps 8 or 9 miles come rain or shine. We also practised map reading and would drive out of Aldershot, two drivers to a truck, to some remote spot where our officer had led us and where we would then be given a six figure map reference, different for each truck, and our task being to find our way there and then return to barracks to report exactly where it was we had been.

It was also our lot to do guard duties. Three differing duties existed, the most arduous being the Main Gate Guard which, although there was no actual gate as such, was carried out at the Guard Room located at the approach to the Barracks from the town. This was the real thing - full field kit (webbing, respirator, small pack, ammo pouches, steel helmet - all newly blancoed and polished brasses), and rifle complete with military pacing up and down and associated foot stamping.

The other two duties were not quite so disciplined, the MT Yard one involved touring round the yard with rifle slung over shoulder guarding against intruders. The last duty was performed down at the Company Workshops where there was a gate of sorts and a sentry hut to stand in during your stint outside.

All guards were manned by six men, two actually being 'on guard' at any one time, while the remaining four rested or slept (not undressed). The system was common to all units in the army - two hours 'on guard' and four hours 'off' over a twelve hour period. The Main Gate Guard and the MT Yard one rested in the Main Gatehouse whilst the lower yard guard had a hut at their disposal.

As some of these duties were shared with other units I seem to recall that your turn for duty came around every eight days or so but I can't be sure. One thing is for sure though and that is there was no relief from normal day time duties after you had been on guard. No following morning lie in!

I think it must have been during September that mum and dad came to Aldershot to see me. They only stayed one night and I remember when they went home I got a pass and escorted them to London on their journey home. I do know that after I had seen them off I went to the Odeon, Leicester Square and had an upper circle seat, can't recall the film though.

I am sure that I went on leave during late October but cannot verify this as the entry in my Soldier's Service and Pay Book, to give it it's full title, otherwise A.B.64, which I still have, contains some date errors. This book is endorsed as a 'Certified True Copy' which confirms that my original book was lost or replaced for some reason and the act of copying was not as true as stated.

Almost before we realised, Christmas was upon us and Christmas Dinner was something else. Army tradition is that on this one special day of the year, officers serve dinner to other ranks and this they did. I don't think we had turkey but it doesn't matter, it was the novelty that made it for us.

As part of the celebrations over Christmas our platoon officer suggested that some of us might put on some form of entertainment for the rest of the platoon. We had a piano player and I suppose someone could juggle. Myself and a guy called Fullerton decided to do a sketch. Now Fullerton was a bit of a wild card in that some time earlier in the MT Yard he had been verbally laying into a little guy - I think it was a kid called Cummings, but no matter, I was witness to this and although I did not consider myself a violent individual I squared up to him and told him to tackle somebody his own size! Believe it or not he simply backed down and from that day we were bosom mates or nearly so. (He actually insisted on standing near to me when we had the platoon photograph taken). Back to the sketch. It was very brief and the only thing that I can remember with any accuracy is that we did a take off of an American commercial, thus:

Me: (in pseudo American accent): "Ladies does your husband come home and say"

Fullerton: (in real yob voice): "What - meatballs again "

Me: "Ladies - get Grant's Gritty Granules for Grander Gravy"

It obviously carried on but that's all I recall, but it went down well.

If there was one thing that I detested about Aldershot it was the 'bullshine' or in old soldier's parlance 'spit and polish'. It was a peacetime Garrison Town and many of the peacetime traditions and attitudes prevailed. As part of South East Command it was notorious for the presence within the Command Structure of a Colonel Gates who became infamous for his love of 'bull'. Stories of coal stocks being painted white were rife but turned out to be true! He allegedly introduced a form of greeting between officers where one party would say: "Hi-de-hi" and the other party would respond with: "Hi-de-ho"! Oh what a lovely war!

We had our own private version of Colonel Gates by way of Captain Fuller who was the Company Adjutant. Before we went about our daily driving routine we were required to drive down to the MT Yard where Workshops was located. He would inspect us and our trucks and one of his favourite habits was to run his finger along the top of the chassis under the load body. On finding that it came away dirtier than when it went in, he would class the vehicle as being filthy and order that it should be brought back at, say 18.00 hours for a further check. There was no answer to this but you returned at the specified time after stopping off some two hundred yards short of the yard and wiped dust off the chassis.

One other wonderful effort demonstrated that some people in authority were on a different planet to the rest of us was the morning parade, which in itself was part and parcel of normal army practice and was in effect a roll call in that each platoon officer or NCO would report in turn that his lot were: "All present and correct, sir" at the appropriate moment. Now, in peacetime it appeared that on some ceremonial occasions, drill movements, such as coming to attention and sloping arms (putting your rifle on your shoulder, in simple terms), would be carried out to the sound of a sequence of beats on a drum. So, this is what we found ourselves doing! In 1943? All this led credence to the adage 'if it moves salute it, if it doesn't, paint it'.

At some time that I cannot give a precise date to, I suffered from some skin infection which necessitated spending ten days or so in an isolation unit, along with two or three other guys. All meals were brought to us and we lived the life of Reilly for the time we were there, but we were still pleased to be discharged and back to normal duties including a new issue of blankets to negate possible reinfection.

After Christmas we settled down to a regular routine of driving and vehicle maintenance as well as weekly drill to ensure we retained our military image, plus most weeks a route march come rain or shine. Guard duties were not forgotten as was the odd Sunday morning Church Parade in the Garrison Church. On a normal Sunday we bought our newspapers from a van on the road outside of our barrack room and settled down for a quiet Sunday morning. An unwritten army rule was that on Sunday afternoons you were either in bed or out of barracks.

As the year progressed to spring it became obvious that momentous events were about to unfold. Increasingly we gazed skyward when working in the MT Yard to see hundreds of American Flying Fortresses and Liberators on their way to bomb Germany. We were also amazed witnesses to the test flights of the first jet powered aircraft flying from Farnborough, although we didn't know what they were at the time.

We did manage to enjoy some leisure activities, mostly at weekends, as during the week by the time we came off duty, had washed and eaten, it was easier to go over to the canteen than dress up to go out. At the weekend we had the choice of cinemas in Aldershot which was a bit of a non starter as several thousand off duty troops had the same idea. I was not a pub man so if we went into town it usually ended with just walking about. Our favourite was to go out to the nearby village of Fleet and take a rowing boat or canoe out on the canal. Many a happy hour or three was spent there.

The high spot of this time was when I was detailed to go to Bordon Camp (in Hampshire), which was where a large supplies depot was located to pick up a load of large pulleys and then deliver them to some dock in Hull. I was accompanied by a Lance Corporal Haslar and we took it in turns to do the driving. We had only driven about 30 miles or so and we suffered a rear wheel puncture and it was then, when we had to jack the truck up, that we realised that it was severely overloaded. A lot of trouble later we had managed to change the wheel and resume our journey.

L/Cpl Haslar knew that I came from Goole and we obviously had to pass there to get to Hull. He suggested that he should drop me off at home while he carried on to Hull and then pick me up on the way back to Aldershot. In Hull he had to wait to be unloaded and also get the puncture repaired and it was two days before he appeared at 88 Marshfield Avenue, Goole, so I had managed nearly three days unofficial leave. He was a great guy and although he was much older than me he remained a good mate until I left Aldershot.

The tremendous news that D-Day 6th of June had arrived came to us over the radio in the Mess while we were having our breakfast. The previous late evening had made us aware that something was afoot as large numbers of aircraft towing gliders had passed overhead. A short time after this our platoon moved to Plumpton Racecourse near Lewes in Sussex from where we would operate for the foreseeable future.

Plumpton was (and still is I suppose) a small course - over the sticks - with a grandstand to match under which our cooks set up their gear. Our Mess was the steps of the stand itself - it was not equipped with any seating. We slept on bunk beds which had been installed in the Tote building, quite comfortable and better for not having to make up our beds in the usual Aldershot manner. The distance round the course was two and a half miles and a number of us did run round it more than once, usually before breakfast, missing out the fences of course.

Our task was to convey troops down to Newhaven where they embarked on Landing Craft bound for the beaches at Arromanches in Normandy, France. We had to collect them from special camps in the area in which they had been held for some time prior to 6th June. These camps were spread all over the southern counties of England and the ones we collected from were identified by the code letter 'J', mostly they were located in wooded areas to camouflage them from observation from the air, and once the troops were inside, the camps were sealed and no contact either from or with the outside world was permitted.

Troops and supplies being loaded onto Landing Craft bound for the beaches in Normandy

We would drive into a camp, drop the tailboard and twenty or so men would climb in, tailboard up and off we drove. As we passed through villages on the way to Newhaven the troops would throw out all their English money to civilians who had become accustomed to this generosity which, however, never came our way. Still a lot of the troops would not survive to spend it even if they had hung on to their cash so I suppose we could count ourselves lucky that we were not boarding along with them.

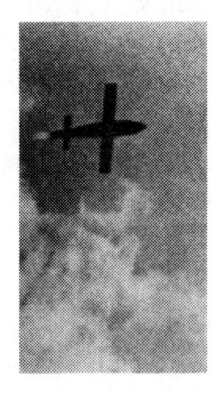

There was no set pattern to our trips to Newhaven and we had to be ready to go at a few minutes notice. A lot of our waiting time at the race course was spent lying on top of the truck canopies watching Doodlebugs (V1s - see picture left) flying over on their way to London. Not all of them made it and we saw a fair number shot down by fighters - usually Hawker Tempests as they were possibly the only plane capable of matching the V1's speed of 400 mph or so. More often than not when the fighter got in a good shot the 'bug' would explode in mid air.

We did manage a few visits to Brighton although the sea front was barbed wire country and the beach not accessible, with buildings along the front devoid of civilian inhabitants as they had been since 1940 when the south coast and other areas had been prepared for the expected German invasion. (Operation Sea Lion). One venue I do recall was The Dome which was a superb dance venue having a great band and a ceiling full of twinkling lights. After this I never again succeeded in reconciling myself to a Saturday night in Goole Market Hall.

July saw us back in Aldershot but routine as we had previously known it was at an end and we undertook longer journeys and moving in convoy. Convoy driving leaves a lot to be desired, the theory is fine in that the lead vehicle, usually the officer's pickup, motors at a steady 30 to 35 miles per hour which seems to imply that the rest of the thirty odd vehicles follow slavishly at that speed. Don't you believe it! The effect can be best compared to the action of a concertina in that as the front vehicles meet with some delaying factor the rest of the convoy closes up reducing the usual 60 yards between vehicles to something much less. As the front vehicle clears whatever brought about the delay and starts to speed up each following truck suffers some delay in getting under way. The further down the line you are the compounding effect necessitates the need to speed up more and more to catch the truck in front.

The effect of this is that the last truck ends up doing the maximum that the vehicle is capable of until catch up is achieved and then the whole process is repeated time after time throughout the entire journey. Thus the road length of the convoy is forever shortening and lengthening. At night this can be a nightmare as headlights are not used and you follow the vehicle in front eyes glued to the light illuminating the white painted rear axle differential of the vehicle in front of you. Usually we were accompanied by a couple of dispatch riders on motor cycles who would ride ahead if we were driving through a built up area and stop at junctions or cross roads to signal the direction to be followed. If the convoy stops during a night drive and you relax for a few moments, before you realise it you are asleep and awake suddenly to see that the vehicle in front isn't there any more! Panic! Saved by the dispatch rider who suddenly appears and indicates to follow him. I remember this happening to me somewhere near Honiton in Devon and that's all I can recall about that particular trip.

We did one delivery to the Rolls Royce factory in Derby of bogie wheels for tanks. Part of the journey took us through Leicester and five or six of us got detached from the main body and stopped off when we saw a night watchman, (yes, they really did exist once upon a time), outside of some building site, to enquire if he had seen a convoy go by, yes. he had, about five minutes ago. It only took us that long to arrive back at his site to realise that we were chasing ourselves. Perhaps I should mention at this point that RASC drivers were not permitted to load, or unload, their own vehicles, this task being performed by factory personnel when loading or unloading from a civilian installation, and by men of the Pioneer Corps at military locations.

During August it all became rather frenetic - it was the time of the Falaise Gap battle in Normandy and the allied armies were breaking out of the slow grinding conflict that they had been involved in since D-Day. Our forces urgently needed fuel and our company, along with others, was needed to transport it from fuel dumps to an airfield near Swindon in Wiltshire where it was loaded into Douglas Dakotas (DC3s) flying it to France. I do remember that we were given more than one issue of Benzedrine tablets to help us stay awake.

Aldershot and 'home' again by the beginning of September. I took advantage of a weekend pass to join a guy called John Ryan to go to his parent's home in London and was there when we saw the armada of gliders and towing planes heading for what we later found out was operation

John Ryan, his father and I in London, September 1944

Market Garden during the weekend of the 16/17th September - the attempt to secure three bridges across the rivers Rhine and Waal in Holland. This as we all know only partially succeeded and the story of the 'Bridge too Far' at Arnhem is well documented.

A few days later on the 19th of September, we said goodbye to Aldershot and entrained as a platoon for Bradford. We were transported to a street near to Clayton Park where a number of houses were being used by the army as temporary accommodation for us. Slept on the floor on a palliasse, (like a six foot long sack), filled with straw, along with two or three blankets.

Foden DG6/12 10 ton, 6 x 4

The following morning we were marched to Clayton Park where thirty odd Foden 10 ton trucks were parked. I was allocated a vehicle and Sid Pritchard was nominated as my co-driver. It is only now that I realise that our platoon must have been nearly doubled in size to permit the double manning of each truck but I don't know where the other personnel came from. Events were moving rapidly and when this happens you tend to lose track of event/time relationships.

We spent the following days checking over the trucks, 'getting to know them' as it were. During this time I did manage to get a day pass to go to Goole taking with me John Ryan and Sid Pritchard. I could not tell my parents what we were going to be doing or where we would be doing it as I didn't know myself.

We were now C Platoon, part of 917 Company RASC, a new company formed to meet the urgent need to move supplies from the beaches in Normandy through France and into Belgium as the port of Antwerp was not yet operational. (We did not know this at the time).

On the 25th we set out for London on the way to London Docks. The progress of the convoy, which must have been composed of over 130 vehicles, was very slow and at the end of the first day's driving we staged somewhere near to Leicester. The following day saw our arrival in Epping Forest where we staged overnight. I seem to recall that this area was 'secure' in that we were not allowed out nor anyone in! It was here that we were issued with 200 French Francs - so we now knew where we were heading.

I seem to recall that we were also given some literature which sought to put us in the picture relative to certain misfortunes which could overtake young soldiers in France through contact with the fair sex. I still have a mostly intact French and German phrase book issued to the Canadian Army which must have come into my possession at this time. (See right). A small booklet explaining the controls of German vehicles was also issued to us and this is also still in my possession.

The drive down had been an education in that the Foden was no Bedford three tonner. The truck was six wheeled with two rear driven axles, nearly thirty feet long and of 'cab over' design, that is the engine was in the cab and didn't you know it! Top speed was 32 miles an hour, the power unit was a Gardner 6LW six cylinder diesel. Brakes were hydraulic with no vacuum or air assistance and power steering was unheard of never mind being fitted. The gear change, through a two and a half foot long lever, was so slow that you could light a cigarette (I was told as I didn't at this time smoke), waiting for the revs to drop back before the next gear could be engaged. It was a very difficult truck to drive.

The last two nights we had experienced sleeping in the back of the trucks which turned out to be a foretaste of things to come. On the 28th therefore, we drove to the Royal Albert Dock where our trucks were loaded with cased food and then driven out to the dock side and with nets under the wheels craned up and into the ship's hold. Our vessel was the Sampep an American built 'Liberty' ship of some ten thousand tons. (See picture on next page). The first lot of vehicles were lowered down into the bottom of the hold and wheels chocked against movement after which decking was put in place over them and a second layer of vehicles loaded onto that.

Some space in one of the holds was given over to sleeping areas - no beds - but hammocks, which when we got out to sea swung in unison and in so doing reduced to some degree the sick inducing roll and pitch of the ship.

We sailed on the 29th and received a good send off by the Ford factory at Dagenham as we passed down river heading towards the English Channel and, eventually, Normandy where we would become part of the British Liberation Army.

Example of an American built 'Liberty' ship - some 10,000 tons

RASC badge

The card showing the Cap Badge etc. was hand painted by a German POW for the price of a few cigarettes.
The badge itself was shiny brass (not worn on berets whilst on active service overseas).
The inscription - 'Honi soit qui mal y pense' - (French) means (I think), 'Banned be the one who thinks evil'.
The shield to the right was the insignia of the 21st Army Group - a light blue cross on a red background.
The shield to the left was that of the 2nd Army - a gold sword on a light blue cross on a white background.
The diamond at the top - a white arrow on a red background - is the insignia of the 1st Corps.

CHAPTER 3
1944 - 1945
MONTY'S LIBERATION ARMY

The formation of the new 917 Company at Bradford in September 1944 did, at that point in time, make me as a member of that company, a part of Montgomery's 21st Army Group. On the 6th of June 1944 - 'D-Day' - the Allied Forces landed on the beaches of Normandy. The objectives of this Army of Liberation were twofold, initially to free the people of mainland Europe from German occupation, which they had suffered for four long years, and secondly to destroy the armed forces of Germany. General Montgomery's Army Group contained British, Canadian and American troops for the initial assault under the overall command of the American General Eisenhower. Following arduous weeks of combat in the Bocage countryside of Normandy, the allies eventually broke out and stormed across northern France and into Belgium. The capture of Paris was achieved by the Americans during late August, followed by the British entry into Brussels during the first week of September. With supply lines stretching back to the beaches of Normandy (the port of Antwerp was not yet usable), additional transport was desperately needed. Our unit was to fill some of this need.

This chapter covers the ensuing year and a half I spent driving the length and breadth of Northern France, Belgium, Holland and north western Germany.

ON THE ROAD

We arrived off Arromanches on the coast of France during the night of the 30th of September 1944 and disembarking of troops started whilst it was still dark. This involved climbing down scrambling nets, hung over the ship's side, into Landing Craft lying alongside. I was snug in my hammock at this time so knew nothing about the events taking place on deck. We did hear later that one poor sod had fallen overboard to land in the water between the ship and the Landing Craft. He was not recovered.

Probably because of the number and size of our company's vehicles we had been loaded on to more than one ship. The effect of this was that there were other units aboard with us and a number of replacement scout cars destined for the Reconnaissance Corps. Some of our drivers were assigned the job of driving these to the inland vehicle park once they had been unloaded.

Scrambling down the nets into pitching and rolling Landing Craft was no easy matter especially when wearing full battle kit as one poor soldier found out - see text.

I must confess to being hazy about the precise sequence of events which followed. I do remember that the weather was anything but fair with low clouds and a very choppy sea. We were anchored one to two miles off shore inside of the artificial breakwater formed by a series of huge concrete caissons which had been towed across the English Channel and then sunk at intervals of 400 yards (I learned much later), to form the breakwater. Outside of these were a number of concrete filled old ships (known as 'Gooseberries', see Appendix K) which had been sunk in shallow water to the seaward side of the caissons. A number of these caissons had been constructed in the docks in my home town of Goole.

Large ships anchored inside of the breakwater off loaded into either Tank or Infantry Landing Craft, which then discharged at one of a series of floating piers linked together and with the shore, and then on to waiting transport. Small coastal vessels moored alongside the piers to discharge direct into trucks. Vehicles were driven off Landing Craft at prepared points on the beach. (See left)

The whole of this construction was the famous Mulberry Harbour, one of two which had been towed across the English Channel to Normandy within a few days after D-Day, the second one located off the American beaches had, unfortunately, suffered irreparable damage during a subsequent storm.

(See Mulberry feature on the following pages and Appendix K).

As our trucks were stowed at the lowest level in the hold, we had to wait to be virtually the last to be disembarked and as our turn drew nearer, the weather grew worse until the point was reached when unloading was suspended. As there was now a reduced number of us on board we abandoned the hammocks and making use of every blanket in sight made up our beds on the deck. For the next few days we waited for some improvement in the weather lounging about in a positively non military manner. There was no shortage of food on board and a total absence of long queues for it. We ventured down into the vehicle storage space and that was where I met Pete Pritchard for the first time. He was in another platoon and after this first meeting I didn't see him again until March 1945 when I transferred from C to B Platoon, but more about him later.

The time must have arrived when someone decided that our ship was needed elsewhere and unloading of the remaining vehicles and troops should recommence. In due course an American Tank Landing Craft appeared alongside and we now became soldiers again in that we were ordered what we were to do. Three of us, myself, John (Richie) Richardson and another were detailed (a good army word) to board the Landing Craft.

MULBERRY HARBOUR 1

Port Winston, the Mulberry Harbour at Arromanches for the British, where men and material continued to pour ashore in July-August 1944. The American harbour at St. Laurent-sur-Mer off Omaha beach never recovered from a big storm and was abandoned in favour of the British harbour.

Strategists on both sides had long appreciated the crucial importance of safe harbours for subsequent waves of troops and supplies. For their part, the Germans concentrated their defences around such ports, placing them almost beyond capture. The Allied solution: to create new harbours! These artificial harbours - code-named Mulberries - would accommodate deep draught ships by enclosing sheltered water with a depth of a least nine metres. This meant the structures would need to be at least 18 metres high.

By 21 days after D-Day, the Mulberry Harbours would have to be ready to receive 12,000 tons of cargo and 2,500 vehicles a day - and have a minimum life span of 90 days. The final concept was described by Churchill as "majestic". The largest of the sections was 61 metres long, 18.3 metres high and weighed more than 6,000 tons.

Altogether, 213 sections were built, using more than one million tons of reinforced concrete and 70,000 tons of steel reinforcement. All around the British coast, dozens of construction companies and 20,000 workers rushed to finish the task in only seven months.

MULBERRY HARBOUR 2

Right: Taking casualties to awaiting ships, Austin ambulances on a 'Whale' floating pier of the Mulberry Harbour near Arromanches, Gold Beach.

Below: The final link to the land: a British Sherman tank rolls ashore along a floating roadway at Arromanches.

Picture showing an excellent view down one of the Whale floating piers looking towards the beach.

MULBERRY HARBOUR 3

A "Phoenix" caisson, major component of 'Mulberry' prefabricated harbour on tow across the Channel (note the A.A.A. on top). Some 150 caissons were built, ranging from 10 of 1,672 tons (the smallest) to 60 of 6,044 tons. The remains of the great caissons can still be seen today.

What the Germans are saying

In Nazi propaganda broadcasts to Britain, William Joyce ('Lord Haw Haw') said of the Mulberry Harbour project: "We know what you're doing with those caissons. You intend to sink them off the coast when the attack takes place... We'll save you the trouble and sink the caissons before you arrive."

Caissons were giant concrete structures manufactured in creeks and inlets around Britain, including Lee-on-Solent near Portsmouth (below), before being towed to assembly points on the South Coast. One such structure was also built at the author's home town of Goole.

MULBERRY HARBOUR 4

A Bedford truck rolls ashore from a US landing ship.

Supplies are unloaded at one of Port Winston's Whale floating piers.

RASC drivers hang around while their lorries are loaded.

The piers that formed part of the Mulberry Harbour offered safe berthing for ships. They stood on steel legs which could be adjusted to allow for the tide.

ON THE BEACH

Columns of trucks of all types arrive on the beaches from Landing Craft at specially prepared points at the waters edge. The shear scale of the operation can be seen by the vast number of ships at anchor in the pictures here, which only show a small part of the operation.
Note the barrage balloons to ward off attack from dive bombers.

RASC   Page 69   Chapter 3 1944 - 1945

Now this warrants some explanation. The ship was fairly stable, probably rolling very slightly, but the Landing Craft was rising on the swell some ten to fifteen feet and to get on to the craft the method adopted was to go so far down a Jacob's Ladder, which was made of two lengths of thick rope with wooden slats at intervals, then on to the Landing Craft. As I got so far down, the craft below me rose and momentarily an American sailor appeared alongside and shouted: "Next time I appear bud, let go the ladder and step off on to this platform." Now so far as I can recall this platform was about two feet square, but before I had time to digest this information he reappeared alongside of me and I dutifully stepped(?) on to his platform, he grabbed hold of me as the craft went down and the Jacob's Ladder seemed to accelerate upward at a high rate of knots (seafaring term).

I was bundled down on to the cargo deck of the Landing Craft which was open at both ends and was awash each time the craft's bow dipped, which it was doing quite often. The other two followed me down and we awaited the next event with some anxiety. As we gazed upwards a Foden truck appeared suspended from one of the ship's derricks, it descended slowly towards us swinging gently from side to side. We grabbed hold of the ropes dangling from it and, following shouted instructions from somewhere on high, looped them through rings set in the deck to steady the truck as it was deposited on the deck with a dull thud. This truck belonged to the unnamed member of our trio and we awaited the unloading of the two belonging to Richie and me.

Meanwhile the Landing Craft was rolling and pitching and each time it did so it crashed against the ship's hull. Since coming aboard we had seen nothing of the crew but somewhere someone had made a decision - we were heading for the shore. We did not land on a floating pier but directly onto the beach on to a prepared area where the truck could be driven off.

A Bedford landing straight onto the beach

At last, on October 3rd, we were on foreign soil! But there was a snag! There we were, three men in one truck and with one man's kit. Primarily this means that we had between us four blankets, one set of mess tins, one each of a knife, fork and spoon, and one enamelled mug. Forget things like razors and towels. Our own kit was safe in our own trucks on board the ship. We were instructed to drive off the beach to the top of a muddy slope and eventually to a vehicle park where we were to stay until the rest of our trucks were unloaded.

Adjacent to the park were the usual facilities - mess, ablutions and canteen (Red Shield - Salvation Army), all under canvas and with barbed wire and signs saying - 'Achtung Minen' (beware of mines) all over the place. Here we stayed for the next three or four days with Richie and me trudging down to the beach every day to see if unloading had recommenced. The one uplifting thing that I remember about the track down to the beach was a Royal Engineer's structure with a swinging sign outside picturing a downward pointing female breast and titled 'The Swinging Tit'. I kid you not! I think it must have been a canteen for sole use of the engineers who were responsible for the maintenance of Mulberry.

During this time the weather was, to put it mildly, inclement, and sleeping in the back of a truck loaded with sacks of potatoes with one blanket wrapped round you, was not what could be called comfortable. However, it could have been much worse as those who had stormed up the beach before us had experienced. We were lucky that we always had a roof over our heads. I think I must have written home from here but I would not have been able to say where we were.

Maybe we didn't realise it at the time but 917 Company was part of the British 2nd Army within the 21st Army Group, commanded by General Bernard Montgomery. At this time the British forces were into Belgium having captured Brussels on the 3rd of September and were advancing into Holland. The port of Antwerp had been captured on the 5th of September but was not usable as a supplying port, nor would it be for a while. There was, therefore, an urgent need for transport units to move munitions and other supplies from the supply dumps back in Normandy up to the forward areas. This was why our Company had been formed so rapidly and why we were here. All vehicles carried the five pointed white D-Day star painted on cab doors and tops.

D-Day star

Eventually our remaining vehicles were unloaded and arrived in our parking area. We then proceeded further inland into another muddy field where we sorted ourselves out and prepared to make up a convoy. Normally a convoy would consist of the 38 vehicles belonging to a platoon. This convoy was, however, made up of vehicles from different platoons, as had previous ones been, in order to clear the parking area as vehicles came off the ships. We would regroup to our own platoons a few days later. All convoys were organised by the Command structure of the RASC - movement orders laid down timing, routes and distances to be covered each day. Staging points were determined and not left to the individual unit to decide. The purpose of these regulations was to keep distance between the numerous convoys running to and fro on the main routes through France into Belgium. Command check points existed along the routes where the officer in charge of a convoy had to report, and should the route ahead having become congested or blocked, then his convoy had to halt and wait until the OK came to continue. There were also occasions where a convoy could be ordered to speed up if it was in danger of being caught by a following one.

Our first experience of overseas driving began as we left our muddy field at 14.00 hours on Monday the 9th of October. We were all given a route card listing the towns we were going to drive through with an end destination of some Fort, which meant nothing to me either then or now. Later on as we progressed along the route it became clear that we were heading for Brussels and this Fort was actually in the city. The immediate concern however, was to come to terms with driving on the 'wrong' side of the road whilst trying to avoid the numerous holes in the road surface. In fact within a matter of hours we suffered a casualty where one driver didn't miss a pot hole and went off the road causing him to break an ankle. No idea what they called him, didn't matter anyway as we never saw him again - home on the next boat as it were!

Normandy had suffered enormously from the battles which had raged here since June and village after village lay in ruins. One place I especially remember was called Tilly-sur-Seulles where the devastation was so complete that the road through had been created by simply bulldozing a way

Tilly-sur-Seulles, southeast of Caen, was devastated by tank battles

RASC   Chapter 3 1944 - 1945

through the rubble. Villers Bocage was another wasteland of rubble which had once been a working village. The town of Caen was almost unrecognisable as it had been very heavily bombed as a prelude to successive attacks. As we had set off after midday, we only drove 45 miles as far as a town called Lisieux where we parked up for the night, at regulation intervals of some thirty yards, which meant that as my truck was number C32 and the cook's truck was at the head of the convoy (where the officer was), I had a walk of some nine hundred yards for supper.

CAEN

Below: When Caen finally fell on July 9th, much of the old city was in a state of ruin. Hardly a building was left untouched by the shelling, and many of the civilian population had died. That the French continued to welcome the Allied liberation despite the destruction wrought by it, is an indication of the extent of their loathing of German occupation.

CAEN

Right: An aerial view of Caen shows the extent of its devastation

LISIEUX

An armoured column of the British 2nd Army in Lisieux, east of Caen, shows how the devastation had miraculously passed by the beautiful and recently built Basilica of St. Therese on the hill.

The mud which plagued the advancing Allied Army is also much in evidence.

VILLERS BOCAGE

An aerial view of Villers Bocage conveys the full extent of its devastation after the RAF had, in their first daylight raid over Normandy, dropped 1,100 tons of bombs on June 30th.

    Villers Bocage was instrumental in Montgomerys plan to capture Caen. It all depended on the 7th Armoured holding, and keeping, the road junction at Villers Bocage and the nearby high ground. It was here though that the British met Lieutenant Michael Wittmann of the Waffen-SS, Germanys most formidable tank fighter of WWII, who held the record for the most enemy tanks destroyed on either side. He was in command of just 4 or 5 German Tiger tanks and with a series of surprise attacks managed to inflict many casualties on the somewhat confused British forces. When Wittmann was eventually beaten, the British had lost twenty seven tanks. Wittmann and his tank crew escaped unharmed.
    Wittmann's actions had stalled the whole advance of 7th Armoured Division, which could otherwise have driven almost unopposed to the outskirts of Caen. The Germans later recaptured Villers Bocage on June 14th and forced the British to pull back and rethink their actions. It would not be until August 5th when the town was finally secured by the British 50th Division.

The cooking equipment was simple but effective. Utensils consisted of a number of 'billy cans' which were stainless steel rectangular containers about 24 inches long, 12 inches wide and 15 inches deep. These sat in a row on supports with space underneath allowing for a petrol fuelled flame, under pressure, to shoot under them and so heat whatever they contained. One was always full of tea brewed from a mixture of tea, sugar and powdered milk, others contained a meat and vegetable stew, out of tins, and if my memory serves me correctly, rice pudding, also out of tins.

Meat and vegetable stew and more often than not rice pudding to follow became the order of the day. There may have been some variation but if there was it can't have been that significant. Our rations were based on 'Compo Packs' (I think), where one pack would feed one man for seven days or seven men for one day and included seven cigarettes per man per day.

British mess tins, 'eating irons', field cooker, and emergency ration packs - including cigarettes, matches, and 'bumf' (toilet paper).

After eating we were allowed to go into town for a few hours which offered the opportunity to mix with the local populace. Not dramatically exciting but at least it was the feel of being in a foreign country and for most, if not all of us, our first visit abroad.

Our sleeping arrangements in the truck were extremely simple but effective. They needed to be so because it was starting to be somewhat cold at night. Our bed consisted of folded camouflage nets, (usually called scrim nets), folded to the size of a bed and overlaid with the truck's bonnet rug plus a couple of blankets. Against King's Regulations we slept two to a bed but as we never undressed it didn't seem to offer any unforeseen hazards. Covering us were the rest of our blankets as well as our great coats. On this first journey we had to sleep on top of the load but on subsequent trips we organised the loading of the truck to ensure that space was retained at the front of the load, which we accessed from the front of the body via the space behind the cab where the spare wheel and other

The Foden 10 ton truck became our home as well as work place.

accessories were kept. This system of loading proved beneficial in that it concentrated weight more to the rear of the vehicle which made steering easier. It also enabled us to move to and from our sleeping compartment whilst we were on the move.

After our night out in Lisieux, we groped our way back to our trucks and fell into bed as we were, apart from taking our boots off. The wake up call the following morning may have come from one of the NCOs doing the rounds or maybe by word of mouth being passed from vehicle to vehicle, but whichever we stumbled up to the head of the convoy for breakfast which consisted of porridge followed by American tinned bacon, which was heated in the cans, in hot water in a billy can, and then out of the can into your mess tin. The bacon was very fatty and was still wrapped in the greaseproof paper in which it had been in the can. Juggling two mess tins and a mug of tea was an art which we acquired very rapidly. The big decision was whether to eat there and then or take it all back to your truck, - eat it now whilst it was still hot or, if your truck (like mine) was half a mile away, eat it cold when you arrived. If it was raining it was a little trickier as uncovered mess tins did tend to fill with water, although this could to some degree be avoided by inverting the tin containing porridge over your bacon. The porridge was guaranteed not to fall out. Think about it! I resolved this dilemma by not having porridge.

Breakfast over - time for ablutions. The nearest ditch solved some of the problems but washing and shaving? The water in the platoon water wagon was for cooking and drinking - definitely not for washing. The only water available was in the truck's radiator which fortunately did not have anti freeze in. Drain some off into your mess tin and that became your wash basin and then your shaving mug! Return it to the radiator when finished. If you desired hot water then start up the truck and run it for a few minutes. This became our ablution practice for the next few weeks.

The following two days we covered a total of 297 miles either passing through places, or seeing signposts to them, which evoked thoughts of the 1914-18 war. Cambrai, Mons, Verdun and Amiens were just a few of the places where heavy fighting had taken place. We staged for the night at the end of the first day at Doullons near Amiens after having driven 160 miles. The nearer we got to our destination which we now knew was to be Brussels, the more we drove along the famous Belgian block paved roads which made for less than a comfortable ride.

Observation of the various signs which we had seen on our journey, made us aware that we had travelled along a specific route reserved for convoys such as ours and our route number was designated as either the 230 or 240. I seem to recall that these two routes used the same roads for part of their length with other parts being one or the other. There was also a difference if you were driving to or from Belgium in that the route number would be for example '230 up' going to Brussels and '230 down' on the return journey into France. This was all part of the convoy management system.

Part of a huge column of trucks that formed the convoys as described in the text.

The only stops we made during the day were those necessary for our platoon officer to report in to the RASC check points along the route, as well as a short halt for a midday 'brew up' and a minuscule meal of biscuits, pat of butter and a spoonful of jam. The biscuits were not what you may imagine biscuits to be, these were as hard as - well they were bloody hard and took a while to eat. We didn't know then but these were to substitute for bread until after Christmas!

As we were taking it in turns - mornings or afternoons to drive, I spent half of my time as a passenger and was able to observe the countryside we passed through. In Belgium, I was particularly struck by the designs of some houses and the use of yellow bricks which were smaller than the ones used at home. Between Normandy and Belgium, the country in north eastern France - the Somme - I didn't find particularly attractive, lots of industrial sprawl.

So it was that after 342 miles we found ourselves in Brussels, capital city of Belgium, after two and a half days travel, to off load at Fort 'whatever it was called'. We had driven for about ten hours each day including a short meal stop at midday, covering an average 150 or so miles a day at an average speed of about 15 miles an hour. It should be remembered that the roads were full of traffic, both ways, and that numerous villages and towns had to be negotiated. We parked in close order along a road outside and gathered for a good 'get together' to exchange experiences, don't forget it was all very new and different. We must have been partially off loaded that evening and completed the following morning when we took to the road again and headed back towards France, arriving at our overnight staging point 18 miles north of Amiens after 136 miles. This was a small village, Domart-en-Ponthieu, where our Company Headquarters had been established. This was a typical rural environment, a one cobbled street village with one café (pub), farm carts, cow pats and a noticeable lack of main sewerage.

The café became our evening gathering place and, as only one platoon of the company was here at any one time, it was large enough for us. I was able to put into use my fairly good French language capability and became very much in demand to act as interpreter, although there were occasions when I was asked to translate some comment to the young girl behind the bar, I was less than accurate as it better served my own selfish interests.

We availed ourselves of the opportunity on the following day to put our dirty laundry in for washing, - shirt, vest, underpants and towel, to be picked up a week later and the procedure repeated. We also made use of the village hairdresser and it was there that I befriended a young French man called Emile Varlet, he wrote to me later and I still have the post card (below) but unfortunately I lost contact with him.

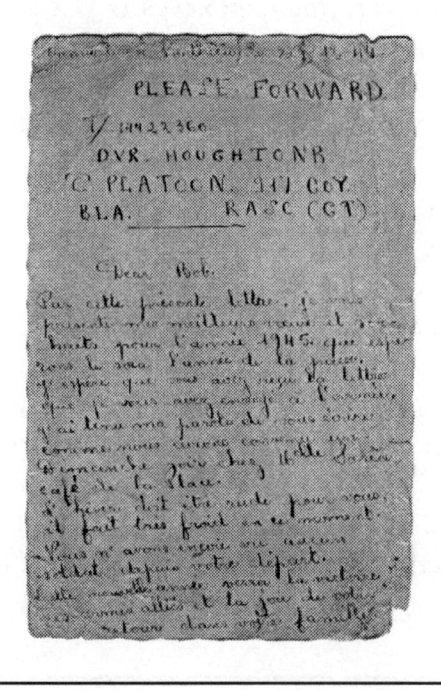

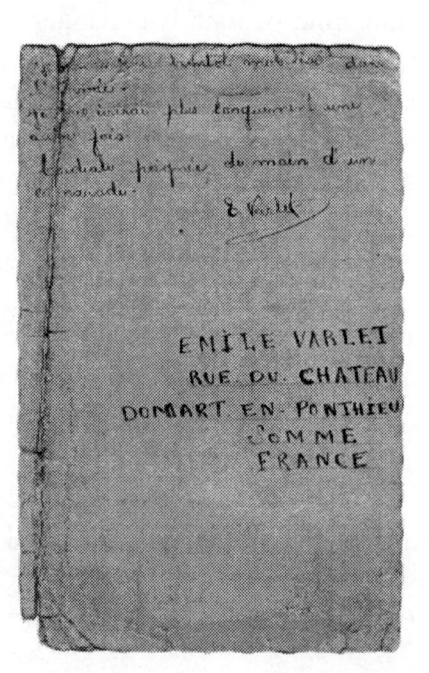

We made several visits to Domart and I remember three of us being invited one time by a French family to an evening meal and a chance to sleep in a proper bed. We enjoyed a superb meal, probably roast pork after which we were ready for sleep. Our bedroom boasted one very large bed into which we fell and slept soundly until sometime near dawn, waking to find that the room did not possess any container suitable to meet our urgent needs! We tossed for it and one boot was selected for our use, the eventual contents being poured through the window on to an outbuilding's roof. Active service ingenuity!

Leaving Domart on the Friday we put 132 miles behind us and Saturday saw us driving 91 miles to Bayeux, located a few miles south of Arromanches, to the 16th Base Ammunition Depot which consisted of numerous stacks of all types of munitions spread over several acres of mud. The objective was to drive to a designated stack and be loaded by men of the Pioneer Corps supervised by a corporal or sergeant belonging to the Royal Ordnance Corps. When loading was completed we had to lash the canopy back into place and then move back to the road to wait until all trucks had finished loading. That was the theory, the practice turned out to be somewhat different. We had sunk, well down to the axles anyway and were totally incapable of moving under our own power. So we sat there sounding the horn and flashing our lights (it was getting near dusk) until eventually we were seen and a Caterpillar tractor was dispatched to tow us out. If my memory can be relied upon our load consisted of hand grenades packed in wooden cases. I have been asked if this kind of load was dangerous. Well, carrying explosives is just a little bit different to having a truck full of loaves of bread, but, to be fair, grenades and artillery shells are not usually primed or fused until they are at the point of use. Rifle and machine gun ammunition is safe so long as you can resist the temptation to hit it with a hammer to test its reaction. Any or all of such munitions can explode if the truck carrying it is shot up by either aircraft or artillery, or is involved in an accident resulting in in the truck catching fire. Danger money is not payable in the armed forces.

Reaching dry land we decided that our skid chains (for use on icy roads) which had been in the back of the truck, but were now in a side rack where they had been put whilst we were being loaded, would be better located in the back of the truck again as we had a need to utilise the rack to carry jerricans of diesel fuel. Now these two chains consisted of numbers of steel pads connected together with what appeared to be anchor chain, and were long enough to mount as some kind of track around both rear wheels on each side of the truck. (The Foden had two rear axles fitted with single wheels and cross country tyres). Our first attempt to throw them over the tailboard failed miserably as did our second and a half hearted third try. By this time our joint army inspired vocabulary had nearly become exhausted, (as had we), so we decided that the front crash bar would make an admirable place to hang the chains on to until we could get them into the truck at a later date. We slung the first set up and over, forgetting that mounted on the bar was the horn which promptly shorted and sprung into action and could only be disarmed by wrenching out the wires to it. We were now cold, tired, muddy and totally 'browned off' (fed up). At this point we decided to implement our Emergency Plan. All trucks were equipped with a shovel and ours was quickly brought into use to dig a suitable hole for our beloved skid chains. They could still be there! They were never missed because we found out later that only a few trucks had skid chains.

Sid's whole demeanour had actually suffered a set back when on our way into the Depot. (Sid was my co-driver you will remember). We had arrived at a T junction and the oft experienced dilemma - left or right? - raised its head. I was driving and he decided to dismount and 'recce' the road ahead. The road was a muddy brown colour and when Sid jumped down (a distance of about three feet from cab to ground), he found that this muddy brown was actually the surface of about six inches of muddy water! He was quite displeased with this. Sid was a Londoner, his parents had the Brown Cow pub in the Mile End Road, and we got on very well together but on this particular occasion we were a little devoid of amiable conversation. I well remember another event on a later trip when he lost his 'irons' (eating irons - knife, fork and spoon). The Foden truck was, as I have said earlier, what was known as a cab over vehicle in that the engine kept you company in the cab. Two large air cleaners were mounted on top of the engine cover which, when the engine was running, were extremely noisy. Our practice was to spread a spare blanket over the cover between the cleaners on which we could carry odd bits and pieces. This was where Sid had decided to keep his 'irons'. The Foden had also a number of other features one of which was the open gaps between some of the controls - brake and clutch pedals and gear levers, thus it was that after a particularly nasty jolt, on an equally nasty piece of road, Sid's 'irons' parted company with the truck through one of these spaces. His scream of anguish was virtually drowned by the noise of the Gardner engine going full crack and it was some time before I understood what all the gestures and mouthing were about by which time it was too late. We would not have been able to stop anyway, being in convoy, but this was no solace to poor Sid at the time. Luckily he was able to replace his loss.

We were back on the road on Sunday and drove 85 miles to our staging point, and the following day a further 127 miles on to Waterloo, (place not station), where we unloaded on to the side of a road which ran in a wooded defile from where we could see the hill top monument to the Duke of Wellington. On the Tuesday we returned to our Company HQ - a trip of 143 miles. We had organised ourselves so that whoever was on morning driving got up for breakfast and brought the other a mug of tea back to the truck, enabling the resting driver to have an extended sleep, going without breakfast, but so what? Halfway through the morning the late sleeper would climb into the cab via the rack behind it while the truck was on the move. We became very adept at this manoeuvre. Whilst sleeping in the truck was not exactly akin to being in the Ritz we managed to create a snug and dry cubby hole complete with lighting from the truck's battery.

The next few weeks were to follow the pattern of the first, a succession of journeys between France and Belgium transporting munitions, fuel and anything else needing to be moved. Pritch and I did one solo trip to somewhere near the Albert Canal in Belgium.

A pungent memory of driving through the French countryside was the stench emanating from the practice of depositing, on the land, the contents of cess pits which were pumped out periodically into wheeled tanks to be towed by either horse or tractor.

We always had a fire going when we stopped for the night managed by half filling an empty five gallon oil drum, (with the top cut off), with water and floating on top a quantity of diesel oil, which once lit with the aid of an oil soaked rag would burn for hours. Gradually the water would evaporate and had to be replaced - not from the water wagon and not from truck radiators but from more natural sources. Think about it! Replenishment of our fuel tanks was done at fuel dumps which were sited along the route, vast stacks of petrol and diesel in jerricans along with supplies of lubricating oils.

One night we had staged for the night on the outskirts of Tournai in Belgium, and we were all standing around our fire when I heard a voice calling out asking if any one here was from Yorkshire. What followed was probably the most notable occurrence since we had landed at Arromanches. Someone directed a man to me who having established that I did indeed come from Yorkshire took me off to his home. There I met his wife, previously named Greensides, who had come from Goole. That night I slept in a brass bedstead that had been bought from Glew's furniture store in Goole. I wrote home about this and excerpts from my letter appeared in the Goole Times.

(See feature on next page).

THE GOOLE TIMES

Friday, 1st December 1944

HOSTESS WAS GOOLE NATIVE

SURPRISE IN BELGIUM

We have frequently published accounts of how local servicemen have met while serving overseas, but a Goole soldier recently experienced a novel meeting of rather a different character. He was being entertained one evening by a Belgium family and much to his astonishment learned that his hostess was formerly a Goole lady. Describing the circumstances the soldier, Driver Robert Houghton (19), R.A.S.C., eldest son of Mr and Mrs R.W. Houghton, of 88 Marshfield Ave., has written to his parents as follows:- "This time I've really got you something to tell you about. Every week you read about servicemen meeting Goole chaps overseas. Well, my experience takes some whacking. We were sitting round the fire one night on the outskirts of Tournai when I heard a voice asking if anyone came from Yorkshire. It was a Belgium civilian who had been in Yorkshire from 1900-20, and above all in Goole! He took me home and then I got the surprise. His wife was a Goole lady - Elsie Greensides. She is the sister of Mr. C. Greensides, the teacher. Was I shaken! I've never been so surprised in all my life. Anyway, I had quite an enjoyable evening, and that night I slept in a bed that came from Glews!"

A single man, Dvr. Houghton joined the Army in April, 1943 and has served with the R.A.S.C. all the time. He landed in Europe about ten weeks ago and is now somewhere in Belgium driving a ten-ton lorry taking supplies up to forward bases. In his letters home he says he is quite happy and well and has been to Caen, Amiens, and Brussels. Dvr. Houghton attended Alexandra Street School.

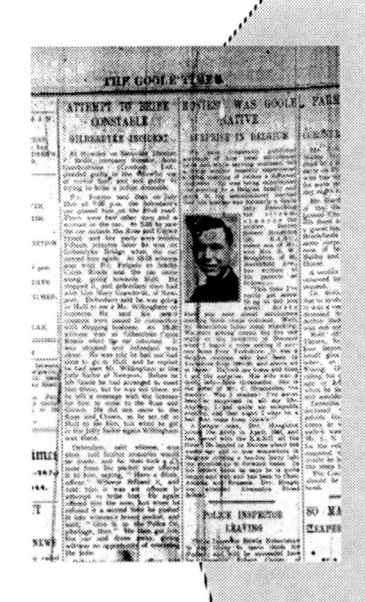

Excerpts from the author's letter home appeared in the Goole Times reproduced here from the original article. (See previous page).

Sometime in early November, we moved into a large country house or hotel near the village of La Hulpe in Belgium, along with a number of French Canadian lumberjacks. They were employed in felling trees which we hauled to a local sawmill, to produce timber to be used in building accommodation for ATS girls, who were manning anti aircraft guns defending Brussels from V1s. Or so we were told.

Below is the actual 'secret' route letter issued for the movement of the logs by the RASC. Note the instructions showing what and how many trucks the convoy is to consist of, the times/dates, route to be taken, equipment required, rations needed and other relevant information.

NO. 14 CANADIAN FORESTRY COMPANY, C.A.O.

SECRET   File: F14-7-7.
                                         8 Dec 44.

                       ROUTE LETTER

PARTLY SQUARED LOGS
Unit Convoy No. 40.

       1.   Convoy, consisting of six(6) R.A.S.C. lorries, hauling partly squared logs to Scierie Brabrants, Rue Claessens, LAEKEN, (North Suburb of Brussels), will leave No. 14 CFC campsite at 0800 hrs. 8 Dec 44.

       2. ADMINISTRATION: ROUTE: From No. 14 CFC follow Route 15 "UP" to Manhay, from Manhay through Bomal, Tohogne, from Tohogne follow Route 34 to Hamoir, follow Route 23 to Huy, Tirlemont, follow Route 3 to Louvain. From Louvain follow Route 51 to Malines, from Malines follow Route 1 to LAEKEN.

                       EQUIPMENT: Blankets, small kit, personal weapons, S.A.A., steel helmets.

                       PERSONNEL: One driver for each vehicle and one N.C.O. i/c Convoy.

                       RATIONS: Sufficient 10-1 Rations for journey will be issued by NCO i/c Kitchen.

                       STAGING: NCO's i/c Convoy will report to Town Major and arrange for overnight staging.

                       CAUTION: Before leaving campsite check your load and ensure that chains are tight. After travelling approximately five miles, stop, check your loads again. Vehicles should stop about every 20 miles and make certain that chains are tight and loads in place.

       3.   Report your return to NCO i/c Shipping, No. 14 CFC and surrender this Route Letter to Him.

                                       _____ Lieut. & Adjt.
                                        (R.E. DARLING)
                             For O.C., No. 14 Cdn. Fsty Coy.

Posing in front of a Foden (nicknamed Denise painted on the front) at La Hulpe, Belgium... author third from right with Sid Pritchard to his right. November 1944.

Our stay here was not uncomfortable as the house was centrally heated and we had the benefit of hot water supplies. The lumberjacks were something else though and had the habit of bringing murderous looking knives to meals and sticking them in the table top - we were not courageous enough to question this practice.

Adjacent to us was a farm where our trucks were parked and we offered to help the farmer out with some timber to keep the home fires burning, so we dutifully arrived one day with a whole tree trunk, about eighteen inches in diameter and twenty feet long. The unloading technique was simplicity itself, rig up a set of 'legs' complete with ropes and pulley block, drive the truck under this set up, ropes under the tree trunk, lift it a couple of feet and drive the truck out from under, then - lower the tree to the ground. We got as far as lowering the load to ground level when the ropes round it started to slip - no real problem except for the farmer who, carelessly one might say, was stood underneath it all. He showed a great deal of alacrity in moving to avoid becoming firewood himself but in so doing left his wooden clogs behind! Before you could blink these were neatly converted to kindling. His muttered: "Oy-oy-oy-oy-oy" lives in my memory to this day. This became a popular saying in the platoon when ever anything went amiss.

One event which occurred while we were in this area was an accident to one of our trucks. Many of the roads were cobbled, extremely narrow and steeply cambered and when meeting opposing traffic, great care needed to be exercised as the road side verges were very soft. Just such a meeting took place one day on one of these roads alongside of which ran a canal. The vehicles front wheel strayed onto the verge and the driver, instead of stopping, carried on motoring with the apparent intention of keeping up his speed to avoid becoming bogged down. He was unsuccessful and I can do no better than quote verbatim from the official Accident Report completed by the passenger.

> "I observed that the vehicle was about to proceed into the canal so I skedaddled"

He did just that - baling out before the truck toppled into the canal finishing up on its right hand side in about eight feet of water. The driver appeared shortly after exiting from the passenger door. The fact that he was only a small guy - about five feet three - made this a feat well worth remembering. The truck was later hauled out and after a good clean and some moderate repair work was (nearly) as good as new.

During March of 1999 whilst I was writing this book, I learnt that a guy by the name of Sid Barnes, who I occasionally see when I visit Cromer in Norfolk, and who was a member of A platoon, 917 Company, vividly remembers the incident. He was the guy who, using the winch which was fitted to his Mack breakdown truck, pulled the Foden out of the canal. He certainly remembers the driver being very small.

Shortly after this, our truck started to develop problems associated with airlocks created by a leak or leaks somewhere in the fuel supply. The engine would tick over OK but as soon as it was subjected to load would cut out. The partial remedy was to open up the engine cowling in the cab (on the mate's side), and loosen off the injector pipes whilst hand pumping the fuel supply and waiting until all the bubbles of air had dissipated. This we had to do so many times it became ridiculous and so on the 20th of November I took the truck into the Main Workshops in Brussels where the fuel system was stripped down completely and rebuilt before the problem was eradicated.

I could have moved into a transit camp to sleep during this time but didn't want the aggravation of moving all my kit so I stayed with the truck in so far as sleeping was concerned. At the end of a week the truck was pronounced 'fit to be let out'. Meanwhile orders had come from my platoon that we had moved into the Ardennes in southern Belgium near the town of St. Hubert which lay about ten miles west of Bastogne (see photo on next page), and I was given route directions to enable me to find them. Now this was December and the Ardennes is not noted for sub-tropical weather at this time of the year so as I drove onwards and upwards, so to speak, the snow got deeper and the air colder and not to forget that no army vehicle that I ever drove was blessed with a heater, I hoped like hell that I would find our platoon before it got dark. Then I arrived, just like that, a line of trucks on the side of the road and halfway up the hill side a large hotel building.

My arrival had been noted and someone sent down the 15 cwt truck to convey me and my gear up to the billet. The place had been luxurious at some time but was looking somewhat less than that now. As I went inside to report and find a bed space, (on the floor), I was advised not to stand up in front of the windows and it was then that I became aware of the bullet

Scene showing the heavy snow conditions in Bastogne January 1945

holes in them, caused by random sniping I was informed although to this day I still can't get to grips with this. I found out that we were attached to the American Army which meant among other things we would have the dubious pleasure of enjoying their K rations. These came in separate packs for breakfast, midday and evening meals, the containers were of a uniform and uninspiring murky brown with I suppose, semi waterproof wax coating. They contained, depending upon which meal, small tins of meat or cheese, biscuits, coffee, soup or lemonade powder, cigarettes, chocolate bar and fruit bar. The last was avoided at all costs as it was designed to help you avoid becoming constipated.

I must confess to some haziness in relation to the precise timing of certain events about this time. It was around the beginning of December and I know I had to go into Company workshops in Fourrieres for something but I cannot recall the details. I can remember us marching to and fro and singing a popular tune of the day - Swinging on a Star - but with some alternate lyrics which eventually became too much for the NCO in charge of us, so we had to desist. This place also saw the emergence of a cartoon character named Chad, his crudely drawn image appearing everywhere, much to the annoyance of all NCOs.

WOT! NO K RATIONS?

RASC   Page 87   Chapter 3   1944 - 1945

When I returned to the hillside hotel it was back to timber hauling again but don't ask from where to where. I can certainly recall that it was damned cold.

The air was full of rumours about German paratroops being dropped and, naturally, everybody was very edgy. This was demonstrated one night when the vehicle guard, down on the road, thought they were being attacked and promptly began firing in all directions. For a short time all hell was let loose until it became apparent that they were shooting at shadows. There was no enquiry into this affair and I suppose the guys involved would have sworn that their action succeeded in dispersing the enemy!

Thus it was that one midday in mid December, parked in the town square of St. Hubert, where Sid and I were consuming our nutritious K ration dinner meal, when we became aware of a lot of fast moving American trucks all heading in the same direction. What we didn't know at that time was that this was about to become the Battle of the Bulge, when the Germans attacked the American line with the objective of breaking through to the port of Antwerp and separating the American and British forces (See map on next page). But we were unaware of any of this, so we quietly finished our meal and got on with the rest of the day's work.

When we arrived back at our base all hell was breaking loose! Get your kit into your truck, load up extra diesel fuel and so on. Our canopies had been dismounted to facilitate timber hauling and we had no time to refit these so, along with the cans of fuel we didn't manage to load we had to set fire to them and moved out a bit sharpish. We did this in twos and threes, after being given a rough route to the village of Bassily, a short distance to the south west of Brussels.

Albion 10 ton truck, written off due to enemy action?

By this time it was dark and I was driving our truck followed by an Albion ten tonner from D platoon. Some time later we arrived at a T junction and stopped to determine whether to turn left or right, I think we decided to turn left which turned out to be the right way because if we had taken the opposite direction we most certainly would have run into trouble. Anyway, after we had made our decision I slammed the gear lever into reverse and backed up to make it easier to take the bend, I just did not know that the following Albion was so near, but it was and its radiator, which was mostly of cast iron construction, disintegrated amidst a combined flood of water and language to suit the occasion. No time to argue who was at fault - the two occupants joined Sid and I in the Foden, somewhat crowded but cosy! I think the Albion was written off as having been lost due to enemy action.

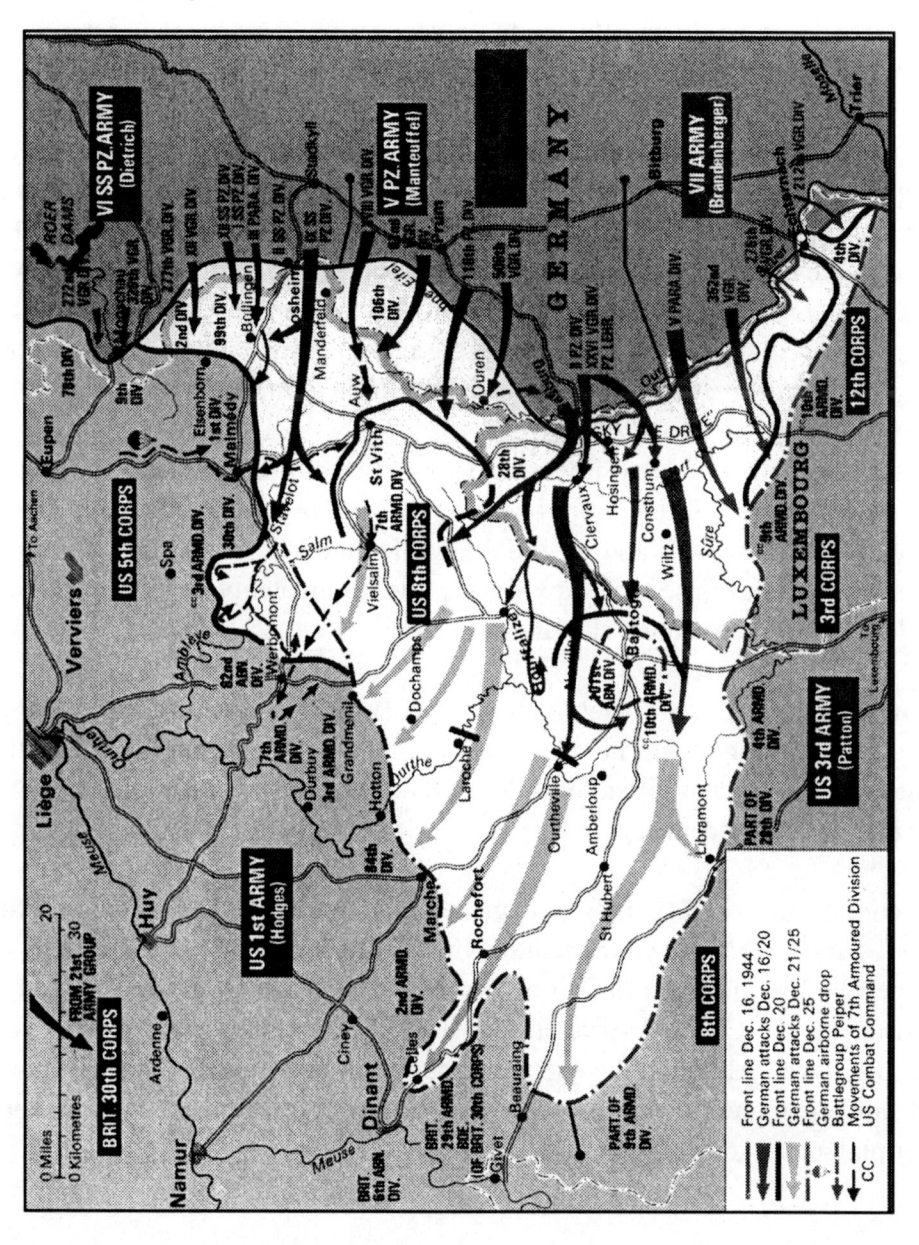

This Ardennes map is showing the extent of the German advance during the first few days of the Battle of the Bulge, bypassing Bastogne and striking through St. Hubert from whence I had left some hours earlier.

Eventually we arrived at Bassily and all our vehicles were parked on roads to the left and right of the main road which was in fact the main road we had traversed back in October from France to Brussels.

I am sure it was now that we lost our co-drivers who were posted elsewhere, because I was billeted in the attic of a house along with John Richardson. If my co-driver Sid Pritchard had still been there we would have stayed together. This attic was so cold it was unbelievable, it had a stone floor! We had to scavenge around for whatever we could find to place under our blanket to maintain reasonable warmth.

If any one knew what was happening back in the Ardennes they forgot to let us know. We were aware that all was not well as we were told that groups of Germans dressed in American uniforms were possibly in the area. So we were not exactly surprised when we were ordered to parade, to be issued with ammunition in preparation to searching a small nearby copse for reported Germans. Whilst ammunition was held by the platoon, it was not normally issued to us excepting in such situations as we were now experiencing. We did, of course, carry our Sten guns with us at all times.

Considering that the field we had to traverse to get to this copse was some six inches or more deep in snow we viewed the entire exercise with some trepidation. Our mood was not helped when one clown fell and in so doing pulled the trigger and let off a shot. Had there been anyone in the copse they would have had no difficulty in picking us off. This is why we drove trucks and others shot guns.

There was one unfortunate event when a member of B platoon was accidentally shot dead by one of his own platoon. I was nowhere near to this tragic event but George Balls, who later became a good mate, has given me a detailed account of the occurrence and this is reproduced as part of the appendices.

It was now coming up to Christmas and guess what we were going to have for Christmas Dinner. Turkey? Not on your life, not with all that meat and vegetable stew in stock, not to forget the biscuits - we hadn't as yet seen any bread let alone eaten any! But the platoon officer and NCOs did serve us. I assume the remaining platoons enjoyed a similar menu and service. Although the entire company was now resident in Bassily we still maintained our allegiance to our own platoon and had little or no contact with members of other platoons.

Bassily was large enough to support two or three cafés and we certainly made use of the one in our territory, so much so that the net effect of our Christmas and subsequent New Year celebrations was to drink it dry of beer, as a result a number of us developed a taste for Benedictine which has stayed with me to this day. After one particularly heavy session Richie and myself were making our way back to our billet more than a little worse for wear; the road back passed over a bridge spanning a small shallow stream which seemed to have an attraction for Richie in that he waded through it instead of going over the bridge. This could have been New Year's Day, as I remember lying in bed trying to get warm and hearing in the distance the sound of aircraft machine guns. (I found out after the war that this had been the time when the Luftwaffe mounted what was to be their last effort in terms of numbers of aircraft employed).

The weather at this time was extremely cold with very hard frosts, with the road from our parking lot down to the main road so icy that we could not attempt it with our heavy vehicles. However as soon as the road was passable we packed up and moved out of Bassily and our platoon retired back into France.

Our new home was in the village of Wimereux - between Boulogne and Calais where some of the platoon moved into a large villa in the centre of the village whilst the remainder occupied a large two storey building on the outskirts. I was lucky and ended up in the villa. This was to be our home until March. Incidentally we were now back to bunk beds but this time they were German ones, different from ours in the UK in that these were capable of being disassembled, the side pieces were clipped on to the upright ends and then wooden slats were placed in between the side pieces to support the mattress. An example of early flat pack.

WIMEREUX - FRANCE

Before the war Wimereux must have been a delightful little seaside place built as it was astride a small river. The bridge which had spanned the river was now, sadly, no more, having been blown up (or even down) during the autumn fighting. The effect of this created two separate villages as the nearest crossing point was upstream a number of miles away. In any event I don't recall that we had a lot of contact with the local populace, in fact when I look back it seems that there had been a noticeable lack of enthusiastic welcome on the part of the French people in general. Perhaps they had exhausted themselves giving their all to those who had fought through this area, but my latest reading of history seems to imply that many of the inhabitants of Normandy and the Pas de Calais (where we now were), considered the Allies as interlopers bent upon disturbing their comfortable existence.

In the cities the people must have experienced some hardship and would have been in closer proximity to large numbers of German troops. Certainly large numbers of men were conscripted to work for the Germans, both in France and elsewhere, leaving their families to fend as best they could, but in the country areas there appeared to be no shortage of food or wine, or indeed beer and such spirits as Calvados (a Normandy brandy made from apples). Meals such as we had eaten in Domart-en-Ponthieu, roast pork a-plenty, did not strike us as being out of the ordinary.

Totally different was the attitude of the Belgians where even when we first drove into Brussels in early October, five weeks after its liberation, the streets were lined with people to greet us.

So we kept pretty much to ourselves. We had a large room in the villa as a recreation room where we were allowed to play Bingo or 'Housey-Housey' as it was known then. Gambling of any kind was strictly forbidden in the army, but this was organised recreation under the supervision of an NCO and no money changed hands! In any event our work took us away from Wimereux for two to three nights each week when we were able to indulge ourselves in other pursuits, although we did enjoy some rather exciting pastimes outside of the village for a while but more about that later.

Our accommodation was warm and reasonably comfortable, which was very welcome and our diet showed some improvement in that we had supplies of bread and, with a more permanent cooking facility, the cooks managed to introduce some variety into our meals.

The task that we had been brought back into France for was to move materials into Calais, which were needed in the construction of a large Transit Camp, which was to cater for troops travelling to and from the UK by way of cross channel ferries to Dover or Folkestone. The camp had to have accommodation to house troops over night if needed and, therefore, suitable ablution (that word again) facilities, mess halls and a canteen.

We were assigned the job of transporting cement from Tournai in Belgium at the rate of three loads a week by each of us, (we were now driving solo, no co-drivers and not in convoy). Tournai was about 90 miles away, 20 miles to the south east of Lille in France. Lille was the designated overnight staging point and, depending on our start time, we either drove to Lille and staged overnight and then on to Tournai the following morning to load and return to Calais, or drove straight to Tournai, loaded and staged at Lille on the way back. Either way we were able to have a night on the town in Lille three times a week. The staging point was in an old French cavalry barracks from where we could take a tram direct into the city centre, at no cost of course, where we were free to indulge ourselves so long as we were back in barracks by midnight.

Lille was very lively. As I recall it had not been severely damaged by the war as the drive through France and in to Belgium during August and early September had been extremely rapid. There was a theatre which we visited a number of times to see visiting artists from the UK including Harry Gold and his Pieces of Eight - a notable jazz group of the day. Cafés were plentiful and no shortage of what to drink. Some establishments offered more than something to drink and on one visit a group of us enjoyed a delightful evening with a group of equally delightful young females.

The coast around Wimereux was heavily fortified with weapon emplacements along the cliff top, (the cliffs were about twenty to thirty feet high if my memory serves me right), and when time allowed we duly explored them. The Germans had left an armoury of weapons and ammunition including grenades. One of our number was smart enough to fuse some of these small egg shaped grenades and we amused ourselves by bombing the beach and when we tired of this, we sorted out some ammo for a machine gun we found in a pill box and tried to explode mines on the beach by shooting at them. However, all good things must come to an end and one day we were requested by a local Gendarme (policeman) to cease. So we did.

Among the bunkers and so forth, there were living quarters which were built so that they did not project above ground level and one day I was walking on the path round one of these and a face appeared at a window. I nearly jumped out of my skin, my immediate thought being that it was a Jerry but it turned out to be a Frenchman who had no other place to live.

We were not far from the infamous Cap Gris Nez where the long range guns which had shelled Dover were installed and one day we decided to go and give them the once over. We drove, in a ten ton Foden, down a road which led off from the main Boulogne/Calais road along which we had to drive so far on one side and then switch to the other and alternate in this manner for about a mile or so. The reason for this was that the intervening stretches of the road sections were mined.

The battery of three guns was housed in three huge round concrete fortifications and each must have measured seventy feet in diameter and thirty feet high with walls probably six to eight feet thick. We ventured into one and saw that on the wall alongside of the doors, was a painted panel depicting the number of shells that had been fired. The shells themselves, laid on a length of railway track, must have measured five to to six feet long. Inside was stupendous, the gun itself was mounted on an enormous steel structure that enabled the weapon to traverse to a limited degree and also to depress to allow loading before elevating to fire. In addition there was all the machinery necessary to handle the huge shells and firing charges. How I would have loved to have had a camera but regulations forbade this.

A massive long range gun at Cap Gris Nez looms from its concrete emplacement dwarfing the German sentry.

Outside, the immensely long barrel of the gun still pointed up at an angle of maybe sixty degrees, probably the firing angle. The top of the entire structure was covered with soil - with grass and plants growing there.

One of the other two emplacements was wrecked and it was only later that we found out that it had been booby trapped. The extent of the damage indicated that it must have been a tremendous explosion. Had we been aware of this we would probably not have embarked upon our expedition.

We were still obliged to do some elements of vehicle maintenance, although not much had been performed to date. We were expected to change oils however, and it fell to my lot to change gearbox and rear axle oils in the freezing temperature which prevailed at the time. We did not have any covered areas to undertake this operation so it had to be done outside on the road, not to forget that the Foden had two rear axles each holding God knows how many pints. The only consolation I got out of this was that the old oil was poured into five gallon drums and with some new oil floated on top, was sold to a café owner somewhere between Calais and Boulogne.

Above: The author on the cab of his Foden truck along with one of his mates.

Left: The author (2nd from the right) and mates doing truck maintenance.

During my over seas service I experienced two unbelievable meetings. The first of these occurred one day when I was driving back to Wimereux from Calais and I caught a fleeting glimpse of the driver of a truck going in the opposite direction. I screeched to a halt and saw that the other truck had also stopped, we reversed back towards each other and - would you believe it, it was George Coult with whom I had joined up! We exchanged a few words and then continued our journeys. It may seen strange but I did not feel as though I now had a lot in common with George.

Our platoon sergeant was named Hyams. I don't know from whom we had inherited him but he wasn't at the top of the popularity stakes. Some of our trucks were parked at the rear of the villa on an area of brick rubble and as I drove in one time, my front nearside wheel caught a piece of metal which tilted up and caught against the front wing. Hyams was standing near and I was treated to the usual stream of obscenities he had at his command, whereupon I dismounted from the cab and suggested to him that he should demonstrate how my truck ought to be parked, knowing that this would needle him as he was devoid of heavy vehicle driving experience. Apparently I had not phrased my suggestion as politely as he would have liked, (my command of language had come on by leaps and bounds during the preceding two years), so I was put on a charge which meant that I would be brought before the platoon officer charged with 'conduct prejudicial to military discipline' or something or other. I was judged guilty and received a sentence of seven days confined to barracks which I spent keeping the platoon office clean.

The one thing that persists in my memory from this time and place was the cold. The Foden was a cold truck to drive and although having the engine in the cab or the fact that the usually hot exhaust manifold was on the passenger's side, did absolutely nothing for the driver's comfort. I can remember once driving to Calais in freezing rain and as the windscreen gradually became thick with ice, the only way I could see where I was going was to open up the top half of the screen. The end result of this was that I arrived at my destination with my beret frozen to my hair.

Progressively I became less enamoured with Sergeant Hyams, (I was not alone), and when he insisted that we blanco our kit I knew my future well being depended on getting away from him.

Early March saw John Richardson and myself having our request to see the Company Commander - Major Frome - approved. He was quite elderly and a very kind man who had us sat down in his office, (I don't know where), while we aired our grievance. We both requested transfer to the Airborne but he said that was not an option and instead arranged for both of us to be transferred to B platoon who at that time were located in Ostend in Belgium.

The author blancoing his kit.

So it was that we left C platoon and all the good mates that we had lived with since July 1943 and departed for Ostend arriving there towards the middle of March.

TOURING HOLLAND

The platoon was about to exchange its trucks as the ones they had been using were developing a serious fault.

The five ton Mack (right) was an American four wheeled petrol fuelled vehicle having rear wheel drive. In common with all American general transport trucks, (up until I went into the army they had always been known as lorries but the use of the word truck seemed to have crept up on us), the vehicle was equipped with high sides to the load carrying area part of which could be dropped down to form seats for troop carrying, this being a feature on all American trucks. In common with both American and British vehicles, the load area was covered by either a steel or wooden frame, in this case the latter, which supported a canopy made of heavy duty tarpaulin like material. This canopy was removable, when desired, to facilitate the carrying of bulk loads such as timber.

The Mack EH 5 ton truck, 4 x 2

The problem with this particular model of Mack was that the rear axle tended to move out of position due to loose spring centre bolts and that caused the entire axle and wheel assembly to slew out of true. This meant that one rear wheel moved forward and the other moved backward. This action was known as 'crabbing'. Needless to say it didn't do a lot in the context of drivability of the truck.

The guys in B platoon who we talked to were more than p****d off with these trucks and couldn't wait to trade then in. Richie and I were in a kind of limbo land for a few days until the time came for the exchange, so we kept out of the way and messed about in some open garages where three or four ERF trucks were parked. We tried to give the impression that we were familiar with these and pretended to be cleaning the engines. We might as well not have been there for all the notice anyone took of us.

After two or three days the five ton Macks were driven off somewhere following which we were all taken to a park to pick up replacement vehicles which turned out to be ten ton Macks (right), diesel powered, and a totally different animal to the five tonners. They turned out to be an absolutely superb truck to drive and although the cab was canvas topped and had only half doors fitted, (the upper half was equipped with a canvas and mica screen), the seating was comfortable and the driving position was excellent, due in no small measure to the fact that the engine was out in front and not keeping you company in the cab. Although top speed was no more than a good 40 miles an hour this was a great improvement on the 32 in the Foden and the gearbox was an absolute joy, - four forward plus overdrive and a transfer box which had the effect of dropping down or up half a gear, usable through every gear - thus we had ten forward and two reverse. A smart operator could change gear in both boxes at the same time with combined hand and foot dexterity.

The 5 ton Macks were replaced with the diesel powered, 10 ton Mack NR, 6 x 4 which was a big improvement and a joy to drive.

When reversing with the transfer box engaged the speed was so slow that it was possible to to stand outside of the cab on the wide running board and steer the truck with one hand. If you wished to be really clever you could actually dismount and walk round to ensure that the direction in which the truck was reversing was clear of obstacles, not to be attempted in enclosed spaces!

The body was the usual American format with high sides which dropped down to provide seating on each side, the canopy being fitted over a series of wooden supports. Two rear axles were fitted with twin wheels giving us a total of ten tyres in all. In army nomenclature the truck was a 6 x 4 - six wheeled with four driven. Brakes were assisted by compressed air and were extremely effective.

As Richie and I had driven heavies when we were with C platoon we were both allocated a truck. Mine was platoon number B28, its army registration number was L6164725 as can be seen on the oil smudged vehicle breakdown card below. (Note the vehicle make/type showing a Mack ten ton.)

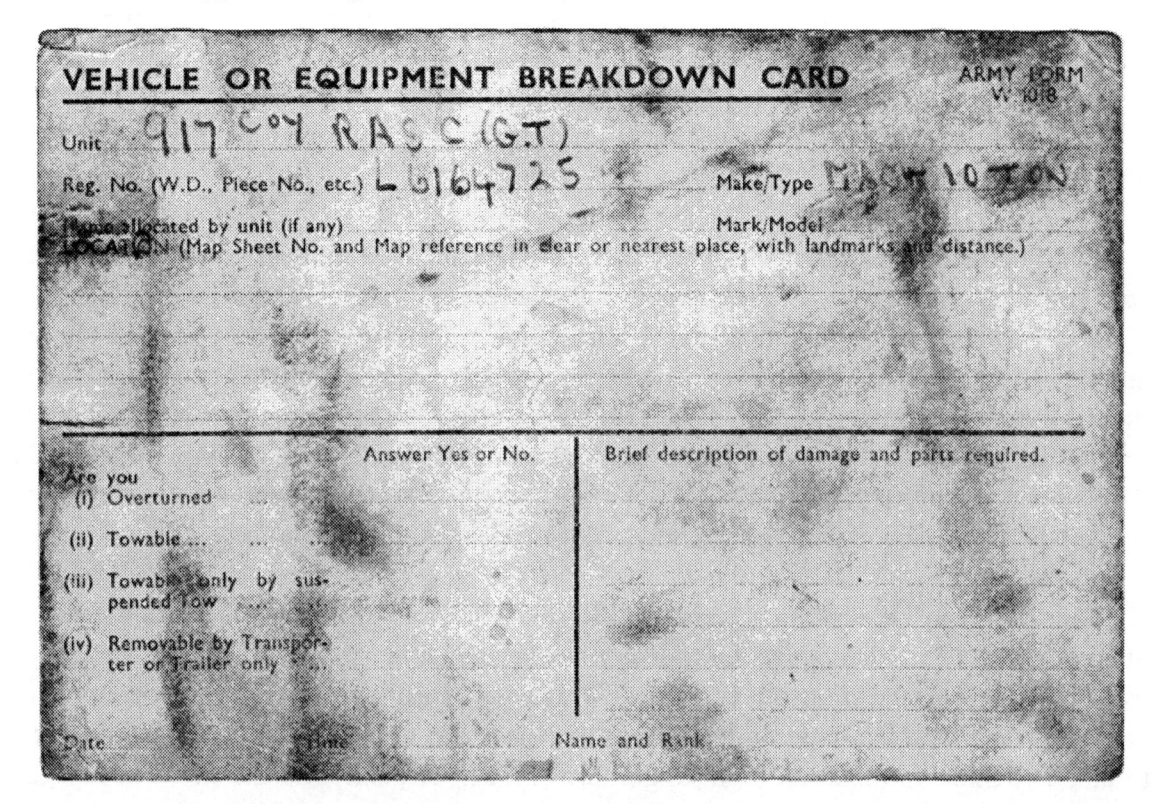

VEHICLE OR EQUIPMENT BREAKDOWN CARD — ARMY FORM W 1018

Unit: 917 Coy RASC (G.T.)
Reg. No. (W.D., Piece No., etc.): L 6164725   Make/Type: MACK 10 TON
Re-allocated by unit (if any)   Mark/Model
LOCATION (Map Sheet No. and Map reference in clear or nearest place, with landmarks and distance.)

Are you   Answer Yes or No.   Brief description of damage and parts required.
(i) Overturned
(ii) Towable
(iii) Towable only by suspended Tow
(iv) Removable by Transporter or Trailer only

Date   Time   Name and Rank

Events moved rapidly from now on and within a day or two we left Ostend, not that this affected me much, and after having loaded munitions, headed into southern Holland to unload them in an ammo dump spread out along a road near a town called Venlo. We made a second trip and following that loaded from Venlo and made our way into Germany. All this fetching and carrying was done in convoy and was in support of the assault across the river Rhine which in this sector was to be accomplished during the 23rd and 24th of March.

The reader should be aware that the retreating German Army had destroyed bridges over virtually every waterway, and so far as the river Rhine in Germany was concerned the only one not to have been completely blown was the famous bridge at Remagen, which did actually collapse after ten days of use by the Americans. Later on during our travels through Holland and Germany, we became very familiar with army constructed bridges. The most numerous was the superb Bailey, which was constructed from a number of lattice type steel side panels, each ten feet long by five feet high, bolted together to provide the required length, rolled over the river, stream, or other obstacle, and then decked with wooden planks. This single span construction could only be used over relatively narrow waterways. Where longer spans were needed the lengths of Bailey would be supported by pontoons floating at intervals. Doubling the height of the side panels had the effect of increasing the load bearing capability of the bridge from 40 to 80 tons. All army vehicles carried an indication of their weight, in tons, painted on a front wing.

The first bridges across wide rivers usually consisted of a number of pontoons, like small boats, having lengths of steel tracks laid over them. These pontoon bridges did not have any sides and were more than a little 'hairy' to cross, as they moved quite dramatically under the weight of a loaded ten ton truck. They must have been more than 'hairy' crossing in a tank! Later, these bridges were replaced by more permanent Bailey bridges constructed with piers situated in the river itself. The only other type of bridge I crossed was one over the Rhine at Wesel in Germany. This was a wooden construction erected by American engineers and tended to flex when you drove over it!

The day when we went into Germany for the first time, probably the first or second of April, was blessed with torrential rain and we arrived at the river Rhine along a muddy track running parallel with the river near the town of Emmerich. The Mack did not possess a particularly good turning circle, or lock as it was termed, and I recall that we had to take two shots to make the right angle turn from river bank onto the pontoon bridge spanning the river. At this point the Rhine was between 900 and 1,500 feet wide and flowing at about five miles an hour and the sight of the first half of the pontoon bridge was somewhat daunting. The remaining half was invisible due to the mist like pouring rain. The river current caused the bridge to adopt anything but a straight line and appeared to us a curve disappearing into the distance.

We were instructed to ensure that we maintained adequate distance between vehicles because as each truck drove onto a section of the bridge, it dipped down causing the sections behind and in front to tip up. The overall effect was somewhat akin to driving along a shallow roller coaster not forgetting that the width of the bridge track was not much more than the width of the truck.

The following pages feature the Bailey, Pontoon and other bridges mentioned here.

BRIDGES 1

Crossing the Rhine

The first stage for all of the Allied armies was to reach the Rhine river. To accomplish that, they had to break through the west wall in the south and cross the Ruhr (Dutch Roer) River on the north. The Germans had flooded the Ruhr valley by opening dams. After waiting nearly two weeks for the water to subside, the US Ninth and First Armies crossed the Ruhr on 23rd February 1945.

In early March, the armies closed up the Rhine. The Bridges were down everywhere - everywhere, that is, except at the small city of Remagen, where units of the US First Army captured the Ludendorff railroad bridge on 7th March. By 24th March, when Montgomery sent elements of the British Second Army and the US Ninth Army across the river, the US First Army was occupying a sprawling bridgehead between Bonn and Koblenz. On 22nd March the US Third Army had seized a bridgehead south of Mainz. Thus, the whole barrier of the river was broken, and Eisenhower ordered the armies to strike east on a broad front.

Two pictures showing Pontoon bridges spanning the River Rhine.

RASC   Page 101   Chapter 3 1944 - 1945

BRIDGES 2

Left: A Pontoon and Bailey Bridge. Note that a Bailey Bridge can be identified by the lattice type steel side panels while the Pontoon Bridge has none.

Right: A Pontoon Bridge

Left: A Sherman tank crosses a Pontoon Bridge over the river Seine, August 1944.

RASC   Page 102   Chapter 3   1944 - 1945

BRIDGES 3

Left: Bridge across the Albert Canal, Belgium to the north east of Brussels, and a natural defence line, was blown up by the Germans as they retreated.

Right: Nijmegen Waal roadbridge
Below: Nijmegen Waal railbridge

Left: Model showing Bailey Bridge sections
Below: Bailey being assembled by British engineers.

With many of the bridges destroyed by the retreating Germans, they had to be repaired or replaced before the British troops could continue the chase. This is where the Bailey played a part. The Bailey Bridge (bottom) was the most versatile military bridge of the Second World War. It was a heavy fixed bridge built from prefabricated parts which were brought to the site in lorries and then bolted together usually within a few hours. Decking was laid on two main trusses built of 10 foot panels pinned together with horizontal cross members (see model). These basic elements, placed in position by hand and machinery often under fire, could be reinforced to carry heavy tanks and guns or other loads up to 100 tons over spans up to 220 feet wide. The Bailey could also be used as a Pontoon Bridge laid on 60 foot pontoons. It was also employed by the US Army Engineers.

Once across we reassembled our convoy and promptly headed out of Germany to unload near to Hengelo not far from Enschede in Holland. This may seem odd but it would have been because Emmerich was our designated crossing point.

The river Rhine near Emmerich, pictured here in 1959, shows how wide it was at this point and emphasises the difficulties encountered by the Royal Engineer bridge builders.

We spent the next few weeks going backwards and forwards in this area, always in convoy, moving munitions, small arms ammunition, grenades and shells (particularly lumpy to sleep on). Towards the end of April we became involved in relief work carrying food desperately needed by the starving Dutch population. I remember driving over the bridge at Arnhem only a few days after it had been captured, where dead cattle were still lying in the fields. Most probably we were on our way up to Zwolle but I can't be sure. Also visible were numbers of gliders which had been used in the abortive attempt to capture the Arnhem bridge during September 1944.

We drove long hours, some of them after darkness had fallen. This did not qualify as my most popular experience. This was a repeat of earlier days in France and Belgium, when we had done this to some extent. In convoy you did not employ headlamps but followed the dimly illuminated white painted rear axle of the vehicle in front. On the odd occasion when I did drive in darkness, not in convoy, it was absolutely nightmarish in that the headlamp masks, with their minute aperture allowing an equally minute amount of light to escape, totally failed to provide enough light to drive safely.

The northern part of Holland was still held by the German Army, and later reading of war history records that dispensation was given by them, to permit the delivery of emergency food supplies into the occupied zone. Some of this relief was provided by air drops, but it seems possible that we were actually operating within this area.

Our base at this time was Enschede in Holland where we were accommodated in some buildings in the town slaughter house. We found that it was less than appetising when, on the way to breakfast, we had to pass an open door through which we could view the whole gory operation. To some extent I had other things on my mind as I had contracted Gingivitis (a gum infection) which made it extremely painful for me to chew food. The cure was to suck foul tasting penicillin tablets for a week or so whilst existing on soft foods.

Some photos taken at Enschede, Holland in July 1945

'Richie' Richardson and author.

Room orderly Winters and author.

Some 'soldiers'?

Midnight on May 8th 1945 brought the end of the war in Europe and during the following day there was wild jubilation among the Dutch population. Curiously, none of us that I can recall, were invited indoors or any where else for that matter to help them celebrate. (In fact the cease fire on the 21st Army front took effect from 08.00 hours on the 5th of May).

At this point we ceased to be the Liberating Army (BLA) and we became BAOR (British Army of the Rhine), although this title did not come into effect until late August.

CHAPTER 4
1945 - 1947
OCCUPATION ARMY - GERMANY

Following the surrender of the German armed forces on May 8th 1945 Germany was divided into four Occupation Zones, Russian, American, British and French. As government in the country, both at national and local level, had virtually ceased to exist, Military Government was established in each of the four zones, having the responsibility to temporarily carry out all government functions. Each city area had its own Military Governor and his word was, quite simply, law! Later the Control Commission for Germany was created which replaced the Military Government, and worked towards the reestablishment of civilian administration. There was much to do for the Occupying Forces, civilian transport was meagre, communications, water and power supplies were non existent in many places, particularly in the Rhineland and Ruhr industrial areas. Providing needed transport was to be the RASC's task.

My later move to an Ambulance Company supported the provision of medical services to the Occupation Army.

NO FIXED ABODE

Other than in the south of the country near Nijmegen, Holland is, to put it simply, flat! It is also a network of waterways and, of necessity, a lot of bridges. A lot of these had not survived in their 'as built' condition and in the majority of cases had been replaced by Bailey bridges. These were the sectional steel structures with wooden decking which could carry up to one hundred tons if needed, though most were constructed to handle forty tons. We still had to negotiate the odd pontoon bridge, at either Zwolle or Zutphen or both, to cross the lower Rhine (Rijn in Dutch) where the current I remember was very swift. On one occasion we had to cross a canal where there was neither a Bailey or pontoon, just a barge in mid stream with some pontoon bridge roadway laid across. This was very 'hairy' and I recall that we had a very excited Dutch audience to witness our efforts to cross, or not? But cross we did!

As we went up into the north of the country, we found numerous people dressed in traditional Dutch costume, not just clogs, which were very prevalent, but women wearing long black dresses and white hats. One place where we first saw this was Assen which was on the way to Groningen where the locals came out to marvel at a heap of burning sand! This was in fact our evening conflagration created by mixing diesel into the sand along with a drop or two of petrol to start it.

As the weather warmed up it became more comfortable as far as sleeping in the truck was concerned and driving was pure pleasure. Dress was very informal - plimsolls instead of boots - cab top rolled back - no hats or jackets, but we moved materials like nobody's business. These were fairly long days, on the road certainly no later than 8am, and often continuing into the hours of darkness. We were moving nearly 400 tons of supplies on each trip and, depending where we delivered to, we could manage two to three trips a week. During the period April to July we must have moved a total of 14,000 to 17,000 tons.

As I have noted the weather was extremely pleasant and June and July became quite hot, so much so that sleeping in the truck was very enjoyable due to the fact that for some of this time we were not carrying our canopies. Cosy sleeping dens could be created by moving the load around, in some of the trucks, to clear spaces into which we could get blankets down for three or four men. On one trip we arrived at a warehouse too late to unload that evening, so, having eaten, we settled down in the manner described for our sleep under the stars. The following morning we were awakened by a babble of female voices and raising our heads we were treated to the spectacle of a cavalcade of women on their way to work in the warehouse. The morning air was rent with screams of laughter as men struggled to get dressed without unduly exposing themselves.

Clean laundry was achieved by washing in petrol, scrounged from the cook's truck, then rinsed in water and dried by simply fastening it to the front radiator grille, when after 20 miles or so it was dry. We had long organised the carrying of water in jerricans for washing ourselves and rinsing clothing.

On the 7th July, I left our base to sample the delights of home for eleven days leave, the first time that I would see home since the one day in October 1944, just before we embarked for France. This involved being transported to Gennep near Nijmegan to board a leave train to Calais in France. Wooden seats - no lighting and a slow and monotonous twelve or so hours journey, arriving early morning. I remember the crossing to Dover being a little rough but I stayed on deck for the entire trip. Arriving in Dover I was amazed to see what was being brought back by troops, radios and radiograms and all kinds of loot (no other word for it) - even motor cycles were being taken ashore.

My family was so pleased to see me as I had not, sad to say, been too prolific on the letter writing front. I could not have told them much anyway due to all letters home being censored. Although the war in Europe was at an end there was still the question of how long would it take to win in the Pacific, and how would the invasion of Japan itself be undertaken, but opinions seemed to be that this was mainly an American sphere of operations. Rationing was still in force and commodities not rationed were in short supply. Cigarettes were very hard to come by unless you were a regular customer at a shop, where you would most likely be served from unseen supplies kept 'under the counter'. But people, although tired of the war and its effects on their lives, possessed a much brighter outlook than I remembered from previous home leaves.

Arriving back from leave, I found that we were involved in transporting loads other than food for the Dutch. For example on one trip we took Canadian bottled beer to a large storage installation. This gave us some problems as the weight to bulk ratio meant that the cardboard boxes holding the beer had to be stacked fairly high in the trucks with the result that odd boxes fell out. Now we had anticipated this and had left one truck free to trail the convoy and pick up these strays which were then recorded as having been lost in transit. So I'm sorry to have to record that we did sometimes 'appropriate' for our own use, but we never reduced the contents of a box or carton, it was always the entire package that was 'lost'.

We moved from Enschede in the last week of July to take up residence in a vacant convent near Nijmegen where we were based for a week or so. Here we were able to enjoy swimming in the nearby canal where the banks had been bulldozed to slopes either side of the water and out into the centre so that tanks and vehicles could cross as the adjacent bridge had been blown.

Other than this leisure activity there is not much more that I remember about this place except driving 'home' one evening I could detect the smell of the ever popular M & V (meat and veg.) in the air. The aroma persisted until we arrived back at base, to find that one enterprising individual had sought to have his evening meal ready for when he arrived by the seemingly simple expedient of placing a tin of M & V on the hot exhaust manifold! Unfortunately the tin had overheated and exploded showering the engine with the contents.

At the risk of being repetitive I have to record that the time during May, June and July were the best that I had experienced since I joined the army. Good mates, lots of travel in good weather, and the feeling of doing a worth while job and a damned good truck to do it in!

It was during this period that I first met George Balls and his mate Stanley Hobson. Stanley came from Beeston, Nottingham which I knew of, whilst George came from some totally unknown village called East Runton near an equally nebulous Cromer somewhere in the outer limits of Norfolk. I think I had gone to the truck in front of me, when we had halted somewhere, to borrow or buy cigarettes. (I had been smoking on and off since the debacle in the Ardennes). This was to be the start of a long lasting friendship with George which has prevailed to this day.

The end of July saw us on the move to new

Stanley Hobson and his mate George Balls

quarters just over the border into Germany in a little village called Kessel, a few houses and a café astride a cross roads. Every building virtually wrecked, no glass in the windows and no working sewage system. We had to dig field latrines and these along with the combination of very hot weather, the general state of everything and a veritable plague of flies resulted in a number of cases of dysentery necessitating hospitalisation for some. Those not suffering so drastically had to make do with the runs.

George Balls stood next to one of the two NR9 10 ton Macks in our platoon. George and I formed a long lasting friendship which has prevailed to this day.

One of our Macks crossing a Bailey pontoon bridge somewhere in Holland.

KLEVE

Our platoon officer decided that this was no place for us and he toured around seeking more salubrious accommodation for us with the result that on August 8th we upped and moved into the nearest town which was Kleve in Germany. Although this place had suffered great devastation during February and March he had located a café which was still whole and had suitable adjacent space for parking the trucks. This was the Café Hebben and we were to enjoy, and I mean enjoy, a stay of some six months until January 1946.

The Schwanenburg in Kleve, West Germany

Schwanenburg translated literally means 'Swan's Place'. Origin: Cleves (Kleve) was the capital of the Duchy of Cleves, where Anne of Cleves, one of Henry VIII's wives, came from. The castle was associated with the legend 'Knights of the swan' immortalised in Wagner's Lohengrin.
I guess therefore that the colloquial translation for Schwanenburg might be 'Swan's Castle'.

The people running the place were offered two simple options; either move out or be forcibly ejected, after all we were the Army of Occupation. They left voluntarily and we immediately began to organise the place. First priority was electricity as the supply to the town was non existent and would remain so for a while. We took ourselves off to the Canadian Army's stores depot outside of Nijmegen where tons of unwanted material was dumped. The reason for this was that come the end of the war, all Canadian troops were shipped back to Canada and demobilisation as fast as transport could be found, hence all these unwanted goodies. Personally we were able to equip ourselves with such things as berets (much better quality than ours), rubber boots, which I still have, and other items of clothing. Our prime target was the acquisition of generating equipment and we succeeded in getting hold of three Petter generators, petrol powered and very reliable.

It is worth recording that of the two bridges at Nijmegen over the river Waal, (the Dutch stretch of the Rhine), the one carrying the railway into Germany had been blown. The centre pier had been partly demolished causing the two far spans to collapse into the river. The road bridge was virtually intact with the exception of a relatively small crater in one carriageway, after a failed attempt to blow it, bridged by a section of Bailey.

Nijmegen Waal railbridge   *Nijmegen Waal roadbridge*

Our unit and I would guess most others, had within it tradesmen from civvy street, electricians, plumbers and joiners. Armed with a list of 'wants' we set out in a truck and toured bombed houses looking for, and finding, pipe work, sinks, timber and electric cable. Bomb damaged properties were abundant as Kleve had suffered heavy air raids and artillery fire preparatory to the crossing of the Rhine. The end result of all this foraging, put together with the expertise and labour of our own platoon was the installation of wash basins, latrines (toilets), and showers including a supply of hot water in an extension to the café, plus our own electric supply from our generators. The truck canopies, which we were not going to need in the immediate future, were pressed into use as roofing and sides to the extension.

The café obviously had a bar and we dispatched a truck to Dortmund to a brewery and as a result ended up with the bar fully stocked. An official requisition form procured a piano from somewhere and we were in business. We were sleeping two or three to a room, the café had actually operated as a small hotel before the war and had ample space for our needs.

When we had first entered Germany the sullen faces of the people had gone hand in glove with the white sheets hanging out of upstairs windows. Since then there had existed an occupational policy of non fraternisation, meaning that we were not supposed to enter into any kind of conversation or relationship with civilians except where necessary in the conduct of military business. Progressively this was relaxed, we were allowed after a while to talk to children and hand out chocolate or sweets although the prevailing request was: "Cigarette for papa", repeated ad nauseum. It didn't take us long to figure out that even if papa existed he had no intention of smoking all, if any, of the cigarettes that young Fritz brought home. They were for sale, sold individually they fetched six or seven Reichmarks each and the mark at this time had an exchange rate of twenty to one pound sterling. Cigarettes sold in packets of twenty changed hands for one hundred marks.

By the time we were well into August the non fraternisation ban was being disregarded and a fair number of liaisons were blossoming.

Our trucks were parked at night side by side reversed up to the wall of the local cemetery which was opposite our billet. We were obliged to set up an armed night guard to patrol the whole area although most nights until late there was always a number of bods (men) around the fire which was maintained during the hours of darkness. This was the usual five gallon oil drum fire, including voluntary effort to maintain the water level below the diesel.

It was as if we knew that we were going to be here for a good while because life became much more settled than hitherto. We had a properly organised kitchen complete with diesel burning equipment, albeit home made, which was much safer than the pressurised petrol burning gear along with a well furnished mess to eat in. Our bar was well stocked and whilst army regulations allowed only NCOs and officers to drink spirits, the fact that our officer had moved to other duties and left us in the hands of two sergeants meant that on occasions blind eyes were turned.

Progressively the social scene changed. We had amongst us Pete Pritchard, (no

Top middle - Pete, below him, George, below him, Jock Cunningham.
To right of Pete (smoking cigarette) Richie.

relation to Sid of earlier times), who was a gifted pianist and became a bosom mate to me. We also had a guy called Roberts who could handle a piano accordion quite well, don't know where he'd got it from but he had one. Jock Cunningham from Glasgow had been a drummer in his dad's band before being called up and he had managed to acquire a bass drum from somewhere, which he modified with some make do wire snare to make it sound like a side drum. This was our band and it provided music for dancing lessons given by Joe Davis, a Liverpudlian, and in turn for the couple of succeeding dances we organised. These naturally called for the presence of females and we had no problem in this direction. We had light, chocolate, cigarettes and booze. Pete's repertoire was somewhat limited as he was not good at playing by ear, he read music expertly and had to rely on his memory of melodies that he'd played previously. No matter, he was an absolutely superb 'boogie-woogie' player and as this kind of music was currently all the rage it was great for dancing.

Away from the social scene we had work to do and it turned out to be timber hauling again. A few miles from us was the Reichswald (State forest) which, as far as we could see, was composed entirely of coniferous trees. Belgian lumberjacks were felling trees having a diameter of about four to six inches and trimming them into fifteen foot lengths or so. These were to meet the urgent need for pit props at coal mines in the Ruhr area of Germany and our task was to convey these where needed.

Initially we worked as a platoon going into the forest around eight in the morning and dispersing to various points to be loaded after which we assembled as a convoy and drove to a designated coal mine. We usually stayed overnight at the mine either before or after unloading. I think we only delivered direct to two or three mines in order to speed up the process of getting coal out as due to the lack of props and other supplies, underground operations had temporarily ceased. One mine I do recall was named Gustav IV and a few cigarettes got us a ride down to the coal face where it appeared to be a pick and shovel operation, not much different from practice in the UK I guess. Glad I managed to get into the RASC and not become a Bevin Boy.

The sounds, smells and feel of the forest during early morning is something I can never forget. There was always a controlled fire, in a clearing, of the lopped off tree tops and the smell of burning pine filling the air was, extremely intoxicating. Any cares that you thought you may have had were rapidly dissipated.

My thoughts often pictured those poor guys who had fought their way through this forest five months ago. During one of my post war visits to Kleve I revisited this area to find a huge War Cemetery covering the ground where I had often stood on a sunny morning in 1945. How very sad and stupid it all seemed to have been.

The Reichswald War Cemetery pictured in 1958, located in the area from where we hauled timber in 1945/6.

We enjoyed one extra special trip which commenced by loading pit props and delivering them to a coal mine from where we loaded coal, which we transported to a cement works at Marburg near Frankfurt. There we exchanged our coal for cement which we conveyed to a factory producing conveyor belting, located in Bremen. Suitably laden with rolls of belting we returned to the Ruhr and delivered them to the mine from where we had picked up our coal, then back to Kleve. We must have clocked something like 700 miles in the six days we were away.

Somewhere along the way, possibly from the Canadian stores at Nijmegen, we had acquired 'one man tents' which were made in one piece to include a ground sheet. I remember that outside of Marburg we pitched camp on the local football field, (just a field - no buildings), in a circle, in true John Wayne fashion with all the trucks and tents facing inwards and a damned great fire blazing in the middle. A crowd of locals turned out to witness this spectacle but we couldn't make up our minds whether it was just natural curiosity or the sight of their goal posts forming part of our fire.

This journey involved a good few miles driving on the autobahns (motorways) with the occasional detour to avoid blown up bridges and/or craters. I seem to recall that German civilian traffic was at that time not permitted to use these roads and I have to say that we were very much impressed with them.

After this splendid outing we settled down to a simple daily routine where we drove into the forest early each morning and loaded up with timber and set off, individually, to designated local railway stations. There, local German labour off loaded into rail wagons for onward transport to the various coal mines. We usually managed to do three loads a day and there was always a scramble each morning to get away early. Any Germans watching would not have believed that we were soldiers as this ill assorted procession of casually dressed men appeared, no hats or belts and carrying sandwiches and mugs of tea leapt into their trucks and with a minimum of delay hit the road in clouds of dust. At the stations there were always several vehicles unloading and we always found something to occupy ourselves with even if it was only setting off fireworks. Fireworks? Well yes, homemade by tying knots in lengths of cordite which were lying around and then lighting the ends so that as the flame reached a knot there would be a sharp explosion. Don't forget that everywhere there were bits and pieces of all descriptions scattered around after the fighting had subsided.

In the early days some of us had to go out to a village called Weeze and pick up German prisoners of war from a tented camp, and take them into the forest to load us with the cut timber. Later on they were moved into Kleve, into one of the two non working biscuit factories which had, miraculously, escaped with only superficial damage.

Later on in life when I was working at International Harvester, a visitor from the Company's factory in Neuss near Düsseldorf, Joseph Müller, told me he had been in the camp in Weeze and he may have even ridden on my truck.

Dinner time (not lunch in those days), we ate our sandwiches, either cheese or more often jam. We did try to enrich these by toasting them over the always present fire, usually in a forty five gallon empty fuel drum, but this procedure was fraught with danger because if your bread and jam fell off your makeshift toasting fork into the fire, everybody, except you, fell about laughing and you didn't get to eat unless somebody took pity on you and shared theirs. It is worth noting that to conserve our meagre supplies of butter the cooks would melt it and then apply it to the bread with a shaving brush.

Apart from the social scene in our café, we did go out to the neighbouring town of Goch where there were two canteens, a NAAFI and a Red Shield (Salvation Army). Both were equipped with a piano so it became mandatory to have Pete Pritchard with us. We were, naturally, allowed to take one of the trucks for these outings.

We had only been in Kleve a couple of weeks or so when Jock Cunningham persuaded me to accompany him to some nearby house where he had a couple of girls lined up for a chat(?). The house we went to was very small - the ground floor of a two storey maisonette, a living room come kitchen with a bedroom off. The cellar was shared with the flat above but two attic rooms were part of the ground floor flat. I found out later that the family living here had returned from Magdeburg near Berlin to where they had been evacuated in February, to find their house a heap of ruins and as Kleve had been very heavily bombed in March they were fortunate to have found their current accommodation.

So here we were in the light of a flickering oil light fashioned from an empty cigarette tin half filled with diesel with a piece of string pushed through a hole in the top to act as a wick. The two girls were called Helga and Marie, Helga was a true Teutonic blond whilst Marie had dark hair. Marie's mother and father were there, he was happily smoking free cigarettes while mother was depositing her share of the cigarette harvest into a drawer. (For later resale it transpired).

Marie and her dad, Wilhelm.

My friend for the night was Helga. No one except me spoke English, (Jock came from Glasgow you remember), so can you imagine the intense conversation with which we whiled away the evening? But sadly it had to end and back to the café and a good wash after the diesel smoke.

A couple of nights later I went visiting, complete with loaded Sten gun slung over my shoulder, this being compulsory at this time, (our rifles had been exchanged for Sten guns, - light automatics - before we left England), but Helga was not to be found. Instead I was invited in by Marie and I found myself at home with the Thielen family joining them for supper. At this point in time I was four months short of my twenty first birthday and Marie would reach her eighteenth in the coming November.

After this I became a regular visitor and I soon realised that Marie was the girl for me and as time went on I knew that one day we would be married. So much so that in November when I next went on leave, I told mum and dad and went the whole hog and bought an engagement ring from a jewellers in Carlisle Street in Goole. Marie and I became engaged but with little hope of marrying in the foreseeable future as Occupation Army regulations did not permit it. I never really knew what my mother and father thought at the time about my intended marriage to a German, but they accepted that if this was what I wished to do, then so be it. When we did eventually arrive home at the end of 1947 Marie and daughter Hedy, along with me, were lovingly welcomed.

Conducting a courtship in conversations made up of snippets of English and German necessitated the possession of vivid imagination on the part of both Marie and myself, but as time went on it did get better. Her parents were sleeping in the next room, along with her one year old brother, so staying late was out of the question. At this time Marie's bed was the couch in the living room. However, one evening I arrived to be told that if I came in I would have to stay all night. Father and a friend were going to be involved in the process of distilling Schnapps which was, and still is for that matter, an extremely potent spirit. I agreed to stay and became witness to intense initial activity concerned with hanging damp blankets over the door and windows to prevent fumes from escaping from the room. I had noticed a wash tub full of potatoes in water alongside the stove during my previous visits and now some of these were put into a large pot on the stove and brought, eventually, to the boil. Then the rest of the apparatus was brought into use, a cover for the pot and an array of tubing which passed through another pot full of cold water with the end protruding, so that as the steam from the boiling pot condensed, the resulting liquid would drip into a conveniently placed bowl.

The process went on for ages until at some time around midnight the spirit began to drip-drip-drip into the bowl. This was duly sampled and father's expression told the tale, this was the real stuff. We all had to taste and pronounce judgment during the next hour or so as the volume of Schnapps increased. At about 5am I was ready to quit and was carefully let out of the door. I couldn't believe the difference in air quality between indoors and outside as I made my way back to the café for a few hours sleep.

Summer passed into autumn and it gradually became colder and the mornings in the forest were not quite as halcyon as they had been. The cab side screens had to be fitted and the gaps filled with spare bits of old blanket on numerous occasions to keep out the cold and the worst of the rain. In addition the forest floor became exceedingly wet and avoiding getting bogged down was a major concern as we had to stick to the recognised tracks and ruts, for it was not so long ago that a Foden from my old platoon had reversed off track onto a mine. Fortunately no one had suffered injury, but, be warned!

My 21st birthday arrived on the 8th of December 1945 and it was celebrated with Marie and family at their home - 18 Dr. Scholtenstrasse - complete with a cake that I had brought back when last on leave. A small but select gathering!

August had seen the end of the war with Japan and as we were now no longer likely to be shipped to the Far East we could anticipate an enjoyable Christmas in not unpleasant surroundings. Quite why I was chosen to go out on detachment to a village near to Recklinghausen (about 50 miles away) was something I could never figure out. I don't even remember what I was supposed to be doing there and about the only memory I have of the place is that I had a bed upstairs over a pub, sharing the room with one other guy and a harmonium complete with foot driven bellows, upon which my room mate played Lady of Spain, followed by Lady of Spain. It was all he could play!

Christmas Eve arrived and I decided that enough was enough. I packed my shaving tackle along with a biscuit tin full of buns Marie's mother had made for me and hitch hiked back to Kleve after about three hours travelling, including a lot of walking. Needless to say I didn't go anywhere near to Café Hebben for the two days I was there. I think the return journey was in a German truck that Marie's dad had 'sussed' out for me. What wonderful effective currency cigarettes were in those days! In any event I was recalled back to Kleve a week or so after Christmas

Sometime towards the end of January my truck underwent a Platoon Inspection and I was accused of falling down on maintenance in that I was told my engine sump bolts were loose causing oil to drip out. To this day I believe I was being 'nobbled' and maybe this had something to do with my declared intention to marry Marie. The army was very much against marriages to German nationals, and even when this attitude moderated at a later date, permission had to be given from 2nd Echelon Headquarters in Hamburg and this could, and did, take a long while. (In our case from application in summer 1946 to approval took 15 months). In many instances while couples were awaiting approval the army would quite deliberately move the soldier to another place and/or unit. A similar tactic was employed if the girl was pregnant and the guy did not intend marriage.

Whatever the motive was, I was taken off driving and given the job of platoon storekeeper. This wasn't exactly challenging, arranging to have boots repaired and issuing the odd pair of gloves was about all it involved. At least I was warm and sheltered and there was no fear of my sandwiches falling into the fire, but I did miss the driving and although I didn't know at the time my love affair with the Reichswald was coming to an end, as was our stay in this part of the country.

The time in Kleve had been extremely comfortable. We had enjoyed a kind of nine to five working pattern with weekends off. We had been able to visit Nijmegen just over the border in Holland, there were the two canteens in Goch and we had, of course our own well stocked bar in Café Hebben. There was a total absence of parades, beds did not have to be made up or kit displayed and a blind eye was turned to 'sleeping out'. The dreaded blancoing was a thing of the past along with brass polishing. We were of course, still soldiers, which meant that you still had to do as you were ordered, guard duties had to be undertaken and whilst there were no formal parades we still had to attend Pay Parade to receive your week's money. (All fourteen shillings - 70p - of it, left after seven shillings allocated to parents). In practice most of us did not draw our pay for weeks on end as our financial needs could easily be met by flogging a few cigarettes. (Tut tut).

I was spending a fair amount of time with Marie and eating regularly at her home but I did manage to contribute money wise so that I was not a drain on their finances. We had long dispensed with the diesel oil lamps as power had been restored to the town not too long after our arrival. The need to carry a loaded weapon when visiting civilian homes had also passed. The German girls were also getting smarter and no longer came to the Café Hebben to ask if Donald Duck or Mickey Mouse was in! Apparently Disney characters were among the unknowns so far as this generation of German youth was concerned.

If I was to ask any member of the platoon for a memory of Kleve I feel sure that a majority would put the Cemetery wall at the top of their list. As I have written earlier our practice was to reverse into our allotted parking space and we got into the habit of doing this very slowly until you felt the slight jar as the rear of the truck came in contact with the wall. Now no matter how gently this was done there had to be some disturbance to the structure with the eventual result that when we departed the top half a dozen courses of brick work had been somewhat modified.

We did, however, bequeath to the owners of the Café our superb ablutions and a number of other refinements we had made to the accommodation. When I visited in later years these had all disappeared. Ungrateful sods.

IN LIMBO

At the beginning of February 1946, we moved a few miles into the town of Goch and were quartered in the margarine works which at that time was not functioning as a factory. The place was actually owned by Lever Brothers and a plaque on the gate recorded that fact. (Amazing that this was still left intact). The actual operating name was, and still is, Van den Bergh. Stork and Flora margarine are but two of their extensive product range. We had quite roomy accommodation, in fact John Richardson and I had a room each. Actually he had organised a lady friend to keep his bed warm for him. He must have been suffering from insomnia because he disturbed me three times during one night, requesting my assistance in the matter of supplies of those items which would avoid his lady becoming pregnant.

Our stay here was short and on the 20th of the month we gathered up our chattels and set out for Duisburg, about 60 miles away in the Ruhr, in the middle of what can only be described as a blizzard. I was detailed to drive the platoon water carrier which was a Bedford 15 cwt vehicle having a water tank mounted instead of a normal load carrying body. It may have had a capacity of 150 gallons but at that time I couldn't have cared less. The truck had, I'm sure, been designed to be employed in a climate where it didn't even rain never mind snow! There was a noticeable absence of a windscreen for starters - just two small windshields each about nine inches high by fifteen inches wide. Cab doors were non existent, just pieces of canvas which were intended to act as half doors. The roof was, of course, canvas to complement the other refinements. The only additional feature was a sort of waterproof sheet that pulled out from under the dashboard and fastened round the driver's neck to afford some protection from the more aggressive elements.

Bedford MWC water tank

After the first ten miles or so the truck and I were totally unrecognisable for what we were, in that we resembled a wheeled avalanche. Snow accumulated in the so called cab until I had to stop and empty some out otherwise I was in danger of losing contact with the controls. I was never so pleased to arrive at a destination as I was that particular day.

I should mention that I was not the only recipient of unmentionable quantities of snow that day. The day before we left Goch we had visited for the last time the Red Shield canteen there. Here it was that Pete Pritchard had boogied that night away as they now say, (but with a slightly different meaning), and it transpired that the canteen was going to close. Actually Goch was not an inspiring place to lodge as it consisted for the most part of piles of rubble infested with anti personnel Schu mines. (Difficult to detect due to their wooden casing). Anyway, the management had decided that they did not want the aggravation of moving the piano, so they gave it to Pritchard!

We had promptly loaded it onto a trailer we had in the platoon, roped it into place ready to be transported to our new abode and taken it back to the margarine factory. It never occurred to any one that it ought to have been sheeted over as the weather was fine. The following day there was far too much to do to leave time to wrap up a piano with the result it was on its own throughout the blizzard.

Our new home was in a barracks, specifically the Flak Kaserne (anti aircraft barracks) in the city of Duisburg. All the accommodation was in two storey blocks, each room holding about six or eight men, no bunk beds - but single ones, double glazed windows, double locking doors and parquet flooring. Some of the floors had lifted caused by the ingress of rain due to the absence of large areas of roof. A large motor vehicle park was within the perimeter fence surrounding the entire establishment.

The author outside Flak barracks, Duisburg.

Marie with Pete Pritchard.

There was also a large parade ground upon which sat one Mack truck and the trailer carrying the piano. The snow of the previous day had not been as heavy in Duisburg and on the following morning, George Balls and I went out to inspect the platoon's property. Quite naturally we set about proving its musical capability and had hardly progressed beyond four bars when a loud scream assailed our ears. This turned out to be Company Sergeant Major Connolly (who had only been a corporal when we last saw him), and he was asking us, no he wasn't, he was telling us: "Get that thing out of here"!

We responded to his earnest request and over the course of the next few days sold the instrument to a local bar, after which we studiously avoided the place as we knew beyond any shadow of a doubt that the piano was inevitably going to suffer severe disruption to its mechanical and tonal capabilities.

Mack NR14 10 ton truck, 6 x 4.

Our stay in Duisburg was, happily, not a long one. Here the barrack square saw us parading under the eagle eye of Company Sergeant Major Connolly, our first real such parade since Aldershot. Within a few days we had driven the Macks to a location in Recklinghausen where we stayed for a day or two and handed over our trucks to a German Service Group, formed from some of the thousands of prisoners of war still held in camps. A very sad day for us all.

The Recklinghausen billet does not have a place in my memory other than the occasion when George Balls and I were going up the few steps to the door and Sgt. Major Connolly stopped me and told me in no uncertain tones to get rid of my jacket. This hurt me because the jacket in question had served me well for a long time. It was in fact a standard issue leather jerkin fitted with sleeves from a great coat, I haven't a clue from whence it came and to be fair it was looking a little the worse for wear so I had no option other than to dump it. The loss of both jacket and trucks within a day or so depressed me and I sensed the end of the good times.

During the next few weeks events moved so fast that I have difficulty in placing them into a meaningful time scale. I contracted tonsillitis and was immediately transported, by Stanley Hobson in the platoon 15 cwt (right), to the CRS (Casualty Receiving Station) at Krefeld. Here I was duly treated with an injection in the backside, stretchered into an ambulance and moved to the 77th British General Hospital at

A Bedford 15 cwt as owned by the platoon.

Wuppertal a few miles away. I spent a week there, most of it in bed, before being allowed up and issued with a set of Hospital Blues. These consisted of blue trousers and jacket and a white shirt - with collar and a red tie, a real smart outfit, for a fancy dress party! I wandered around the hospital grounds for a day and then got my discharge but instead of returning to Recklinghausen, I made my way to Kleve to spend a few days with Marie.

White 1064, 10 ton truck, 6 x 4

It was while we were spending some time with a friend of hers, that a truck appeared in the street with Jock Cunningham and Pete Pritchard and others aboard. They had come to tell me that I need not return to Recklinghausen as 917 Company had been broken up, and a number of us had been transferred to 905 Company which was equipped with White ten ton trucks and stationed at Bedburg, just outside of Kleve. This meant that I could still get to see Marie, who, naturally had been more than a little tearful when we departed for Duisburg, but, unfortunately, no sleeping out!

Our new company was doing the same job as we had been doing with 917 Company but from a different area of the Reichswald, but we could never rekindle the comradeship of those earlier times in Kleve.

Some of the members of B Platoon, prior to break up of 917 Company.

As if this was all I had to concern me! Guess who was the Platoon sergeant - none other than the kindly Sergeant Hyams, from whom I thought I had escaped when I transferred to B platoon back in March the previous year. Can you believe how pleased I was that I was due for twelve days leave on March 11th which I decided to spend in Kleve.

I don't know how I slipped up but I was late back from my leave and Hyams didn't waste any time in putting me under close arrest, after which I was charged, and to cut a long story short I ended up with seven days in the 'nick' at Company Headquarters, some place I can no longer remember. So I celebrated my third army anniversary on April 1st behind bars. (Iron, not drinking).

Within a few days of my release it was moving time again, I can't remember what happened to the trucks or even being bothered, and we found ourselves back in Recklinghausen this time in a part of a block of flats in the Hernestrasse. We were in a state of limbo, almost as though no one knew of our existence, and even if they had, wouldn't have known what to do with us. Marie arrived unexpectedly at Easter and we found her a place to stay for a few days.

During our time here Pete, Jock and I made a nuisance of ourselves by having musical interludes in the dining mess where our only instruments were knives and forks beating on table edges to simulate drums, leaving said tables suitably notched to prove that we had been here!

From the left: Stan Hobson, George Balls and the author.

I think that we had two weeks or so here and then 905 Company ceased to exist and we were sent our separate ways. I cannot remember saying goodbye to any one of the guys that I had lived with through all the good times (mostly) during the past year. This was the army - pack your kit and get on that truck sort of army - which I did and found myself some time and miles later joining 29 Tipper Company, wherever they were, don't ask me! I didn't even have time to unpack my kit as the following day this company broke up and I was on the road again, this time to Iserlohn ten miles southeast of Dortmund (still in the Ruhr).

LUDENSCHEID AND IBURG

Iserlohn was the home of the archaically named - 218 Ambulance Car Company - suitably equipped with Austin K2 ambulances, about which, more later. More importantly was the fact that Stanley Hobson and George Balls had also been posted here, but before we could collect our wits we were on the move again, this time as a platoon, ten miles south to the town of Ludenscheid.

Left: Stanley
Right: George

We were billeted in fairly new two storey flats, in a town that showed none of the scars of war which we had become accustomed to seeing wherever we had previously been. Apparently the allied advance had been so swift in this part of the Ruhr that some people had quite literally been caught with their trousers down.

It was here that Marie came to visit me in early June, with the news that she was pregnant. At the time I suppose the thought of becoming a father so soon in life was not exactly uplifting, but I soon got over that and if we had any misgivings they were offset by the fact that the situation would, and did in the end, prove favourable to our application to get married as and when we were able to submit it.

Two events marked June 21st. The first of these was the issue of BAFVs - British Armed Forces Vouchers - army money to replace Reichmarks which we had been using up to now. It was alleged that when the NAAFI organisation had audited their 1944/5 accounts it appeared as though the forces in Europe had spent more money than they had been paid! Where were they getting all their money from? So the decision had been made to give us our own currency which would be of no use to civilians, and at the same time was to be the only currency acceptable in canteens. Time to light our cigarettes with all the (now) useless twenty mark notes!

The second event was our departure for pastures new, specifically 90 miles north to Iburg a small village near Osnabrück. Here at the top of a hill was the Hotel Huberteshoff, which must have been in earlier times, quite a select establishment. It boasted a large dining or function room, extensive patio and terraced gardens to the rear and more than adequate accommodation for us.

The German manager or owner (I never did find out which), Herr Schaeffer, was told that the property was being requisitioned for military use and he and his family had the alternative of moving out and finding other accommodation, or they could stay, in specified rooms, on the understanding that they made themselves available to provide a service for the platoon officer and NCOs in return for which they would receive all their meals. They opted to stay.

Hotel Huberteshoff was to be D platoon's home for the next six months or so but would be unlike anything I had experienced to date. The company consisted of the usual RASC format with four platoons of ambulances plus headquarters personnel and vehicles. However, apart from the fact that, as in the past we never saw anything of the other platoons, there never was a time when all the members of the platoon or their vehicles came together. Ambulances were 'on detachment' to CRSs (Casualty Receiving Stations) and British General Hospitals over a wide area of north western Germany. The northern most CRS was on the island of Nordeney in the Friesian Islands off the north German coast. To the north east was a General Hospital in Hamburg while to the south of our territory was another hospital in Münster. Company headquarters were at Georges Marrienhütte just outside of Osnabrück. Our area was probably in the order of 150 to 200 miles in diameter over which our thirty plus ambulances were spread.

Iburg was the platoon headquarters with a minimum number of bods in residence, platoon officer, cooks, NCOs and a floating population of drivers in transit going to or coming from home leave, or drivers in with their vehicles for workshop inspection. Those who had found a very cushy (comfortable) station were usually extremely reluctant to be relieved whilst they came into Iburg lest they didn't get back. I recall the tale of one guy whose ambulance suffered a broken rear spring and rather than put his comfortable life style at risk by going into workshops for repair located a scrapped vehicles dump, (there was no shortage of these), dismantled the spring assembly from a wrecked ambulance and replaced his own broken one, unaided!

Where did yours truly fit in here? Very nicely thank you. As a newcomer to the platoon I wasn't immediately given an ambulance but undertook the duties of platoon clerk. These consisted of typing letters and platoon orders, arranging reliefs for men going on leave or coming in for vehicle inspection. I also helped with the distribution of ration cigarettes and NAAFI goods. A fairly cushy number, comfortable sleeping quarters, regular meals and just the odd guard duty to do.

If there was any drawback to this life it was the absence of mates from way back. I got on OK with the guys who were part of the regular establishment but I did not see much of Stanley or George as they were we both out on detachment, with ambulances to hospitals, and as we three were the only ones who had come from 917 Company, it was difficult during the early days at Iburg to really feel at home. It did get better later on and there were some good guys in the platoon, but it could never be like the old days.

We hadn't been there long before Marie came to stay, I had found her a room in a house in the village. The owner had a small workshop upstairs in which he manufactured wooden buttons and was quite friendly (unusual for this part of Germany). Marie's presence cheered me up and we settled down to a reasonably civilised pattern of living. Later on her sister also came to stay for a few days and I recall one particular event that caused some amusement. We had, naturally, a well stocked bar in which rested a piano, upon which George and I (he was in for vehicle inspection), were pounding out some early evening four hands at one piano boogie-woogie. It must have been August, I remember it was hot and the window which looked out on to the street, was wide open. Suddenly somebody shouted: "Bob! Your girl friend's coming up the road!" George and I immediately terminated our relationship with the piano and assumed looks of total innocence as Marie and her sister Stini appeared outside. I was supposed to have gone to the house where they were staying but I had totally forgotten about this arrangement.

I think it worth while at this point to record that since the early days in Kleve, when conversations between myself and Marie, and any one else come to that, were conducted in a mixture of English, German and sign language, my ability to speak German had improved considerably. I had also developed a knowledge of the Kleve dialect and could use it in conversation. In common with most other local dialects there was no written version and according to my friends in Kleve I was the only Englishman they knew having this ability. This obviously meant that when I was with Marie and other Germans we were able to avoid, to a marked degree, time consuming interpretation.

Although the city of Osnabrück had suffered from numerous air raids, the country around showed little signs of the effect of conflict as the allied advance had been just as rapid here as it had through our last location - Ludenscheid. During our time with 917 Company we had driven through France, Belgium, Holland and Germany and, other than most of Holland, had passed through a landscape of wrecked buildings, bridges and cratered roads. This was particularly true in the Ruhr, the industrial heart of Germany, where the sight of the wasteland that had once been the Krupps factories was sobering evidence of the capability of superior air power. Amidst the tangle of concrete and steel, the only structures left standing were dozens of factory chimneys, some with chunks missing from them but still there! The round shapes of these had obviously protected them from blast damage.

Not only did the landscape differ but the people were not like those in Kleve. I learned later that the area we were in - Westphalia - was noted for the surliness of the population, although there were exceptions to the general rule. Kleve was in the Rhineland where the people were noted for their much more outgoing attitudes and apparent ability to surmount difficulties. In Iburg, other than the button maker, I cannot recall any other liaison with civilians except for the people at our hotel and a visiting pianist. Let me tell you about him.

He was a very small guy, wore glasses and was a tremendous pianist, in a more classical style than either George and me or another quite competent player we had in the platoon. He did, however, play other than classical and he had the hilarious habit that whenever he finished playing a tune he would very quickly turn his head round to look at us and give us the benefit of a huge grin. The music publishing industry was now beginning to function in Germany and I remember he brought the sheet music for Violetta with him one evening and rended, sorry, rendered it in his true classical style. He was quite a character and we enjoyed his company on a number of occasions.

We were also entertained by a couple of guys in the platoon (when they were in Iburg for inspection or whatever) who hailed from London, the Smith brothers, Cockneys all the way through, a sort of early day Chas and Dave. By some stroke of fate, or good management, these two along with one or two welcome others were in Iburg for Christmas, but more about that later.

I think it must have been sometime in August that the news came that applications to marry German Nationals could be submitted to 2nd Echelon Headquarters in Hamburg. I immediately submitted my application with the initial response being a visit by the

Company Padre (Army Minister of the church), whose efforts to dissuade me from marrying a German seemed to be so totally lacking in ethical Christian teaching that it severely damaged my belief in the church.

All Marie and I could do now was wait for the official machine to respond. I knew that this would take a while as I was aware that delaying tactics were the order of the day and my major concern was that I would be demobbed (demobilised) before marriage approval came through. My demob number was 52 and I calculated that I would probably be going home for good some time in late summer 1947. (Demob numbers were allocated to all service personnel and were calculated using a formula based primarily upon length of service). By this time the saying 'roll on demob' was heard everywhere and whilst it was an event to be anticipated, I did not wish to be discharged before our marriage application had come through. The problems of trying to arrange a wedding with Marie in Germany and me in England were not to be relished.

Early in November Marie departed for home, she being now seven months pregnant, and I was sent to Lustringen near Osnabrück for a week or so doing I know not what. I was soon back in Iburg and looking forward to December which would bring the opportunity to celebrate Christmas and my nineteen days leave due on the 29th, which I intended spending in Kleve so as to be there when Marie gave birth.

By the time Christmas arrived we had, by a combination of fair and foul means, ensured that those present were those who would bring a little colour to our celebrations. The Smith boys were with us as was George Balls and I seem to remember that we did have a visit from our German pianist. What I do remember without any difficulty is the glorious p**s up we had on Christmas Day night. It went on and on and at 3am we fetched 'Pop' Schaeffer, as we now called him, out of bed to tap a fresh barrel. I don't recall much about Boxing Day events, in fact I didn't know a great deal about them at the time!

I departed on the 29th by train from Osnabrück to Kleve changing at Krefeld. This kind of journey was not official and I travelled on ordinary trains but did not pay any fares. I was, of course a member of the Occupying Army and we were not in the habit of paying to travel on trains, buses or trams. There was no official regulations pertaining to this, that I remember, we just did it. I eventually became quite adept at moving around the country either by public transport or hitch hiking which would stand me in good stead during 1947.

My leave was due to terminate on the 18th of January 1947 and I was due back at Iburg on the 19th. Showing superb timing our daughter Hedy Elizabeth was born on the 16th necessitating a number of swift visits, with Marie's sister Stini, to officialdom in Kleve to register the birth. This done, back home to the attic room that we had furnished in the Dr. Scholtenstrasse, complete with wood burning pot bellied stove. Two days later I was on my way back to Iburg.

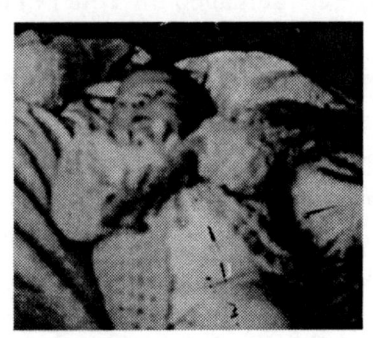

Hedy Elizabeth, ten days old.

Author with Marie wearing a rabbit skin coat, Jan '47.

On my return I learned that the unit had organised a Christmas party for the local children and some forty to fifty mothers and offspring had been well and truly fed and entertained.

Our platoon officer had prepared a surprise welcome for me, he had, in my absence, decided to employ a German secretary person, female of course, to undertake those duties previously handled by me. Maybe she provided additional services that I was quite incapable of offering but I never found out. In addition I was to return to driving duties and be given charge of an ambulance at the CRS in Detmold. I suppose I was ready for a change anyway and I had missed the freedom which came from being behind the wheel and out on the road. Going out on detachment to any location be it CRS or General Hospital did offer a degree of independence away from your own unit officers and NCOs, although you were, of course, under temporary command of the senior RAMC (Royal Army Medical Corps) officer, but as long as you did your job and ensured that your vehicle was available at a moments notice you would be left pretty much alone. At some locations there were two ambulances and this obviously made for improved opportunity on the leisure front.

DETMOLD

Thus I found myself in charge of an Austin ambulance and sent out to 1055 CRS at Detmold which lay about 50 miles south east of Osnabrück. So far as I remember I was the only ambulance there initially but later on a second one was added. The CRS was located on an ex Luftwaffe (German Air Force) airfield which was equipped with semi underground parking for aircraft plus copious accommodation blocks for supporting personnel. Nowhere was there any damage to be seen, not even a broken window.

The aircraft parking areas were full of British tanks, (tracked not water), and the barrack blocks contained a number of units among which were the 1st Royal Norfolk Regiment,

Austin K2, 2 ton ambulance

condemned to a routine of parades and equipment cleaning to keep them occupied until demobilisation time arrived. At this time virtually the whole of the British forces in Germany had nothing to do. They could not be accommodated in the UK so they had, quite literally, to sit on their backsides to await demob. Thinking about it, I suppose that it made sound economical sense to keep them in Germany where they could, as an occupying army, be housed at minimum cost to the British economy.

The only elements of the army which were still working were the RAMC, albeit with dramatically reduced manpower, the Royal Engineers who were involved in bridge construction and maintenance and ourselves. Away from us in the ambulance companies were the general transport units who still had the task of moving the vast quantities of stores and munitions with which the country was liberally endowed.

Our accommodation was in keeping with the nature of our location, four men to a room with single beds (with sheets on them), situated in the two storey CRS building. The medical facilities were all on the ground floor with bedrooms and recreation room on the first floor. Daily room cleaning and bed making was performed by local young female labour as there was no formalised bed and kit layout. We were fortunate to have a superb cook who provided meals which reflected his ability not only to cook army rations, but to use them as barter for more palatable alternatives.

Staff of 1055 CRS (Casualty Receiving Station) at Detmold. Author in back row at left as viewed.

The work load was not exceptionally heavy, light casualties or minor illnesses were handled within the CRS which had eight or ten beds, more serious cases were transported to the 23rd British General Hospital at Bad Oyenhausen which was some 20 miles away. The number of married families now resident in Germany was increasing, the initial influx being officer's wives, and a fair number of these became our passengers to the hospital. They were nearly always accompanied by one of the two Queen Alexandra's Nurses resident at the CRS, and it was on one such journey that one of the wives gave birth, in the ambulance, whilst we stopped on the autobahn (motorway). We had planned to be at the hospital earlier but the journey had been desperately slow due to the icy condition of the roads. There was no gritting service to help us!

The Autobahn (motorway) Ruhr to Hannover.

The policy at the CRS was to ensure that beds were not occupied by patients with illness or injury necessitating a long stay as beds had to remain free for urgent casualties in deference to its title. This need became paramount when a serious accident occurred in the district, where a truck carrying a number of soldiers going out for the evening, went off the road and down a steep embankment at the bottom of which was a small river. All the casualties were brought into the CRS and following treatment the more seriously injured ones were taken to Bad Oyenhausen. I carried four, one of whom was unfortunately dead on arrival.

One of the more mundane tasks we undertook was conveying those unfortunates who had contracted venereal disease to the General Hospital in Münster, which was a 60 mile journey, and it must have been worrying for them to listen to the deliberately lurid conversation between driver and medical orderly concerning the treatment awaiting them in Münster.

During my first two months in Detmold the weather was extremely cold with hard frosts and enough snow for three winters. In fact this was the coldest winter for 53 years. We didn't have anti-freeze in the cooling system in those days! The alternative would have been to drain the cooling system but this would have jeopardised our ability to respond to an urgent call out. Last thing at night we started up the ambulance(s) and let the engine warm up and then put a bonnet rug over it. It was then necessary to get up in the middle of the night, dress and go out to the ambulance and start it up again and let it run for fifteen to twenty minutes.

Snow was particularly heavy at the beginning of February and I drove my ambulance to Hamelin, of Pied Piper fame, to take a fellow RASC driver to see his German girl friend who was ill with diphtheria in an isolation hospital there. A quite dodgy journey using roads cleared by snow ploughs through ten feet high drifts. Had we ditched or suffered any such disaster we would have been for the high jump as this was an unauthorised journey! We were lucky and got back to Detmold unscathed.

The Austin K2 ambulance was a fairly decent vehicle to drive being fitted with a powerful Austin built petrol engine, which was the power unit fitted to three ton trucks. Four casualties could be carried, the beds at each side could be hand wound to an elevated position enabling two casualties to be accommodated at the lower level as well as the two higher up. With both side beds in the lower position, eight or ten sitting passengers could be carried. Inside at the front was a door to the drivers compartment which had a hinged seat attached to it for the medical orderly's use and with the door open, the seat made it possible for three people to sit up front. The K2 was fairly light, and as the engine was not fitted with speed governors it could motor at a fair rate of knots. Care needed to be taken when cornering as, of necessity, the springing was very soft and so the vehicle did tend to 'lean over' somewhat when speed was combined with a tight corner. As a driver you became accustomed to this behaviour but passengers new to the vehicle did tend to grab for support at times. It was said that if you possessed long arms you could actually lean out and strike a match on the ground as you took a left hand corner.

The only vehicle that I had driven to date that managed to keep out the elements was the Bedford I had in Aldershot. Since then I had felt cold air blasting me through gaping holes in the floor, where the clutch and brake pedals protruded from in the ten ton Foden. The Macks we had driven for twelve months during 1945-6, good as they were, did not have a decent cab, and there is nothing more I can, or will say, about the water truck I drove from Goch to Duisburg in February 1946! Now here I was in 1947, in winter, and does the Austin have a cab? No it doesn't! It is equipped with those good old canvas screens which imitate the bottom half of a door, and the canvas and mica screens for the top half of the door. Refinements such as heaters and screen demisters were unheard of, and radios, - in trucks? Please, do me a favour.

We were issued with leather jerkins (a sleeveless jacket) and gloves, as were all drivers, but they struggled to alleviate the sometimes biting cold, particularly where your hands were concerned, they being more or less fixed on the steering wheel for long periods. It was on one journey to Bad Oyenhausen, on a bitterly cold day, that when I arrived there and felt the need to relieve myself, I found that my fingers were so numb and useless that I was quite unable to undo my trouser fly buttons! I had to find a willing bystander to assist me and then realised that I was totally unable to manipulate my wedding tackle in the necessary manner. Willing bystander to the rescue again!

As the weather warmed up, life, especially the driving, became more pleasurable. We could for example take advantage of the large garden which backed on to the CRS or, during weekends and providing that one ambulance with driver was at the CRS, the other driver was allowed to spend the day out. This arrangement would be very beneficial to me later on in the year. The onset of warm weather did bring one slight problem with it.

View from billet of the large garden at 1055 CRS.

It was habitual to leave the windows in the toilets open at night. It was also habitual in the army that after lights out time had passed they stayed out. If perchance a visit to the toilet became necessary during the night then you found your way by touch and experience and the dim emergency lighting. So far so good. But open windows and background illumination provided a natural target for a species of flying beetles which had the habit of hurling themselves through the windows and hitting the opposite wall. Progressively through the hours of darkness the floor became covered with beetle carcasses, so, make sure you wear something on your feet during your nocturnal wanderings

Across from the CRS was a parking area full of no longer needed RAF vehicles including a couple of fire engines. (The RAF had occupied part of the barracks for a while after hostilities had ceased). The other ambulance driver and I dismounted two of the electric bells from these and fitted them on to our own vehicles with a simple push button control fixed to the dashboard. Driving through the town sounding your bell had a very marked effect on traffic flow, even if we were only going down to the canteen in town. The schoolboy in us came to the surface when two ambulances approached the crossroads in town where, at certain times of the day, a traffic policeman was on duty. When I say approached, I mean from different directions. Use your imagination!

After nearly fifty years have elapsed since a particular event took place, one's memory is bound to play tricks, and during the past few weeks I have wracked my brain and searched diligently for some recorded proof of an occurrence which I am sure took place in Detmold.

Detmold possessed a theatre and during the spring of 1947 was host to the Sadler's Wells Opera Company enacting Madam Butterfly. We decided to go in the context of improving our cultural standards. Now, in the armed forces when you go to places of entertainment reserved entirely for forces personnel, you sit where you are told to sit! This I did and sat down next to some character who turned round to me and said: "Hello Bob" and I replied, in equally nonchalant manner: "Hello Wallace." He was Wallace Utting who I had worked alongside in the Goole Co-op offices back in 1942. (He had been called up earlier than me). We exchanged a few pleasantries, enjoyed the opera and went our separate ways. Can you believe such coincidences, first meeting George Coult (from Goole), in France, sleeping in the bed from Glew's furniture store in Goole during one of our stops in Belgium in 1944, and now meeting with Wallace Utting?

Some fate of organisation had brought George Balls to Detmold for two or three weeks in the spring which pleased us both, he and I and two other drivers shared a room. One of the others was a small guy from some other unit and he drove the officer's car, a VW Beetle (Volkswagen). He had a great knack of imitating Hispanic Americans, - we called him Sad Sack (see picture right), after the American cartoon character. The other driver was (Blondie) Nicholls but I can't recall a great deal about him.

During February and March I had been able to visit Marie as the RAMC Lieutenant was a good guy and let me have weekend passes to go to Kleve. (I still have a couple of these in my possession such as the one pictured below).

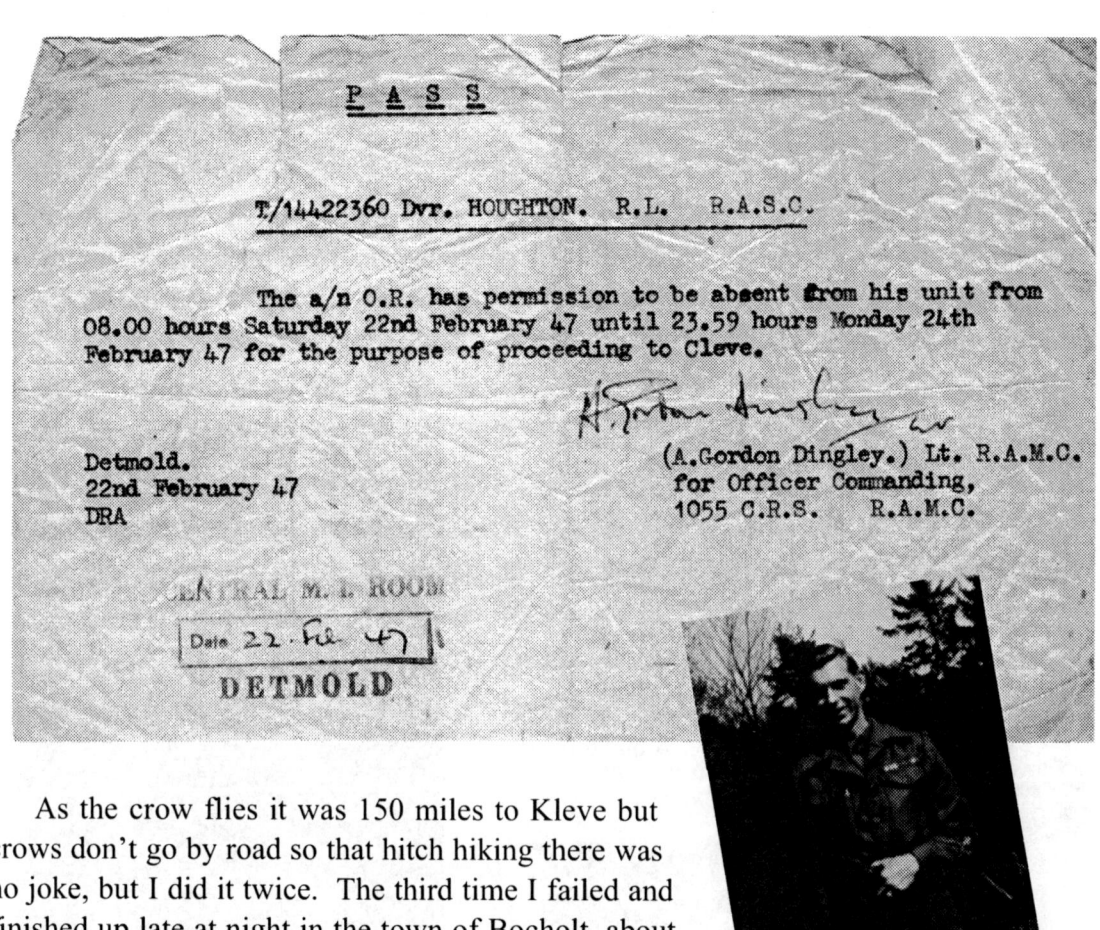

```
                        P A S S

        T/14422360 Dvr. HOUGHTON. R.L.   R.A.S.C.


             The a/n O.R. has permission to be absent from his unit from
    08.00 hours Saturday 22nd February 47 until 23.59 hours Monday 24th
    February 47 for the purpose of proceeding to Cleve.


                                         (A.Gordon Dingley.) Lt. R.A.M.C.
    Detmold.                              for Officer Commanding,
    22nd February 47                      1055 C.R.S.    R.A.M.C.
    DRA
```

CENTRAL M.I. ROOM
Date 22 Feb 47
DETMOLD

As the crow flies it was 150 miles to Kleve but crows don't go by road so that hitch hiking there was no joke, but I did it twice. The third time I failed and finished up late at night in the town of Bocholt, about 40 miles short and spent the night in a police station. Cigarettes on parade again. The following morning I decided to cut my losses and headed back to Detmold. My journey back to Detmold from Kleve had usually been by bus to Emmerich and across the Rhine by civilian ferry, (there still existed restrictions against some civilian traffic using the army built Rhine bridges). From Emmerich I could catch a train to some point near to Detmold and hitch hike the rest, but this time I had to hitch the whole way back and it must have taken me hours.

Author - dressed for pleasure.

My most successful foray to Kleve from Detmold was to have one of the other drivers take me to Bad Oyenhausen where I knew a Brussels bound leave train stopped. Now this town housed the BAOR (British Army of the Rhine) Headquarters so it was awash with Redcaps (Military Police). I had a pass from 1055 CRS but not to go to Brussels. My plan was to wait until I saw the train pull into the station from the vantage point of the nearby canteen, then run on to the station just in time to board. It worked perfectly as when I ran through the subway to the platform I spotted an MP and went straight up to him, panting, and asked which platform I needed to be on for Brussels. Without hesitation he told me and suggested I move a bit sharpish otherwise I would miss it. I made it with seconds to spare. Now I obviously had no intention of going to Brussels but I knew that the train would be stopping at Krefeld and this is where, carefully avoiding MPs, I changed trains for Kleve.

a) Young love
b) Marie - author's favourite picture
c) Marie with daughter Hedy and brother Willibald
d) Marie and Hedy

One of the funniest events, more so at the time, happened when I was driving into Detmold town and a Fordson 15 cwt truck came out of a side street and struck my ambulance on the driver's side at the point of the pretend cab. The driver leapt out hurling abuse at me when I was not even at fault, asking what was I intending to do concerning his starting handle which was now locked into his engine? (Fordsons had a starting handle which was permanently in position held out of mesh with the engine by a strong spring). You should have seen his face when my passenger, - an RAF Wing Commander popped his head out from the door connecting the cab to the rear of the ambulance to ask if there was a problem. End of story.

Ford WOT2 15 cwt 4 x 2 truck.

Marie came to visit for a few weeks during late May and into June, (her mother looked after Hedy) and we managed to see each

A day in the country near Detmold with Marie, 1947.

other nearly every day including some good days out in the fine weather, which was the norm in this part of Germany at this time of the year.

As the size of the occupying forces began to diminish, units were in a continuing state of reorganisation and at some point during the spring, 218 Ambulance Car Company ceased to exist. Its vehicles, and personnel, were incorporated into new companies which were composed of mixed types of vehicles, - general load carriers, ambulances, petrol tankers etc. Prior to this, companies had consisted of just one type of vehicle, but the new approach did make sense as it could be seen, for example, that a company consisting entirely of bulk petrol carriers did not have a place in post war occupation. Our new identity was 507 Company and as such was part of the famous 7th Armoured Division. (The Desert Rats - see inset). The platoon Headquarters had moved from Iburg to Georgesmarienhütte. I wonder what happened to the officer's secretary bird?

June saw me at odds with the military machine once more. The senior officer at the CRS was a Captain Kent (RAMC) and he had decided that a morning parade of the personnel under his command was desirable. His personnel included (temporarily) us RASC drivers so each morning we turned out along with his RAMC soldiers. Now I use the term soldiers rather reluctantly as virtually all of them had only been in the army for a few months and as peace time soldiers they had become accustomed to parading at the drop of a hat, as it were. One morning I decided not to go on parade as I had attended a call out during the night. The result of my non appearance was to be put on a charge and brought before Captain Kent. He wasn't prepared to listen to my defence and finding me guilty, commenced his little speech which would have given me a 'confined to barracks' sentence of probably seven days, which in itself would have been a bit of a laugh, me being an ambulance driver.

However, I was feeling in a particular anti military mood that morning and I interrupted him to say that he had not asked me if I was willing to accept his punishment. This was Military Law when you were on detachment to a unit other than your own, and after four years in the army, and as an 'ex con', (Sergeant Hyams and all that), I was not lacking in knowledge of these things. I thought he was going to explode but he did manage to ask the question whereupon I said that I did not wish to accept! He had me placed under immediate close arrest and detailed an RAMC corporal, name of Abbot, (nicknamed Bud of course), to accompany me, in my ambulance, back to Osnabrück where company headquarters was now located.

At the time this was, to say the least, inconvenient, as Marie was still in residence in Detmold. One of the medics said he would get word to her to make her way back to Kleve. Later my presence in Osnabrück would reap dividends in terms of our marriage application but more about that later.

OSNABRUCK

Headquarters in Osnabrück was reminiscent of Aldershot. It was in a barracks named Kaprivi Kaserne. Huge two storey blocks plus basements dating from the last century with barrack rooms to sleep thirty or forty bods, and no sheets either. In addition, horror of horrors, a spacious parade ground echoing to the sound of marching feet and shrieking NCOs. (Well to be honest not all the time). A guard house at the one and only entrance completed the picture associated with a peace time army. (An oft quoted extract from a fictitious letter home springs to mind, - 'Dear Mum it's a b*****d', and the return missive 'Dear son, so are you!')

My old friend Sergeant Major Connolly was pleased to see me and he had very kindly arranged for me to see the Commanding Officer the following day, although he didn't quite explain it to me in this manner. The meeting duly took place and I was sentenced to seven days confined to barracks (jankers) with its usual complement of cook house fatigues of cleaning utensils and so forth. In addition I was obliged to parade each evening along with the duty fire piquet and main gate guard for inspection by you know who's favourite Sgt. Major. At this time in our career we were obliged to wear medal ribbons in respect of the campaign medals we had been awarded. These were; The 1939/45 Star, The France and Germany Star, The Defence Medal earned with Home Guard service and The 1939/45 Medal. (See Appendix C for picture). Eagle eyed Connolly spotted a loose thread on one of my ribbons and pulling gently on it succeeded in unravelling the whole damned ribbon! I'm sure he could see the gratitude in my eyes for his action in drawing to my attention this slight lapse on my part by coming on parade incorrectly dressed.

He must have taken a shine to me, or more likely he didn't know what to do with me because at the end of my seven days penance I was told that from now on I was to be Company Clerk. I installed myself in the Company office and immediately reaped the benefit by being told that there was no need for me to grace the morning parade with my presence.

I was very conscious of the fact that my demobilisation time was virtually upon me and still no marriage approval. I had no option therefore other than to take advantage of a scheme to extend my service by three months. This was known as a 'Gentleman's Agreement' or GA and was only available to RASC and I believe Royal Engineers in consideration of the continuing need for transport and constructional skills. Believe it or not but this GA could be terminated by either party by giving ten days notice!

Marie came over to Osnabrück to stay for a few weeks with a family not too far from the barracks and she was there when George Balls came into barracks ready for his journey home, for his demob on the 4th of August. The advantage of being in the Company Office together with my now extended service, enabled me to get to grips with the question of approval for Marie and I to marry, and I requested a forty eight hour pass to go to Hamburg to attempt to speed events along. The 2nd Echelon Headquarters in the district of Altona in Hamburg was mainly staffed by members of the ATS (Auxiliary Territorial Service - women's army), and I hung around there while they lethargically sorted out my file. I got the distinct impression that there existed deliberate tardiness in dealing with applications (why does he have to marry a German girl?), but I stuck to my guns and eventually they found my file and I left with the assurance that it would now be processed.

Author and George Balls leaving canteen.

Back in Osnabrück I was approached by Sgt. Major Connolly suggesting that I should sign on for further service, but this time in terms of years not months. I must confess that I was tempted as he assured me that I would receive promotion within a very short time and ought to make Staff Sergeant in a couple of years. However, I had in my mind's eye the notation in my Soldiers Service and Pay Book (AB 64 - see appendix C) that I was available for Far East posting and that was something I did not fancy at all. Later on in the 1950s when we had moved to Doncaster, South Yorkshire, we were visited by a couple who had, like us, married in Germany. This guy had signed on for longer service, in the RASC, and he made it to Staff Sergeant.

Author, 1947

They had enjoyed a good life living in married quarters all over the world with a good standard of living. Sounded good but the question remained - what do you do when you come out of the army aged around forty five with no property and probably no skills directly usable in civvy street?

It's hardly worth noting that we had ceased being 507 Company and we were now 951 Company. Same thing, just a different number. I was fortunate to be given the opportunity for one last driving job before demob arrived. I was detailed to take a replacement ambulance, a Humber as it happened, out to the CRS on Nordeney which was an island in the Fresian Islands, in the Heligoland Bight off the North Sea coast of Germany. The island had been an important seaplane base during the war and it was from here that aircraft were dispatched to sow mines in English waters. How often had we listened to the wartime news, with (probably) Alvar Lidell reading it including items concerning air activity in this area.

Humber FWD, 8 cwt, 4 x 4 - ambulance version.

The journey north was accomplished in two legs, the first of these was to Oldenburg, where we had two ambulances stationed at the General Hospital, for an overnight stay. The following day took me through Emden and then to Norden from where I took the vehicle ferry out to the island, to complete a total of some 160 miles from Osnabrück. The weather was brilliant and the sea trip a superb experience and from what I could see as we came to our destination, no evidence whatsoever that the military installations had suffered any damage.

The reason for me having to bring an ambulance out here was that the Austin there was due workshop inspection, and to have the resident driver take it into Osnabrück for that purpose would obviously have left the island without an ambulance for anything up to four days. Quite aside from that reason the accommodation this driver had was unbelievable, private room complete with 'room service', fresh flowers all over the place and a beach within walking distance. Before the war Nordeney had been a holiday venue, now it was totally bereft of tourists, other than me. No wonder he didn't want to leave!

I spent a very pleasant day on Nordeney and considerably refreshed and having signed over the Humber I departed with the Austin to retrace my route back to Osnabrück.

Mid October brought the news that I had been waiting so long for. The approval for Marie and I to marry had arrived. Our platoon officer called me in to tell me the good news and when he looked at the details of my GA Agreement he realised that I should have gone home two weeks earlier. He advised me to get organised and arrange the marriage as soon as possible and then get ourselves back to England. His command of language in making the last point was far and above what I had come to expect from him as an officer and a gentleman.

The next few days were a blur. I purchased a fruit cake from the NAAFI canteen and the company cook volunteered to ice it for me. At the same time I arranged for dozens of cakes to be obtained from the same source by the two guys who were going to Kleve for the wedding. We had to solve the problem of transport for them and the food and this was where cigarette currency really came into its own! German Service Groups (staffed by POWs), were operating large numbers of ex RASC trucks and we managed to find one who was going to Krefeld about 40 miles south of Kleve. He was plied with enough cigarettes to sink a battleship and agreed to transport bods and cakes all the way to Kleve.

That left the marriage ceremony itself to be organised and when I arrived in Kleve (don't remember how I did this), Marie and I set out to find a church and priest. Everywhere we went we drew a blank, all the churches in Kleve were Catholic! In desperation I went to the CCG (Control Commission Germany) which had replaced the Military Government put in place on the cessation of hostilities. CCG was loosely interpreted as 'Charlie Chaplin's Grenadiers' by all those not part of that organisation. They were very sympathetic and immediately lent us a car and driver to assist in our quest, suggesting that we try to arrange the ceremony to take place in a Garrison Church within an Army Barracks. The nearest appeared to be Hilden near Düsseldorf some 60 miles away so there we went.

The end result was that the two of us and one witness, - Joe Catterall from Great Yarmouth, - and the CCG driver crammed into a VW Beetle and set out for Hilden, where we were married during the late morning of November 1st. Because the church was inside the barracks we were not allowed to have any non military personnel with us and photographs were not permitted. The service was conducted in both English and German with the help of a German lady interpreter and the second witness we required was the first decently dressed soldier who passed. Marie wore a full length blue silk dress which I had brought from home some time earlier.

We all piled back into the Beetle for the journey back to Kleve and arrived at the single carriageway Bailey bridge over the Rhine to find that it was being used by traffic from the opposite direction and we were told that this would be the case for another half hour. We promptly took ourselves off to the NAAFI sited next to the bridge and our health and future prosperity were toasted in canteen tea!

Eventually arriving back in Kleve in the late afternoon we found that friends and neighbours had decorated outside of the house with small

A view of the river Rhine from the railbridge near Düsseldorf during the early 1960's, when the original single track Bailey bridge had been replaced by this simple structure.
A modern suspension bridge has now replaced this.

evergreen trees and we were greeted by a host of people as we made our way indoors. Inside they had constructed a kind of throne for us to sit upon suitably garnished with greenery and what followed was a celebration I shall never forget. It went on long into the night and included an impromptu cavalcade along the street at about 2am.

Around 4am Marie and I decided we had had enough, or perhaps Marie decided that I had had enough and we made our way up to our attic bedroom. Reaching the top landing I reached out for the door knob, (both of them), missed and fell backwards down the stairs, limply! Marie's dad came and picked me up and threw me into bed. End of Wedding Day!

We stayed on in Kleve for two or three days packing, and then Marie and I along with the two mates (Caterall and the other driver) took the train to Krefeld and from there to Cologne where we would part company, us to Hamburg the others to Osnabrück. We boarded the train in Cologne and but for a casual enquiry I made, we would have been on the way to Prague in Czechoslovakia. The Hamburg train was at the opposite platform about to depart and the next few minutes were a blur of motion as we scrambled out and across to the right train.

As we were now a married family we had the right to occupy hotels which were reserved for families, and across the square from the railway station we booked in at the Graf Möltke Hotel, where we planned to stay for a few days. We had chosen to come to Hamburg so that we could go to Headquarters in Altona, a district of Hamburg, and obtain travel documents to England for Marie and Hedy, which we managed to do the following day. After having had two nights at the hotel, we took the train to Osnabrück where Marie's mother and father awaited us with Hedy and the rest of our luggage, which included a large wooden chest containing a double bed size feather quilt.

We had only two days in Osnabrück and with our luggage loaded, including baby carriage, we bade a tearful farewell to Marie's parents at the railway station as we departed aboard the Nord Express to the Hook of Holland, travelling first class. At the Hook transit camp there was good married family accommodation, including a cot for Hedy and we were quite comfortable for the two days we spent there. We were not allowed to cross to England on the same ship, I sailed aboard a normal (all male) troopship whilst Marie and Hedy were on a Dutch ferry carrying civilian personnel and members of the women's forces. Both ships docked at Harwich and I didn't see my family until I met them at Liverpool Street station in London. The army provided transport (a good old Bedford three tonner) to ferry us across to King's Cross. It was about 8pm when we eventually arrived in Goole to be met by mum and dad, (I had telephoned dad at work before we left London). It was November 10th.

I was now on three months end of service leave (actually known as Python leave as I had been overseas for three years), which would end on the 14th of February 1948 one day short of five years service when I officially became a civilian. I would, of course, be paid whilst on leave and my daily pay had, by now, risen to the princely sum of four shillings and six pence. (Twenty two and a half new pence). This would be paid weekly through the Post Office as would my lump sum Gratuity (redundancy money if you like) of £72.

Virtually my last act as a soldier was to go to York and receive my demob clothing issue, - suit, shoes, shirt, tie, raincoat and a hat. I was allowed to keep my uniform, - tunic, trousers, great coat, beret, boots, belt and gaiters, kit bag, small pack and such oddments as shaving gear. In fact the army only retained the webbing straps and ammo pouches, large

Demob.

The author's last trip in an army truck was in a Bedford QL troop carrier pictured above.

pack and, of course, gas mask, steel helmet and sten gun, these items having been left in Germany. Now the time had come to take my last ride in an army truck to the railway station. Quite sad in a way, I already had the feeling of not 'belonging' any more. I was now within a short time of becoming a civilian and during the next few weeks would feel the loss of identity quite markedly.

Since that first day of April 1943 my life had most certainly changed!

ARMY BOOK X801

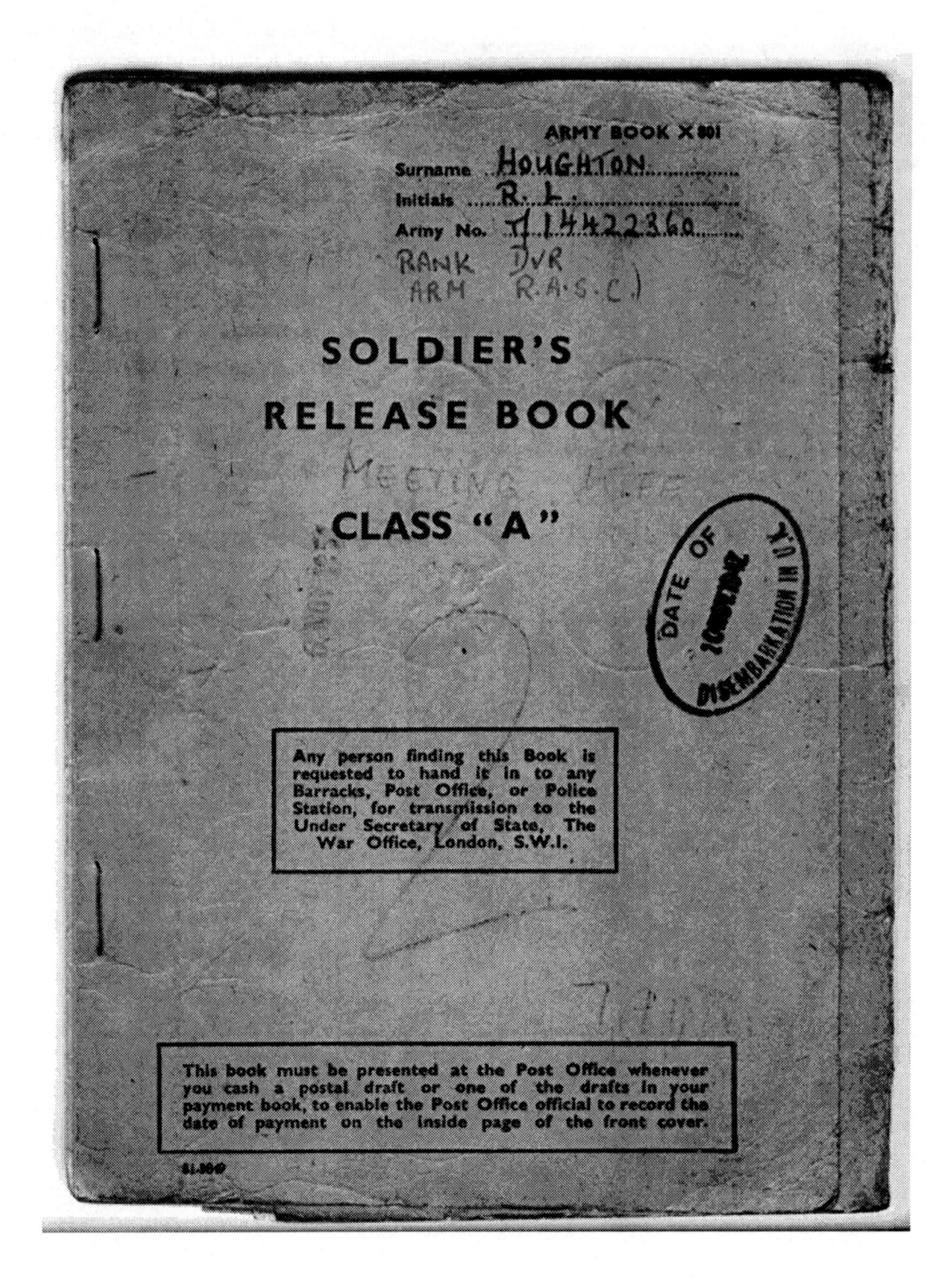

Surname **HOUGHTON**
Initials **R. L.**
Army No. **T/14422360**
RANK DVR
ARM R.A.S.C.

SOLDIER'S RELEASE BOOK

CLASS "A"

DATE OF DISEMBARKATION IN U.K.

Any person finding this Book is requested to hand it in to any Barracks, Post Office, or Police Station, for transmission to the Under Secretary of State, The War Office, London, S.W.1.

This book must be presented at the Post Office whenever you cash a postal draft or one of the drafts in your payment book, to enable the Post Office official to record the date of payment on the inside page of the front cover.

289001   Army Form X 202B.

CERTIFICATE OF TRANSFER to the ARMY RESERVE

Army No. T/14422360 Rank DRIVER

Surname (Block letters) HOUGHTON

Christian Name(s) Robert Leslie

Regt. or Corps R.A.S.C.

The transfer of the above-named to the appropriate Class of the Army Reserve (see note below) is confirmed with effect from 15.2.48.*

*The date to be inserted here will be that following the day on which Release Leave terminates, including any additional leave to which the soldier may be entitled by virtue of service overseas.

Note.—The appropriate Class of the Army Reserve is as follows:—

(i) Royal Army Reserve—in the case of a regular soldier with reserve service to complete:

(ii) Army Reserve Class Z (T)—in the case of a man of the Territorial Army, including those called up for service under the National Service Acts:

(iii) Army Reserve, Class Z—in the case of all other soldiers not included in (i) or (ii) above.

Record Office Stamp.

R.A.S.C. RECORDS
20 NOV 1947

for Col. I/C R.A.S.C. & A.C.C.
Officer i/c .... RECORDS Records.

Date ....

Warning.—
Any alteration of the particulars given in this certificate may render the holder liable to prosecution under the Seamen's and Soldiers' False Characters Act, 1906.

If this certificate is lost or mislaid, no duplicate can be obtained.

Wt. 37285/90 1,000M 12/45 KJL/1515/16 Gp. 38/3
Wt. 40009/240 1,000M 2/46 KJL/1722/32 Gp. 38/3

Back to civvy street as husband and wife with family.

EPILOGUE

I have, to the best of my ability, told this brief history of my life during the period between the declaration of war with Germany in 1939 and the end of my military service in early 1948. Memory can play funny tricks on you. Just when you think that you have recalled a past event or situation to perfection, a niggling doubt assails you and poses the question, 'have I got it right?' The further back in the past you are trying to remember the more fact tends to blur with something less than factual. I have, however, been fortunate in having at my disposal a number of original documents and letters which, in combination with my fairly good memory and the recollections of others, have enabled me to be reasonably accurate with dates, people and places.

I suppose that some future reader may express an opinion that my story is not very exciting, lacking as it does the thrill of fast and furious action. I wouldn't argue with them, for many people the whole war was, to some extent unexciting, but there was no escape for them. Conscription not only inducted citizens into the armed forces, it placed them into factories, farms and coal mines, moved people away from their home environment and into occupations that had no attraction for them whatsoever. The country and its populace were the subjects of the 'State of Emergency' which the Government had declared on the outbreak of war. It is worth noting that my Army Pay Book is noted 'duration of the emergency', not 'duration of the war'. In theory, therefore, there was no guarantee that you would be free to return to normal civilian life even when the war eventually came to an end.

Perhaps you can imagine my feelings when, on April 1st 1943, I was introduced to the joys of service life. The initial culture shock was, I suppose, the sharing of my bedroom with numbers of total strangers. Rough blankets instead of sheets, strange noises during the night and even stranger ones at the crack of dawn. The loss of personal freedom to go here and there as desired, the submersion of individual identity and the uniformity of appearance created by everyone being dressed alike. Wake up when you were told, eat when you were told and do virtually everything else when told to do so.

Gradually, however, the fact that we were all in the same boat saw the emergence of a form of comradeship, particularly following my posting to Aldershot, which I became part of and learned to live, eat and sleep in the company of other men. I learned tolerance of other's failings as they did of mine. I honestly do not recall that stealing from each other took place, beyond the odd instance of petty pilfering, and I cannot recall any real fights having taken place.

There did not seem to be any expressed interest in what any of us had done in 'civvy street'. We were all equal, as soldiers, and at that point in time, earlier careers had no relevance. Not only that, but I found that my attitude to the future gradually changing, in that I might sometimes think about going on leave, but because the army was going to decide what your future held, there was little point in grappling with forthcoming events beyond tomorrow.

Once I had become accustomed to the regimentation of army life and the consequent loss of personal freedom, I found that there was some compensation. This was owed in no small measure to being in the RASC which not only offered the opportunity for travel, but ensured that our vehicles always provided a rainproof place to sleep.

I had mixed feelings concerning the attitude of the people we came into contact with during our time overseas. Many, but not all, of the French population seemed less than enthusiastic at being 'liberated'. Perhaps this was a trait peculiar to Normandy, but as I have recorded, the Pas de Calais area populace didn't exactly fall over themselves to welcome us. Belgium and Holland were different, especially the people of Brussels who greeted us with real enthusiasm.

The Dutch and the Belgians greeted us with real enthusiasm.

Attitudes in Germany were mixed. In those places which had been most damaged the people were, quite naturally, tired of it all, and once they were sure that we were not out to rape and pillage, accepted our presence as a sign that their privations were coming to an end. In other parts of the country where war damage was minimal, or non existent, we found ourselves among some very surly, non communicative people, again this may have been symptomatic of those particular areas. There certainly was a difference between the people of the Rhineland compared to elsewhere.

In the whole of the Ruhr the destruction was enormous. In every town and city we passed through buildings were demolished or damaged beyond repair, whole streets blocked, wrecked vehicles everywhere and the peculiar smell which always pervades wrecked buildings. To say that we became immune to these scenes of desolation would be wrong, but we had seen so much that perhaps we became accustomed to it all to the point when it became normality. When we moved into Westphalia we found small towns and villages totally untouched by either bombs or conflict. It was here that we found the populace less than friendly.

I got the impression that the Germans were a very law abiding people, they seemed also to be dependent on leadership, and after the end of hostilities, the Military Government set up by the occupying powers was the only leadership immediately prevailing. I suppose we were regarded as part of that organisation and we were, therefore, treated with some deference. It should not be forgotten that for most of the war the Germans were convinced that they were going to win, and in place of the arrogance that went hand in glove with this attitude, they had to come to terms with defeat and the acceptance of an Occupation Army.

Wherever we were our life was brightened by the presence of either NAAFI or Salvation Army (Red Shield) Canteens. These provided the opportunity to meet men from other units, to be entertained by some wizard of the keyboard, (there was always a piano available), or to just enjoy a quiet drink. The canteens varied from temporary tents, as was the Red Shield one at Arromanches, to requisitioned buildings, prefabricated wooden premises or the superb 21 Club in Brussels that I visited during late November 1944. Brussels was a short leave centre and this club, all two storeys of it, was beyond belief, complete as it was with umpteen piece swing band, dance floor, decor and furnishings to grace any capital city. After the cessation of hostilities and we were able to conduct a more settled existence, we became avid listeners to both AFN and BFN, (American and British Forces Networks), pouring out copious amounts of big band swing.

Probably one of the most tragic aspects of the time immediately after the cessation of hostilities was the sight of thousands of people attempting to make their way back home. Germans who had been evacuated away from the Rhineland during the early part of 1945, when that area became the arena for the quite titanic struggle to drive the German forces eastwards over the Rhine prior to the assault on that river, had the shortest journeys.

They were outnumbered by the vast army of those from lands outside of Germany, the ex inmates of forced labour camps setting out to leave Germany and attempting to return to their homelands. Crammed into trains, even hanging on to the outside of carriages, but mainly walking. These were the 'Displaced Persons' (DPs) of Europe, living off the land with nothing except what they could carry. A distressing sight.

In addition were the huge numbers of German Prisoners of War, housed initially in tented camps until more suitable accommodation could be found for them as they were not to be immediately demobilised. They were to be used, temporarily, as 'Service Groups', a source of labour to assist in bringing some normality to life in Germany.

My first wife Marie and I were married on November 1st 1947 and within a few days we were homeward bound to Goole in Yorkshire. After the first two or three weeks at home I began to feel a sense of loss, I felt disorientated in what seemed to be unfamiliar surroundings. My friends from before my service days were no longer around, not that I ever sought them out, my true friends were now, like me, mostly out of the army and lost over the length and breadth of the British Isles. I haunted the local Red Shield canteen for a number of weeks but found it impossible to recreate the environment that I had grown accustomed to, large numbers of service mates with whom I could exchange experiences and viewpoints.

I very much regret that either through lack of foresight, or circumstances prevailing at the time, I failed to record the names and addresses of a lot of good mates. There were occasions when we were split up and posted to new units, at extremely short notice, even being denied the opportunity to bid farewell to each other. I have kept in touch with one army mate, George Balls from Norfolk, and we do visit each other on a regular basis and often recall those days from long ago.

Prewar photo of the German town of Kleve, the home town of Marie, showing the main shopping centre before it was bombed.

ACKNOWLEDGEMENTS

This book could not have been written without the encouragement and assistance of family and friends.

Foremost among these is my son John, whose long expressed desire that I should record my wartime experiences has finally been rewarded. His enthusiasm, extensive research and computer competence has made possible the final product.

My wartime mate George Balls has guided me where my memory may have been lacking in the context of accuracy of certain events.

Thanks are also due to my wife Dorothy and John's wife Fiona, for their support and tolerance of the long hours John and I have spent on the phone and in front of our home computers.

Kind words and guidance from Mike Marsh, a Goole born author of a number of local history books, have proved invaluable.

Some of the photographs are used courtesy of the Imperial War Museum, Chronicle Publications Ltd. of Goole and Battle of Britain Prints International Ltd for material from Bart Vanderveen's 'Historic Military Vehicles Directory'.

The Imperial War Museum

Pages 11, 12, 13, 14, 24, 29, 55, 63 to70, 72 to75, 78, 87, 101, 102 and 103

Chronicle Publications Ltd

Pages 21 and 22

Battle of Britain Prints International Ltd

Technical data and vehicle photographs in Appendix G and elsewhere in the book.

BIOGRAPHY

The author Robert (Bob) Houghton was born in December 1924 in Goole in what was then the West Riding of Yorkshire. He was the eldest of three children having a brother and a younger sister. He completed his education at the town Grammar School at the end of October 1940 and from then until April 1943 experienced employment with a local shipping agent, the LMS Railway Company, (where his father worked), and Goole Co-operative Society. From February 1941 he became a member of the LMS Home Guard until joining the army in April 1943.

Driver Robert Houghton No. T/14422360

Other than the first six weeks of training, he spent the whole of his five years service with the Royal Army Service Corps. Following driver training he was posted to Aldershot in Hampshire, peace time home of the British Army, where he remained until September 1944 when he embarked for France. For the next three years he drove through France, Belgium, Holland and Germany including a short spell in the Belgian Ardennes during December 1944.

Returning to civilian life at the beginning of 1948, Robert and his wife Marie, from the German Rhineland, later lived in Doncaster, South Yorkshire, with their two daughters and later, a son. Sadly, following a short illness, Marie died in 1982 shortly after Robert had retired from full time employment.

He had spent the majority of his working life at the local factory of an international tractor manufacturing company, initially on the assembly line, and later, in the field of Materials Management specialising in computer systems development.

Robert now lives in North Yorkshire with his second wife Dorothy.

Anyone wishing to e-mail Robert either as a long lost friend or perhaps regarding the book may do so on the following address:- robert@milford24.freeserve.co.uk

new e-mail address

roberthoughton24@o2.co.uk

APPENDICES

CONTENTS

APPENDIX	REF.	PAGE
MAPS	A	165
WHEN AND WHERE	B	171
KIT INVENTORY	C	175
RASC HISTORY & LOGISTICS	D	185
VEHICLES - AUTHOR'S NOTES	E	195
HISTORY OF BRITISH VEHICLES	F	203
VEHICLE TECHNICAL INFO	G	209
GEORGE BALLS	H	233
ALDERSHOT REVISITED	I	237
GLOSSARY	J	241
LATE ARRIVALS	K	243

APPENDIX A

MAPS

UNITED KINGDOM

FRANCE

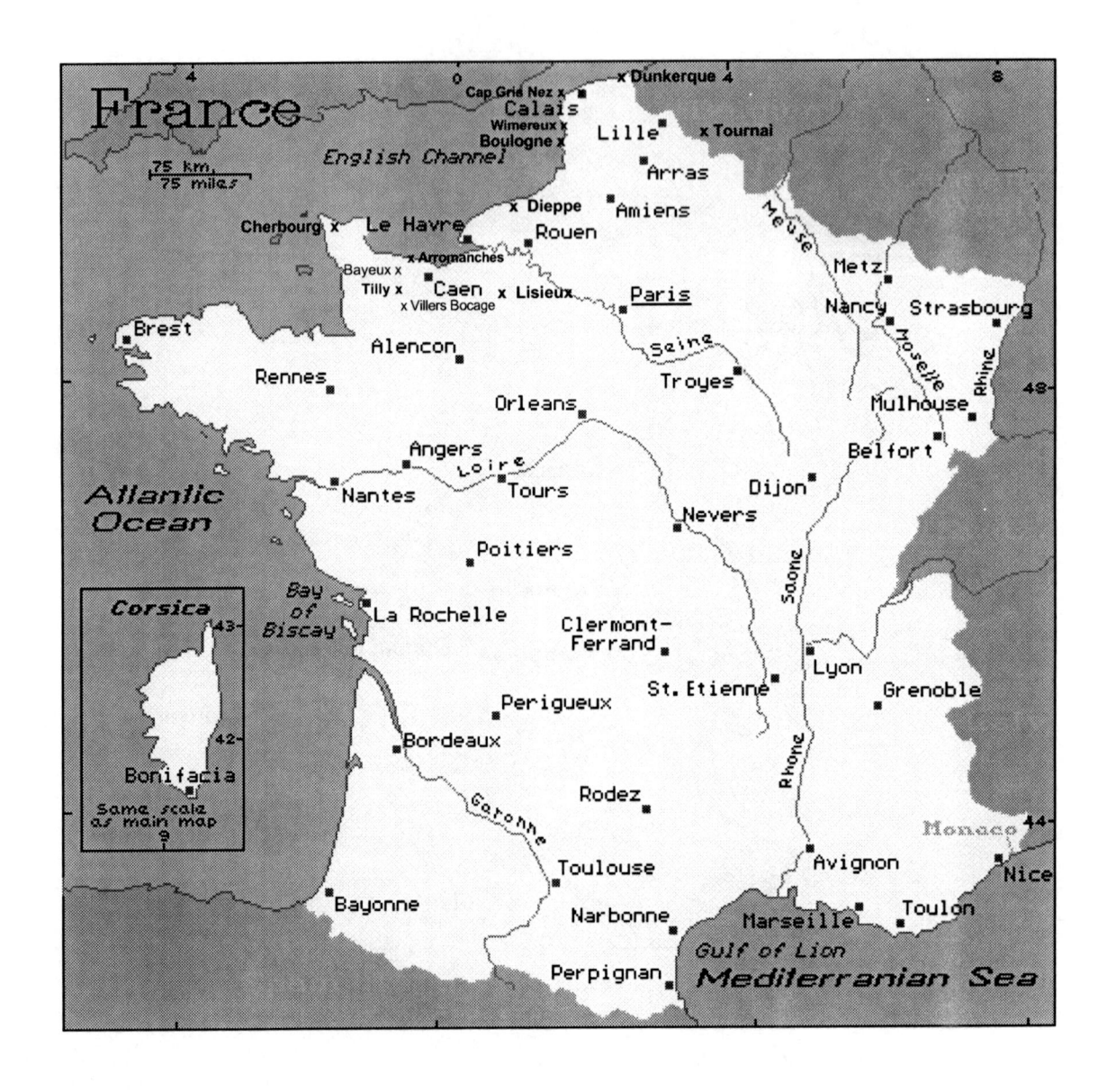

BELGIUM

NETHERLANDS

GERMANY

APPENDIX B

WHEN AND WHERE

The intention behind this particular appendix is to provide the reader with a chronological summary of dates, places, activities, events, vehicles and close mates which span the five years the author spent in the army between 1943 and 1948.

April 1943 - May 1943	19 Infantry Training Centre, Formby, Lancashire. Basic training in foot and rifle drill. Further weapon training - Bren light machine gun, PIAT anti tank mortar, (Projectile infantry anti tank), Mills hand grenade and rifle grenade. Anti gas techniques. Assault course, route marches and how to blanco kit and polish brass work. *Mate* - George Coult from Goole.
May 1943 - July 1943	RASC Driver Training Centre, Brampton, Carlisle, Cumbria. Theory and practice of vehicle maintenance. Driving instruction on various trucks. *Mate* - George Coult.
July 1943 - Sept 1944	B Platoon, 270 Company, RASC (Command (Mixed) Transport), Clayton Barracks, Aldershot, Hampshire. Driving Bedford 3 ton General Service truck (R/H drive). General transport duties in and around the Aldershot area. Training in map reading along with some moderate drill. Weekly route marches to keep us fit.

	During the summer of 1944 we moved (temporarily) to Plumpton near Lewes in Sussex and became involved in transporting troops to the port of Newhaven for embarkation to France. Later we moved thousands of gallons of petrol to an airfield near Swindon in Wiltshire for onward flight to France during the time of the Falaise Gap battles.

Mates - John Ryan, Sid Pritchard, John Richardson, Corbett, Fullerton and Lance Corporal Haslar. |
| **Sept 1944 - Dec 1944** | C Platoon 917 Company RASC Divisional Transport within 2nd Army, 21st Army group. Living in our trucks somewhere in France.

Driving Foden 10 ton diesel truck (right hand drive) with co-driver Sid Pritchard.

Moving munitions and other supplies from beachhead depots in Normandy, France, to Belgium. Later bulk timber transport in Belgium and Belgium Ardennes.

Mates - John Richardson and Sid Pritchard. |
| **Jan 1945 - March 1945** | Retired back to Wimereux in the Pas de Calais area of northern France.

Still driving the Foden, transporting cement from Tournai, in Belgium, to Calais.

Mates - John Richardson. Sid Pritchard, along with others, posted elsewhere as now no need for co-drivers. |
| **March 1945 - July 1945** | Transferred to B Platoon in 917 Company.

Driving Mack 10 ton truck (left hand drive). |

Moving munitions between Belgium, Holland and Germany up to the end of the war on May 8th.

Billeted in the slaughter house in Enschede, Holland for a while whilst carrying relief supplies to civilian population throughout Holland.

Mates - John Richardson, who had transferred with me from C Platoon, George Balls and Stanley Hobson.

Aug 1945 - Jan 1946 Moved into Germany into the town of Kleve.

Still driving Mack 10 ton.

Conveying timber out of Reichswald (State forest) to either coal mines, or railway goods yards for onward transport to mines, for use as pit props.

Mates - John Richardson, George Balls, Stanley Hobson, Pete Pritchard, Jock Cunningham and a whole lot of good guys.

February 1946 Moved to Goch near Kleve for two/three weeks then on to Duisburg in the Ruhr. From there to Recklinghausen where Macks were handed over to German Service Group.

March 1946 917 Company disbanded and I moved to 905 Company located at Bedburg near Kleve hauling timber and doing same job as 917 had done.

Driving White 10 ton truck, much the same vehicle as the Mack but with the advantage of a closed cab.

Mates - George Balls, Stanley Hobson, Pete Pritchard and Jock Cunningham.

April 1946	905 Company disbanded. Posted to 29 Tipper Company which also broke up within two days of my arrival.
	Posted to 218 Ambulance Car Company at Iserlohn, eastern Ruhr, and then on to Ludenscheid in Westphalia.
	Platoon equipped with Austin K2 Ambulances (right hand drive).
	Mates - George Balls and Stanley Hobson who had also been posted to 218 Company.
June 1946 - Dec 1946	Platoon moved to Iburg near Osnabruck.
	Doing job as Platoon Clerk.
Jan 1947 - June 1947	Detached to 1055 Casualty Receiving Station at Detmold in Westphalia with Austin ambulance.
	Conveying accident victims or seriously ill patients to General Hospital at Bad Oyenhausen.
	Mates - George Balls for a short time at Detmold as he, like others, had been attached to a CRS elsewhere.
June 1947 - Nov 1947	218 Company disbanded and platoon incorporated into 507 Company RASC (Occupational Divisional Transport).
	I returned to Osnabruck and was given the job of Company Clerk. 507 Company disbanded and platoon now part of 951 Company (ODT).
November 1947	Home to enjoy three month's leave.
February 1948	To York to be officially demobilised and issued with civilian clothing. Last ride in an army vehicle - Bedford QL Troop Carrier.

APPENDIX C

KIT INVENTORY

This inventory is set out in time honoured army fashion where the noun is shown first followed by relevant adjectives.

All items had to be signed for and, if lost, paid for by deductions from pay.

I may have missed the odd item but it is fifty six years ago.

DESCRIPTION	QUANTITY
Tunic, wool, khaki	1
Tunic, denim, khaki	1
Trousers, wool, khaki	1
Trousers, denim, khaki	1
Braces, trouser	1
Forage cap, wool, khaki	1
Forage cap, denim, khaki	1
Cap badge, RASC, Brass	1
Jerkin, leather, brown	1
Greatcoat, wool, khaki	1
Boots and laces, leather, black	2 pairs
Gaiters, (anklets) webbing, khaki	1 pair
Gloves, wool, khaki	1 pair
Gauntlets, leather, brown	1 pair
Socks, wool, khaki	2 pairs
Shirts, wool, khaki	2
Vests, cellular, white	2
Drawers, cellular, white	2
Pullover, wool, khaki	1
PT shorts, cotton, blue	1
PT shoes, canvas, khaki	1 pair
Towels, cotton, white	2
Anti gas cape, oilskin, olive green	1
Ground sheet. rubber, khaki	1
Blankets, wool, grey/blue/brown	4
Helmet, steel, non reflective	1

DESCRIPTION	QUANTITY
Helmet scrim net	1
Respirator, two eye piece type	1
Goggles, anti gas	1
Ointment, anti gas	1 tube
Belt, webbing, khaki	1
Pack, small, webbing, khaki	1
Pack, large, webbing, khaki	1
Pouches, ammunition, webbing, khaki	2
Straps, support, webbing, khaki	2
Bayonet holder (frog) webbing, khaki	1
Bottle, water, felt covered metal, khaki with webbing holder	1
Jack knife	1
Dressing, field, muslin	1
Tins, mess, aluminium	2
Mug, enamel, brown	1
Knife, fork, spoon (each)	1 of
Emergency rations, chocolate	1 tin
Sewing kit (housewife)	1
Razor, safety and brush, shaving	1
Brushes, boot and button	1 set
Button stick, brass	1
Bag, kit, canvas, khaki	1

DESCRIPTION	**QUANTITY**

Weapons:

Rifle, Lee Enfield .303 calibre with sling.......................... 1
Rifle cleaning kit, - consisting of: pull-through, gauze, oil, flannelette. (Stored in compartment in rifle butt).................................. 1
Bayonet, steel................................ 1

OR (instead of rifle)
Sten light sub machine gun 9mm..... 1

Soldier's Service and Pay Book AB 64.. 1
(See next page)

Identity discs................................. 2

Example of a personal hygiene kit.

Products for soldiers' personal hygiene were often manufactured by household names under contract to the military authorities.

This kit may have been issued later but not to us.

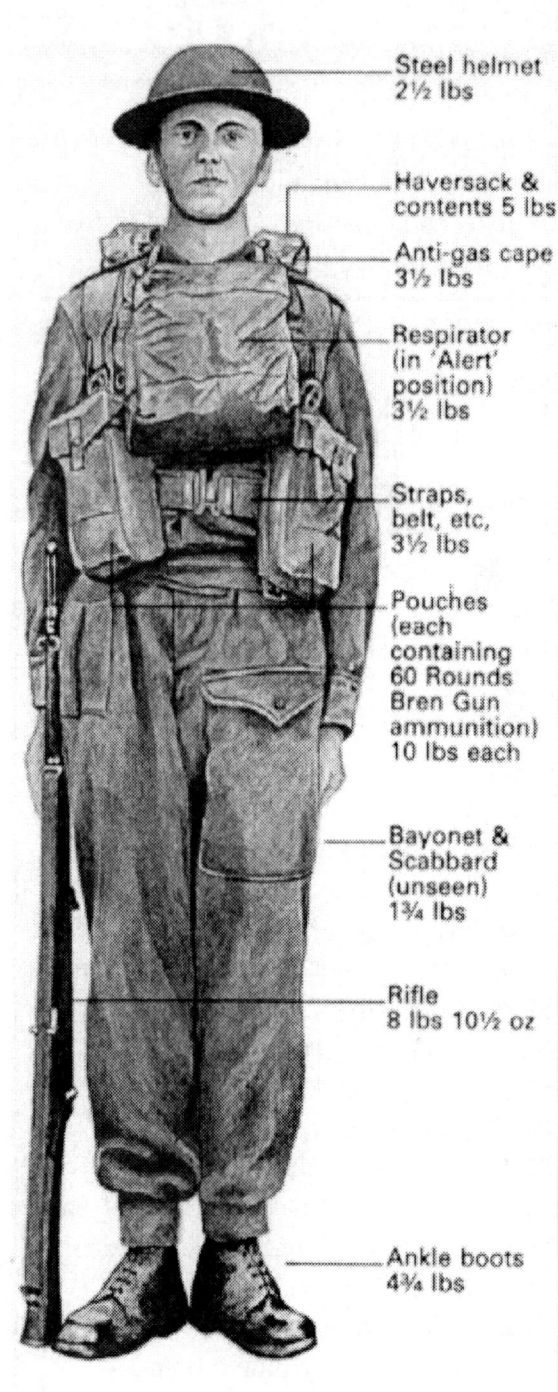

- Steel helmet 2½ lbs
- Haversack & contents 5 lbs
- Anti-gas cape 3½ lbs
- Respirator (in 'Alert' position) 3½ lbs
- Straps, belt, etc, 3½ lbs
- Pouches (each containing 60 Rounds Bren Gun ammunition) 10 lbs each
- Bayonet & Scabbard (unseen) 1¾ lbs
- Rifle 8 lbs 10½ oz
- Ankle boots 4¾ lbs

What the British Tommy is wearing

Soldier's Service and Pay Book
Army Book 64

The Soldier's Service and Pay Book served primarily as the soldier's Identity Card and as such had to be carried at all times. It identified the physical characteristics of the soldier as they were at enlistment including any distinctive marks or minor defects which could assist in identification in case of death in action.

The book carried details of medical category, protective inoculations, specific training and qualifications, decorations awarded and privilege leave granted.

The book had to be presented at weekly Pay Parade. No book, no pay!

Finally, the last few pages of the book were a form of 'Last Will and Testament" - just in case!

UNIFORM AND EQUIPMENT

General

Ranks and duties of the wartime soldier were indicated by sleeve insignia patches and tabs. The dress uniform was not used in wartime, and the usual dress for officers was service dress for evening wear, and battle dress (adopted in 1939) for daytime. This latter uniform was the same for officers and enlisted men, and the only official dress for enlisted men.

Below: Cloth shoulder flash (yellow R.A.S.C. letters on a deep blue background), sewn to the top of each sleeve on the best battle dress as shown by picture bottom right.

Yellow and blue colour bar

Directly below the shoulder, on the upper arms, all ranks wore Corps/Regimental and divisional insignia.

See next page also.

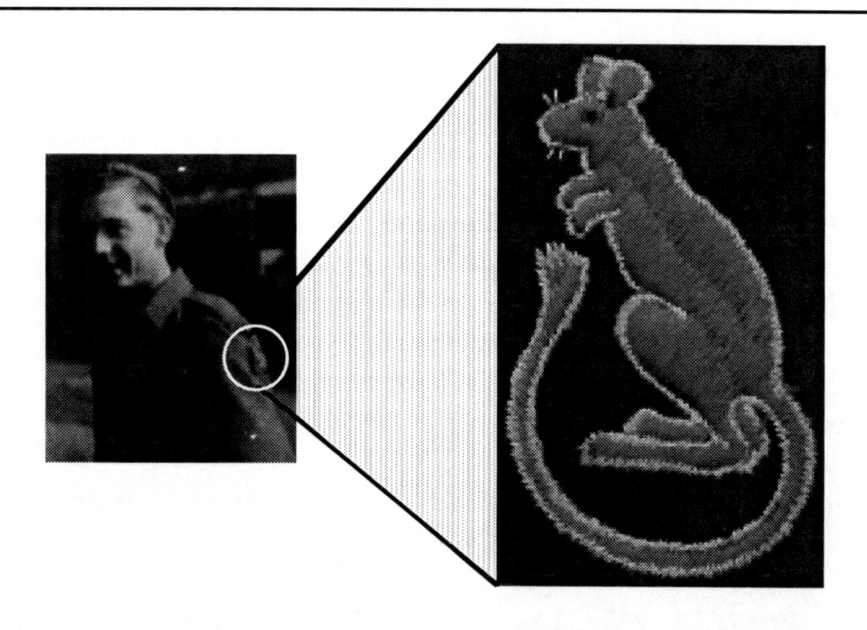

Divisional Insignia sewn under the RASC flash.

In the example pictured above, the 7th Armoured Division Desert Rat was placed with the Rat facing forwards on both sleeves.

The yellow and blue colour bar (shown under the RASC shoulder flash on the previous page) was mounted under the Divisional Insignia with the yellow facing forwards.

Ribbons (left and above) were worn just above the left breast pocket
These reflect the ribbons of the medals shown on the last page of this appendix.

Also worn on the sleeve was the 'Driver's' insignia - a 3 spoked wheel which was located above a Chevron - an inverted shallow 'V' - which was awarded after 2 years service.

Battle Dress

Two piece khaki serge, long, rather baggy trousers with web anklets, worn. with the blouse fastened to the throat, was waist length, with two breast pockets and made of the same khaki serge as the trousers. This blouse fastened to the inside of the trousers, and was taken in at the waist by a right hand fastening cloth belt. A collarless khaki shirt was worn under the blouse. Officers wore collared shirts with a khaki necktie with the top two buttons of the blouse undone. Enlisted men have the blouse buttoned to the throat. Head dress of a field service cap, (forage cap) was replaced under active service or when ordered by a steel helmet.

On the field service cap, regimental or Corps badges were worn.

Inscription 'GR VI' = King George Rex 6th
The inscription - 'Honi soit qui mal y pense' - (French) which means, 'Evil to him who evil thinks'.

Above: Brass cap badge worn on either forage cap or beret of 'best' battle dress, but not on denim work uniform. Forage caps were worn until we went overseas, when berets were adopted as seen in inset photo left.

Forage Caps

I have not been able to establish why this form of head gear was so called. The dictionary merely records that it was a form of cap worn by infantry when not wearing 'dress uniform'. Dress uniform was that uniform worn when off duty or for specific parades. This must have its origins in peace time soldiering when for example, the 'best dress' for the RASC consisted of a natty jacket and trousers coloured dark blue with, probably, a white stripe down the trouser sides. I would guess that headgear would have been a peaked hat similar to that worn by officers. However the forage cap came to be worn by all ranks up to, and including Platoon Officers, during the 1939-45 war, in all units of the British Army and Air Force, until replaced by the beret.

My initial kit included two forage caps, one denim for everyday working and one wool to be worn with 'best' battle dress tunic and trousers. The brass cap badge was worn with the latter cap except when on active service abroad during war time. As a point of interest the cap I can be seen wearing in the photograph (below left) was a form of 'best' forage cap, coloured deep blue with white piping, which I had acquired from I know not where and which I only wore when on leave in the UK in the early days of my army career.

Forage caps were worn as well as berets and came in two styles.

Left: (The author) Best, RASC navy blue with yellow piping and gold buttons

Right: Normal issue.

The photograph of 270 Company in Appendix K clearly shows the rakish angles that caps were worn at. I think that the correct way was to have the cap so positioned so that the buttons were above the right eye. I seem to recall that the challenge was to see exactly how far to the right the cap could be worn before it fell off. When we were issued with berets a similar attitude prevailed, in that the edict that they were to be worn so that the cap badge was positioned over the left eye was seen as a challenge to position the beret as far to the right and rear as possible. It must have cost the army thousands of wasted hours by NCOs and officers ordering us lesser mortals to "Put your hat on correctly lad!"

Two examples of how, or in most cases, how not to wear berets.

And the winner is...

The front of the cap was adorned with two buttons, brass in the case of 'best' versions and a form of plastic on denim ones and apart from decoration they did have another function. On each side of the cap, hidden from immediate view, were brass hooks locked into eyelets. When these were undone the cap opened out into a form of 'balaclava' which covered the ears whilst the front part with the two buttons formed a chin strap. I don't recall this facility being employed by myself or those around me as I seem to remember that the effort expended in reassembling hardly made the exercise worth while.

Author's medals from left to right:

The 1939/45 Star (Bronze)
    Ribbon - deep blue/red/pale blue - represents Royal Navy, Army & RAF
    Awarded for 180 days operational service between these years

The France and Germany Star (Bronze)
    Ribbon - Deep blue/white/red/deep blue
    For all who saw service on the continent during the war years

The Defence Medal (Silver)
    Ribbon - Flame coloured centre edged with green and two black stripes.
    Issued to some 7,000,000 persons for military, naval, air force, or civilian
    service during the war. This one was for service in the Home Guard

The 1939/45 Medal (Silver)
    Ribbon - Red/deep blue/white with red stripe/deep blue/red
    Issued to all service personnel in Europe at the end of the war

APPENDIX D

RASC HISTORY & LOGISTICS

BRIEF HISTORY OF THE RASC

Before the 16th century, armies were supplied on a plunder basis, with each man searching the surrounding area for provisions.

This later became an official function with a foraging party searching the area just ahead of the advancing army, to procure the day's requirements.

During the early history of the British Army, the provision of transportation was a Commissariat function and they contracted for services, as required.

As armies became more sophisticated and ceased to live off the land, their transportation requirements also increased. The need for a dedicated and reliable military transportation organisation became obvious.

The first unit formed was the Royal Waggoners, which existed from 1794-1795.

The Royal Wagon Corps was then established in 1799 until 1802.

This changed to The Royal Wagon Train in 1802, and this unit served during the Napoleonic Wars in the Peninsula and at Waterloo. It was disbanded in 1833 as part of peacetime economies.

The next period of conflict was the Crimean War. The troops in the Crimea suffered dreadfully during the winter of 1854/55 because there was insufficient transport to move their supplies eight miles from the harbour to their encampments. This led to the formation of the Land Transport Corps in 1855. Working side by side with the Commissariat, which controlled the provision of stores, they quickly proved their worth by capably supporting the British Army during the remainder of the Crimean War.

Following the end of the war, the LTC was reorganised as the Military Train in 1856. Service in this title was seen at Luknow and Peking. The next thirty years saw several name changes occur as the departments wrestled with the relationship between the civilian Commissariat (later militarised) which controlled the supplies and the military transportation unit which moved them.

The transport and supply services were united in 1869 into the first Army Service Corps.

This was reorganised into the Commissariat and Transport Corps in 1881.

They finally formed the second Army Service Corps in 1888, which combined the responsibility for both the provision of supplies and their carriage into one military organisation.

At the end of the 1914-18 war, it was awarded the Royal prefix as a reward for the part played in the conflict. The Corps had been able to give tangible proof to the wisdom underlying its original charter. This implies that for an army to be successfully maintained with supplies and transport, the Corps responsible must be fully combatant, with both officers and men fully trained soldiers and fully trained in their particular skill areas.

The Corps incorporated with other units to form The Royal Corps of Transport in 1965, following reorganisation and rationalisation of the Armed Services to meet the modern international requirement.

The modern day Royal Logistic Corps was formed in April 1993 with the amalgamation of four corps (the Royal Corps of Transport, the Royal Army Ordnance Corps, the Army Catering Corps, the Royal Pioneer Corps) and an element of a fifth (the Royal Engineer Postal and Courier Service). The Corps has a total of 16,500 officers and soldiers, equating to 16% of the Regular British Army. This is further strengthened by 11,000 personnel within the Territorial Army.

EVOLUTION

To summarise the previous two pages:

Royal Waggoners...1794 - 1795

Royal Wagon Corps..1799 - 1802

Royal Wagon Train..1802 - 1833 Waterloo

Land Transport Corps..1855 - 1856

Military Train...1856 - 1869 Luknow Peking

Army Service Corps...1869 - 1881

Commissariat and Transport Corps......................1881 - 1888

Army Service Corps...1888 - 1918

Royal Army Service Corps...................................1918 - 1965

Royal Corps of Transport.....................................1965 - 1993

Royal Logistics Corps..1993 - onwards

Some of the more recent badges

RASC & RCT Association

For anyone interested there is an RASC & RCT association that you can join. Membership of the Association is open to anyone who has served in the RASC, the RCT or has been attached to units of the RASC or the RCT while serving in the ATS or WRAC and offers the opportunity to associate with those with whom you have plenty in common.

Applications for membership should be addressed to:

> The Controller
> RASC & RCT Association
> Dettingen House
> The Princess Royal Barracks
> Deepcut
> Camberley
> Surrey
> GU16 6RW
>
> Telephone: 01252 340891

The Function of the R.A.S.C.

The RASC was charged with the responsibility for the storage and issue of stores and supplies. This also included the responsibility for certain phases of their transportation, including the vehicles assigned for that purpose, and for the administration of barracks and quarters. It supplied the daily needs of the soldier, by supplying food, ammunition, petrol and lubricants, for all normal and battle requirements.

History provides ample evidence that, whereas battles are won by leadership and bravery, wars are more often won by superior logistics - the practical, highly skilled and often imaginative art of moving fighting troops and keeping them supplied.

General Organisation of the R.A.S.C.

The RASC was organised into two branches, supply and transport, which were coordinated under a directorate, the head of which, a major general (Director of Supplies and Transport) (DST).

The supply and transport services, under the DST, are controlled by the Quarter-Master-General (QMG).

The supply branch was responsible for the supply of food, forage, fuel, light, disinfectants, medical supplies, petroleum and oils for vehicles.

The transport branch charged with the provision and operation of all vehicles in RASC units or driven by RASC personnel, and with the provision of spare parts, miscellaneous mechanical transport stores (MT stores), and materials, equipment, and tools required in the operation and maintenance of these vehicles. The maintenance and repair of these vehicles was shared by the RASC and Royal Electrical and Mechanical Engineers (REME).

A Division

The strength of the division was approximately 17,500 officers and enlisted men. Within army troops and occasionally Corps troops there are a number of troop carrying companies of the RASC. Each RASC Company being capable of carrying one infantry brigade.

Transport

In the First World War the Corps operated about 90,000 load carriers and 35,000 light vehicles and motorcycles. At the end of the Second World War the number of vehicles in depots and units was nearly 1,500,000, and of those with units roughly 40 per cent were in the hands of the RASC. These numbers owed much to the existence of the Canadian and the United States motor industries. As the war progressed an ever growing proportion of vehicles were of North American origin.

In 1941 a start was made on a complete reorganisation of the transport units of the Corps, adopting as sub-units the platoon and section, almost exactly comparable in size to the infantry platoon and section, thus producing a unit whose size was immediately appreciated by officers (especially staff officers) of other arms, and one, moreover, which could be switched readily to an infantry role when required.

A section comprised of seven vehicles, with a section commander mounted normally on a motorcycle. The platoon consisted of a platoon officer, a platoon sergeant and a fitter and four sections. The total strength of the platoon was 30 vehicles. This platoon was not only the exact counterpart of the infantry platoon but also, if equipped with 3-ton lorries, it could carry in one lift the marching portion of an infantry battalion. This made troop carrying a simple matter to plan and execute. Mobile workshops were similarly organised on a platoon basis. The company consisted of a headquarters, one or more workshop platoons, and as many transport platoons and composite platoons as were necessary for it to fulfil its role.

Whilst the preceding two paragraphs may have been correct in 1941 it is obvious that some rethinking had taken place by 1943. The Transport Company I joined at Aldershot in July 1943 (see Chapter 1 page 48), was organised in a different manner in that it comprised six platoons, Headquarters, Workshops and four Transport). Each transport platoon comprised thirty three load carrying 3 ton Bedfords. This increased number of vehicles provided the ability to have thirty vehicles on the road at all times. Each month every vehicle had to undergo one Workshop Inspection and one Platoon Inspection.

These inspections were carried out in the UK between Mondays and Fridays as Saturdays were reserved for exercises, route matches, map reading and some drill, whilst Sundays were usually days of rest apart from the odd Church Parade. This meant that (usually) three vehicles were 'off road' each day of the month. The 'task' maintenance system was operated by drivers as a preventative system which sought to avoid breakdown or minimise the need for repairs. (See page 42). Overseas this degree of maintenance and inspection was dramatically curtailed due to the demand on transport units although some degree of driver maintenance was practised, particularly in terms of such tasks as battery top up, oil levels and periodic changes. Tyre pressures, including spares, were, of course, very important although as every vehicle was equipped with a mechanical tyre inflation system (engine driven air pump) this was not difficult to ensure.

In the early days overseas vehicle cleanliness took a back seat and even in Germany in 1945-6 we were far too busy to be able to afford time for truck washing. Later when I was driving the Austin Ambulance during 1947, when we had more time, we were instructed to keep our ambulances clean on the outside as well as the inside.

FIELD LOGISTICS

Logistics is the term to cover the maintenance of an army's combat power in the field. It includes the supply of ammunition, fuel and food, the three essential commodities without which an army cannot fight: the repair and supply of vehicles: weapons and equipment: and the evacuation and care of the sick and wounded servicemen.

The radically increased mechanisation of the Second World War over that of the 1914-18 war presented the logisticians with enormous problems. Both in the North African desert and during the early part of the war on the Eastern Front, the attacker was invariably forced to halt because he had outrun his supplies. Likewise, the Allies quickly ran out of fuel during their drive across France in summer 1944.

Another significant aspect was the more sophisticated the army, both in its equipment and the living standards of its men, the more elaborate its logistic system had to be. Thus the Western Allies needed many more men to support the soldier in the front line than the Japanese or Russians did.

The systems shown were those used by the British Army during the war. Yet, whatever the system, it had to satisfy five basic principals in order to work. It had to be as simple as possible and employ economy of effort. The system had to be flexible and have good co-operation among all agencies involved. Finally, logisticians needed foresight and anticipation to support the commander's plan.

General supplies: The four lines to keep an army on the move.

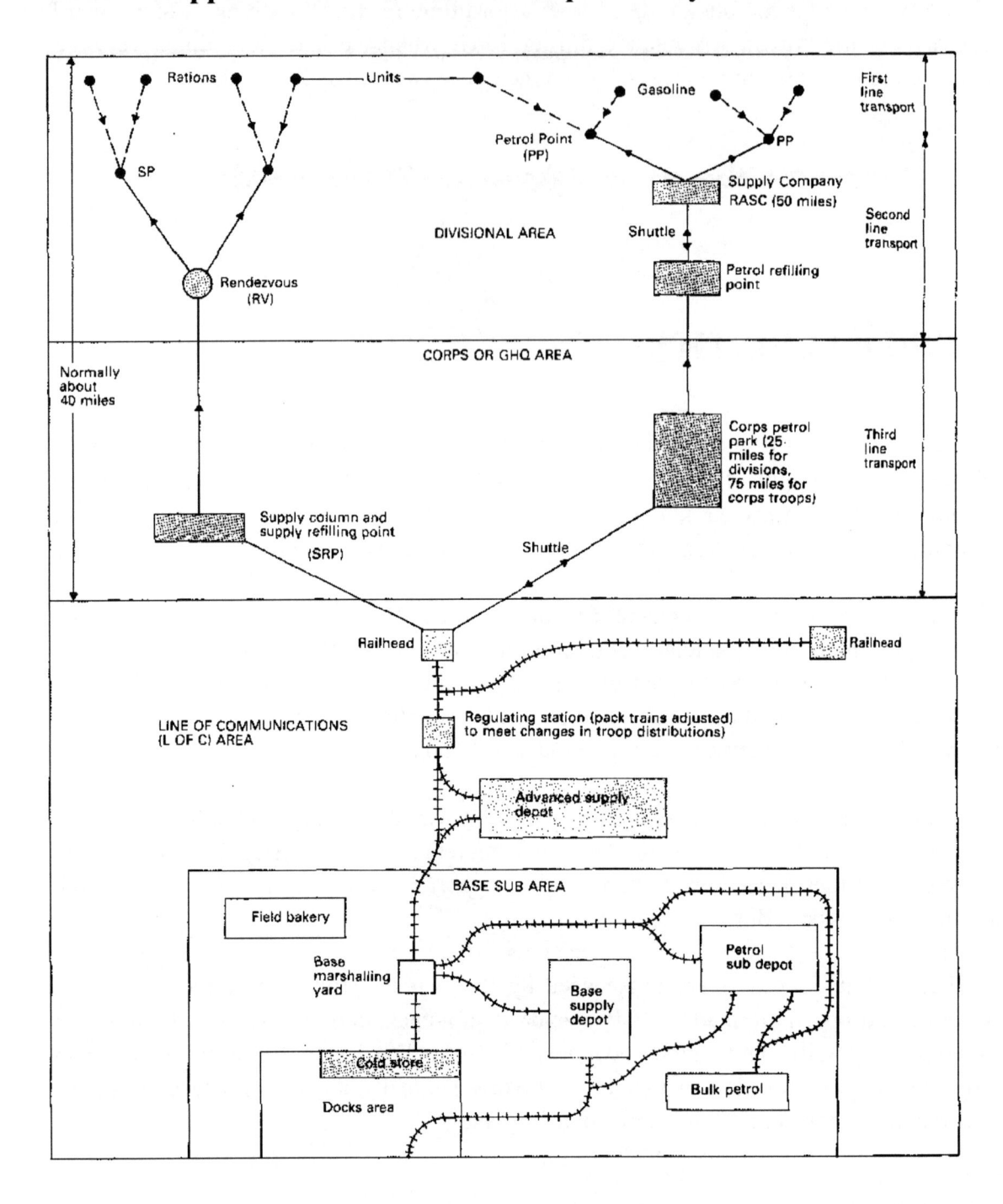

Field Logistics (*continued...*)

The diagram opposite shows the system used, in theory, to maintain the British expeditionary force of a corps consisting of two divisions. The key point to note is how the transport to bring the supplies up to the front line was organised. First line transport was that provided by the battalions. This went back to supply and petrol points to collect the stocks which had been dumped there by the second line transport organised by the division. Corps transport (third line) brought the stocks forward to each division. It was usually not possible to use the railways to ferry supplies from the ports because either they did not exist (frequent in North Africa) or they had been destroyed. Hence additional transport, known as the fourth line was required.

When the breakout from Normandy took place in August 1944, a more streamline system was introduced; it was known as through running. Under this system for maintaining supplies, the trucks drove straight from the beaches and port of Cherbourg to the divisional area. The wear and tear on vehicles and their drivers was the drawback, especially since a division needed 650 tons of supplies per day!

APPENDIX E

VEHICLES - AUTHOR'S NOTES

None of the vehicles I drove were equipped with heaters, screen demisters or washers. Controllable air vents were unknown but this did not mean that there was an absence of a supply of fresh air. Lack of cab sides or, particularly in the Foden, sizable gaps in the floor where clutch and brake pedals were located, provided more than adequate ventilation, whether desired or not! Some vehicles, for example the Austin Ambulance, did not have proper cab doors. Instead canvas screens were fitted which were usually rolled up in the manner depicted in the picture right and on the next page. This facilitated quick exit and

The Austin's cab was very basic as they were in most trucks. Notice the fire extinguisher and rolled up canvas screen by the right doorway.

entry from and to the vehicle when attending casualties. As and when needed the canvas screen could be unrolled and attached to the vehicle body to form a simulated half door to provide some protection against inclement weather. Vehicles having this particular feature did impress upon drivers the absolute necessity to hang onto the steering wheel to avoid the possibility of falling out when cornering or driving over rough terrain, safety belts were non existent. Passengers were left to make their own arrangements!

The Foden and the three ton Bedford did possess closed cabs which, whilst unheated did manage to exclude the worst of the weather. The ten ton White which I drove for a few weeks in 1946 also had a closed cab, but as the time was late March it was irrelevant.

Windscreen wipers did not perform as well as they do these days, particularly when they were driven by a partial vacuum generated by the inlet manifold on the engine. The army did, however, ensure that all vehicles carried a fire extinguisher, filled with liquid fire suppressant, (could have been tricho-ethylene), which turned out to be a first class cleaning agent for stained clothing! The effect of this facility did tend, as time passed, to reduce the number of usable extinguishers. An extinguisher can be seen on the far side of the Austin cab picture on the previous page.

With the notable exception of the Foden all trucks were fairly easy to start provided that you observed the correct use of the choke (petrol engines), or, in the case of the Mack, effective use of the preheat system. The Foden was something else! In cold weather, (and we had our share), it was necessary to make use of the valve lifting mechanism activated by a lever adjacent to the fixed starting handle. This allowed the engine to be turned over by the handle with all cylinder valves lifted, thus there was an absence of compression allowing relatively free movement of pistons. The engine could then be started, either by handle or starter motor, whilst at the same time moving the valve lifting control to a position which moved the valves on two cylinders into normal operating positions. Once the engine fired the valve mechanism was moved to normal operating position. It was a two man job and not particularly exciting on a cold winter morning.

Double declutching was taught and practised. This is where the clutch pedal is depressed to move from a particular gear into neutral, then released whilst in neutral and then depressed to allow selection of the next gear. This technique was probably most useful when changing down rather than up, in order to make use of engine compression as a braking aid to compensate for less that effective braking systems. (The good old Foden again).

Tyre inflation was not a problem as every vehicle I drove was fitted with an engine driven air pump. I only experienced one flat tyre during my five year's service. (Aldershot 1943). Tyres were very heavy, so called cross country, with a large thickness of rubber between road and tube, (no tubeless). We did, however, practice dealing with flat tyres. The wheels on Bedford trucks were the split wheel type where, after having dismounted the wheel from the vehicle and released the air pressure, a set of nuts was undone to release the two halves of the wheel, (one half of the wheel had a set of studs or bolts fitted). The important discipline here was to ensure that the pressurised air content of the wheel was relieved first! Tubeless tyres were unknown and great care had to be exercised when reassembling a wheel to ensure that inner tube, protective gaiter and valve were all correctly located.

The Bedford type split wheel was easy to deal with because the only tool you needed to change a tyre was a normal wheel brace and so this could be done anywhere without the need of a garage. The American split rim did need an extra tool - a tyre lever - to remove the outer rim and then to lever off one side of the tyre so that the tube could be extracted. I only ever did one for practise.

The Austins split wheel system with outer red and inner white nuts. Notice the rolled up canvas screen.

The Austins huge spare wheel mounted immediately behind the driver's seat.

This split wheel system pertained to all Bedford vehicles I had experience of as well as the Austin ambulance. The picture shows the front wheel of an Austin Ambulance and the two sets of nuts can be seen. The inner white ones enable the wheel to be dismounted and the outer ring (in practice painted red) secure the two halves of the wheel together. It was the same on the Foden and Albion trucks. American trucks employed a different method.

Wheels on the Mack were simply rims on which the tyre was mounted and then fitted to the wheel centre, which was part of the stub axle, held in place by a number of metal 'dogs' or wedge like pieces which fitted over the protruding bolts and were then locked in place by nuts. The rims themselves were of the split rim type where the outer edge of the rim was a separate piece which when levered away allowed the tube to be extracted. Not as easy to deal with as the split wheels.

Trucks of one and a half tons or more carried spare wheel(s) mounted behind the cab. In the case of the Austin Ambulance the spare was mounted within the body immediately behind the driver's seat and this can seen in the pictures on the previous page and in Appendix G. Mechanical assistance was fitted in some cases to enable safe lowering and raising of wheels out of and into storage positions. This took the form of a sort of 'jack system' where the turning of a handle transmitted the force through a worm drive and gearing to move the wheel holding cradle downwards or upwards. This was similar to the system used in some cars today where the spare is located under the boot. Without this system it would have been extremely difficult, if not impossible, to handle the spare manually. The 10 ton Mack carried two spares in recognition of the number of wheels on the vehicle. Smaller trucks and utilities etc., carried their spares slung under the cab or on the roof of the cab.

Some vehicles had fittings which were specific to the operational area they were intended to be employed, or the point in time of their production. The Bedford 3 ton I drove when I was at Aldershot had a circular aperture in the cab roof on the passenger side. Normally this was covered by a canvas screen but removal of this enabled a passenger to stand on the seat and operate a Bren machine gun as some form of protection against air attack.

Close scrutiny of the pictures in Appendix G of the Foden and Albion ten tonners will reveal that they were

Mustard gas detector on a Foden DG6/12

fitted with a thin metal plate protruding from below the windscreen on the passenger side. This was coated with a dull yellow paint which was capable of detecting Mustard Gas and signal such detection by changing colour, but don't ask me what colour! These were the only two vehicles types that I can recall seeing with this feature but I feel sure that there must have been others which had been built either prewar or early in the war when the use of gas weapons may well have been seen as being possible.

All vehicles carried indication of their gross weight (i.e. when fully laden). This took the form of a black number on a yellow background either on a circular plate affixed to the right hand wing (offside) or painted onto the wing itself. All Royal Engineer constructed bridges carried indication of their weight carrying capability - 40, 80 or (exceptionally) 100 tons. Thus a Tank Transporter driver driving a fully laden truck and trailer, possibly 60 tons or so over a 40 ton Bailey bridge, would lay himself open to disciplinary charges always assuming he survived the drop when the bridge collapsed!

One of the more laborious tasks whilst at Aldershot was the practice, during winter months, of draining the cooling system at the end of each day's work. Anti freeze was not available. This involved draining not only the radiator but the cylinder block as well, and then filling up again each morning. Overseas this was not undertaken as perhaps the size of the engine on the Foden precluded freezing for the few hours that it was at rest. I have a faint recollection that with the Macks, the night guard may have had the task of starting up each truck during the night if there was a risk of hard frost. In any event, at least before the war ended, it would not have been sound practice to delay getting on the road in a morning whilst radiators were being filled up. Later on when I drove an ambulance, it was the custom, in very cold weather, to get up during the night and start up and run the engine, to avoid the risk of freezing and also to ensure that the engine would start more easily if needed during the night.

Filling up with fuel was either at designated civilian filling stations (in the UK), or, specified fuel dumps when overseas, and later at barrack fuel points. Overseas it was by way of Jerricans, (a German design thus the name), which held twenty litres, equal to approximately four and a half gallons. Refuelling could involve a fair amount of effort. For example the ten ton Mack had two fuel tanks each with a capacity of seventy five gallons (342 litres approx). A major refuel could necessitate the handling of up to thirty odd Jerricans of diesel each weighing in at forty five pounds, (20 kilograms). This could mean a total weight of twelve hundredweights (six hundred kilograms) having to be lifted and upended over the tank neck. Needless to say we replenished tanks more frequently to spread the effort.

All load carrying vehicles were fitted with a canvas canopy which was supported by a removable framework. British vehicles utilised a tubular steel frame, (usually 1" diameter tube), welded to form a rigid structure which was then bolted to the load body. USA vehicles made use of a number of separate wooden hoops which fitted into slots located on the body sides. Canvas covers were fitted over the supports and in the case of British ones, which were longer than the support frame, were folded and roped front, rear and sides. On USA vehicles the canvas was made to just fit over the hoops and separate 'curtains' were fitted front and rear. Obviously the USA version could be dismantled or fitted by one man whilst the British type needed four or more pairs of hands to dismount or mount the steel frame. When hauling timber both canvas covers and frames were dismounted. Part of Chapter 3 records that when we left the Ardennes in somewhat of a hurry our dismounted canopies were left behind. The effort involved in remounting frames on to the Fodens would have kept us occupied up to the time of our probable capture by the advancing German Army.

As a trained RASC driver you were expected to drive any wheeled vehicle the army decided it wanted you to drive, from officer's car to tank transporter. (Maybe some added training for the latter). Thus it was that in September 1944 we 'lost' our Bedford three tonners and acquired ten ton Fodens without any training or familiarisation, this we gained during the two day journey from Bradford to London.

A comment in the context of speed. Other than the Austin ambulance, which could, of necessity, motor fairly quickly, all vehicles I drove were governed so that they could not be driven to relative destruction. This meant that convoy driving for this and other reasons was a slow procession. A typical 1944 convoy of Fodens in France and Belgium might average 15/20 mile and hour, as opposed to 25/30 in the UK driving Bedford 3 tonners. The important strategy was to arrive at a destination with all vehicles and loads intact. In Germany a convoy of Macks could manage 25/30 mph after the end of the war as there was less traffic on the roads.

Whilst the speed of the vehicles I drove may not seem to be fast by current standards, Bedford 3 ton - 40 mph, Foden 10 ton - 32 mph, Mack 10 ton 40 mph, it is worth noting that until well into the fifties the speed limit in the UK for heavy vehicles was 20 mph! Relatively low speeds did present some difficulty when driving in convoy in that if the vehicle ahead of you overtook another vehicle (not one of your convoy of course), then by the time you had ascertained that the way ahead was clear your convoy had moved on a mile or two. This involved foot hard down on the accelerator to play 'catch up'. (See Chapter 1, pages 56/7). We developed a cunning ploy to deal with this problem! As the truck in front completed overtaking and provided that the way ahead was still clear, its moving back to the correct side of the road was delayed so that the following vehicle's driver was aware that the way was clear for him to also overtake. This process was repeated as necessary so avoiding the convoy being too segmented. This technique became invaluable when driving the right hand drive Foden in France and Belgium on the right hand side of the road.

Night driving was not exactly popular. Wartime regulations required headlamps to be 'masked' to reduce the light emission and this was accomplished by the mask having either one 'hooded' slit in it (about 4 inches x half an inch), or a number of smaller slits. Whichever system was adopted the resulting illumination of the way ahead was abysmal. Whilst I was in Aldershot the only night driving I did other than convoy work, was transporting troops from the railway station to their respective barracks.

Most of my driving overseas was done in convoy. All army vehicles were fitted with a light which illuminated the rear axle differential housing which was painted white. This was not visible from the air. No other lighting was permitted (except for the lead vehicle) and you had to make sure that you kept to the regulation distance from the vehicle in front, which I remember as being thirty yards, (day time distance between vehicles was sixty yards). This practice demanded a high degree of concentration to say the least. Lack of sleep combined with the hypnotic effect of gazing at the ill lit patch of white in front of you resulted on more than one near miss as you suddenly realised that the vehicle in front of you had stopped!

The halting of the convoy generated another evil. It was so easy to 'nod off' then awakening to the furious banging on the cab door by a despatch rider who had come back to look for you (and the others behind you). If you became detached from the vehicle in front, for whatever reason, then it was usual to stop and await the ever busy despatch rider (usually a Section Corporal) to come to your rescue.

The end of the war in Europe brought relief to these difficulties in that headlamp masks were rapidly thrown on the nearest scrap heap (never far away as large parts of the landscape were 'scrap heaps').

As I have recorded in Chapter 2, convoy driving restricted the ability to cover long distances during the course of a normal 10/12 hour driving day. As explained in the chapter the very nature of the convoy system itself prevented this. No small part of the problem was, of course, to do with the condition of the roads, in that apart from having been subjected to damage from shelling and/or bombing, they were having to withstand the wear and tear of thousands of vehicles passing over them. Demolition of bridges by the retreating German Army meant that replacement structures were, in most cases, single track. These factors along with the fact that engines were governed, meant that a daily mileage of 150 was considered to be the norm.

Readers interested in viewing some of the vehicles referred to may like to visit the

Museum of Army Transport in Beverley, East Yorkshire

or the

Muckleburgh Collection at Weybourne in Norfolk.

Both have an excellent selection of WWII trucks, tanks and other military vehicles.

Bedford 15 cwt

APPENDIX F

HISTORY OF BRITISH VEHICLES

The following is an extract from the book 'Historic Military Vehicles Directory' by Bart Vanderveen.

In spite of shortage of funds and non-co-operation from many quarters, the British during the inter-war period turned out a fair number of military pattern vehicles. In the 1920s a range of 30-cwt and 3-ton 6x4 chassis was developed by the War Office and the motor industry. Commercial users were lured into buying these by the attraction of a subsidy scheme, which helped to swell their numbers. During the 1930s the ubiquitous 15-cwt was devised, using mechanical components of heavier commercial vehicles, thus ensuring a sturdy design and off-the-shelf availability of parts. Four-wheel drive vehicles were also produced especially for artillery towing in which role they supplanted the heavier and larger 6x4 types as well as some full-track designs. Considerable quantities of these vehicles were purchased, along with adapted commercial models. Many of them, together with armoured cars of several types, served with the British forces in the Middle East, India and other places; others were exported all over the world, particularly to Commonwealth countries.

In the evacuation from Dunkirk in May/June 1940 a large proportion of Britain's MT fleet was left behind and industry worked flat-out to replace these losses. To supplement output, the Canadian industry was engaged in producing a diversity of types which were designed to British specifications and requirements and in addition thousands of vehicles were purchased in the United States. Later, under the Lend-Lease arrangement, many US military pattern vehicles were supplied, ranging from Jeeps and trucks to AFVs of numerous sorts. In addition there were the so-called 'ex-French Contract' vehicles: when France fell to the Germans in 1940, many of the thousands of vehicles ordered by the French in the United States were either en route or had not been shipped yet and most if not all of this material was taken over and diverted to Britain. In turn, many British vehicles - including AFVs - were supplied to allied forces, including the Soviet Union. From 1942, the US forces in Britain also used numbers of British-built vehicles (e.g. ambulances); these were supplied under what was known as reversed Lend-Lease.

When the war started in September 1939, the War Department held a total of about 85,000, vehicles, including more than 26,000 impressed ones. Included also were some

21,500 motorcycles and many trailers. By VE-Day the number was in the region of <u>one and a quarter million</u>, excluding AFVs.

The vehicles used by the British forces were divided into the following categories:

(a) Army 'A', 'B', 'C' and RASC vehicles (WO, War Office)
(b) Royal Air Force (RAF) vehicles (AM, Air Ministry)
(c) Royal Navy (RN) vehicles (Admiralty)

'A' Vehicles. This category comprised all AFVs, wheeled and tracked: scout cars, armoured cars, tracked carriers, LVTs, tanks and their derivatives (e.g. SPs. APCs, ARVs, BARVs). Exceptions included light reconnaissance cars, US-built half-tracks, armoured trucks.

'B' Vehicles. Grouped under this heading were motorcycles, cars (including utilities and light recce cars), ambulances, amphibians (except LVTs), trucks of all types, tank transporters, artillery tractors, breakdowns/wreckers, gun porters, trailers.

'C' Vehicles. Special-purpose vehicles as used mainly by the Royal Engineers (RE, or 'Sappers') e.g. mobile cranes except when on truck chassis), earthmoving equipment (excavators, graders, etc.), dumpers, industrial-type tractors. This classification was introduced later than the previous two, 'C' vehicles becoming more numerous as time went on.

RASC Vehicles. Prior to WWII the Royal Army Service Corps was the largest user of MT vehicles, in the British Army. The RASC was responsible for all 'second line' vehicles, including ambulances and fire engines; these were termed 'RASC vehicles'. The Royal Army Ordnance Corps (RAOC} was responsible for 'first line' vehicles - including AFVs - for the Army's operational units. The enormous growth of Army mechanisation during the early war years called for reorganisation of vehicle supply, maintenance and repairs. Thus, from 1942 all 'RASC vehicles' were included in the 'B' vehicle classification. The Ministry of Supply (MoS) was formed as a provision agent for all vehicle types the Royal Electrical and Mechanical Engineers (REME) for all the Army's electrical and mechanical maintenance, repair and rebuild activities. The RAOC became the exclusive source of vehicle supply, with headquarters and main depot central Ordnance Depot at Chilwell in Nottinghamshire.

RAF Vehicles. The Air Ministry looked after the supply and development of vehicles for the Royal Air Force until early in 1941, after which there was close co-operation with the War Office. Before that date the RAF (originally RFC) had their own distinctive vehicle types, which were usually of different make and type from those of the other services. Examples were the Albion AM463 and certain models of Crossley, Dennis and Ford(son). After the outbreak of WWll the RAF acquired many vehicles which the Army also used, including Canadian and US Lend-Lease types. Used almost exclusively by the RAF were the Ford WOT1 range and Crossley 4x4s; these were standardised RAF chassis and used for the mounting of a great variety of both load-carrying and specialist bodies. In RAF parlance a truck was known as a Tender (Van if under 1-ton payload rating). special-equipment and special-purpose vehicles were referred to as 'technical types'. From 1935 to 1965 the RAF vehicle fleet grew from 2,000 to 22,000, although during WWll well over 100,000 vehicles were in service.

RN Vehicles. The Royal Navy used comparatively few MT vehicles and the majority of them were commercial types with only minor modifications. Bodywork was in compliance with RN requirements. Special types included ammunition vehicles and torpedo-carrying semi-trailers.

Between the wars, British MVs carried civilian-style number plates, but during the 1930s these were supplemented (and in WWII replaced) by a new numbering system. These new registration numbers were carried on both sides of the bonnet or cab and on the rear of the bodywork, or in equivalent positions. Those on Army vehicles were known as WD or census numbers. Normally comprising white 3.5 in. figures, they were prefixed with a letter denoting the vehicle type, as follows:

A	Ambulances	**P**	Amphibians
C	Motorcycles	**S**	SP mountings
F	Armoured and Scout cars	**T**	Carriers, Tanks
H	Tractors (inc. Breakdowns)	**V**	Vans (RASC)
L	Trucks of 1 ton and over	**X**	Trailers of all types
M	Cars (inc. Light Utilities)	**Z**	Trucks of under 1 ton

RAF and RN had their own numbering systems, with the letters RAF and RN respectively. The letters RN appeared either before or after the number.

From 1949/50 all vehicles then in service were renumbered with the now familiar system of two digits, two letters, two digits. Only the Royal Navy (and Marines) still used four-digit numbers with RN in front or behind. New vehicles were, of course, also provided with the new registration numbers, whereby AA-AY were reserved for the RAF and RN for Navy and Marines. Ex-WWll Army vehicles were given numbers with letters from towards the end of the alphabet.

After 1945 many surplus vehicles were transferred to other United Nations countries, others were demobbed and sold via auctions to civilian users. Within a few years the first orders were placed for new vehicles, mainly of commercial (CL) type. New tactical types were also designed and prototyped. A number of these were put into quantity production during the 1950s. The latter were of two classes: GS and CT. GS types were modified commercial vehicles, with all-wheel drive and other special features specified by the military authorities. CT vehicles were government designs, developed in conjunction with the motor industry; they were powered by Rolls-Royce B-series petrol engines with four, six or eight cylinders, depending on application, and very advanced. Several of these CT types also went into series production but they were expensive to manufacture and production was curtailed when it was found that the GS types were quite up to the job, much cheaper to procure and maintain, easier to repair and generally simpler to operate.

In addition to the soft-skin vehicles, the British in WWII had a vast arsenal of AFVs. Numerous wheeled types appeared during 1939-41 but only a few were made in fairly large quantities: 4x4 scout cars by Daimler and Humber (i.e. Rootes), reconnaissance cars by Humber and Morris and armoured cars, again by Daimler and Humber, with heavy types of the latter by AEC. The tracked carrier was also mass-produced. Some of Britain's tanks were developed from pre-war designs but there were notable exceptions like the Churchill and - just too late to see any active service of importance - the Centurion. The 'Cent', however, went on to be the mainstay of the post-war Army and was developed and improved through many marks. In addition to their own, the British employed a considerable number of US-built light and medium tanks, supplied under Lend-Lease. The nation's domestic tank production during WWII amounted to nearly 25,000.

Wheeled armour was largely replaced in the 1950s by new 4x4 and 6x6 designs exemplified by the Ferret and the Saladin and their derivatives. All of these were used at home and abroad (and by other nations), some until well into the 1980s.

Meanwhile, numerous historic British MVs have been salvaged, restored and preserved for posterity. The Military Vehicles Trust (previously MVCG) and other organisations cater for their owners in the UK and overseas, and there are also some first-rate official and private collections, the outstanding one being the Tank Museum at Bovington.

The following section (Appendix G) is a collection of vehicle technical information for the trucks covered in this book. In the title bar for each truck is the name of the truck along with the weight and 2 numbers describing the wheel arrangements eg. 6 x 4. If you are familiar with this system then you have no need to read further, if not and you want to know more then carry on reading.

Wheel Arrangements

The method of describing vehicle wheel arrangements used by the Military has become the standard throughout the vehicle industry. The system identifies two characteristics, the number of wheels, and the number of these that are 'driven', that is connected to the engine via a drive shaft or shafts and one or more gear boxes. In this context the fitting of dual rear wheels to one or more axles is not recognised.

Therefore a vehicle shown as a 4 x 2 identifies it as having four wheels, two of which are driven (rear - unless indicated otherwise).
A 4 x 4 recognises a vehicle with 4 wheels and a four wheel drive.
Other combinations follow, thus: 6 x 4, 6 x 6 etc.

As an example, the 10 ton Mack shown right, is a 6 x 4. The dual rear wheels count as one wheel therefore it has 6 wheels of which 4 are driven.

Mack NR 10 ton truck, 6 x 4

APPENDIX G

VEHICLE TECHNICAL INFO

The following pages contain general data, dimensions, weights, and technical details along with photographs of the vehicles covered in this book. There is also an 'Author's opinion' on what they were like to drive.

Acknowledgement is given to the book 'Historic Military Vehicles Directory' by Bart Vanderveen from which the majority of this technical information has been obtained.

Additional vehicle information can be found on the Internet where many MVPA (Military Vehicle Preservation Association) sites exist. A good starting point for this is at the address:- http://www.mvpa.org

This web site provides an online links page to well over 300 other World Wide Web Internet sites to be found on this and other related subjects. Although a lot of these are American, there is a vast amount of useful information to look at.

Some links to be found on the MVPA Online web site:-

MVPA ONLINE

Lightweight Vehicles	1/4-ton Trucks
1/2-ton through 2-ton Trucks	2 1/2-ton and Larger Trucks
Armoured and Tracked Vehicles	Other Vehicles
Miscellaneous	Businesses
Events	Groups and Associations
Museums	Publications - On & Off the Internet
Reference	Search Engines
U.S. Army	U.S. Government

Hillman 10 HP

Below: Light Utility Mk 1.
Bottom left: Convertible Van.
Bottom right: Ladder Van.

Car, Light Utility, 4 x 2   Hillman 10 HP

GENERAL DATA:

One of the most numerous wartime 'Tillies', the Hillman Minx-based models appeared in six marks, all differing in detail. They were 2-seaters with a pick-up type body integral with the open-back cab. A canvas canopy was carried on three hoopsticks. Some had folding seats in the rear. Late production vehicles had a wire mesh radiator grille. Made also as Convertible Van (estate car) and Ladder Van, both for the RAF in 1941/42, in addition there were the basic saloons, used as staff cars.

TECHNICAL DETAILS:

Own 4-cyl, side-valve liquid-cooled petrol engine. Cubic capacity 1185 cc Maximum output 30 bhp at 4100 rpm. Dry plate clutch. 4F1R gearbox. Rear-wheel drive, 6.57:1 axle ratio (late production models 5.37:1). Mechanical brakes. Unitary body-cum-chassis construction. Rigid axles with semi-elliptic leaf springs. 6.00-16 tyres (late models 5.00-16). 12-volt electrics. 8-gallon fuel capacity.

DIMENSIONS AND WEIGHTS:

Wheelbase 92 in. Overall length 151 in., width 63 in., height 75 in.
Ground clearance 7.5 in. Weight 2350 lb, gross 3240 lb.

AUTHOR'S OPINION:

I drove one of these or similar during driver training. Just a car, nothing special.

Humber F.W.D.

Below: GS Truck.
Bottom left: Ambulance.
Bottom right: BBC Recording Van.

Truck, 8-cwt, 4 x 4   Humber F.W.D.

GENERAL DATA:

Throughout WWII Humber Ltd produced a range of military pattern vehicles based on a common 8-cwt 4 x 4 chassis. Included were a heavy utility car (qv), a field ambulance, a truck and some armoured types. The truck had a standardised WD body with three seats and a superstructure with folding legs that could be used off the vehicle as a tent. The FFW version had two seats in the back and a No. 11 radio. The British Broadcasting Corporation employed some converted ambulances as recording vans for war correspondents in combat areas.

TECHNICAL DETAILS:

Own 6-cyl, side-valve liquid-cooled petrol engine. Cubic capacity 4086 cc. Maximum output 85 bhp at 3400 rpm. Dry plate clutch. 4F1R gearbox. All-wheel drive, 2-speed transfer box with front axle disconnect. 4.88:1 axle gear ratio. Hydraulic brakes. Independent front suspension with transverse leaf spring. Rigid rear axle with leaf springs. 9.25-16 tyres. 12-volt electrics. 16-gallon fuel capacity.

DIMENSIONS AND WEIGHTS:

Wheelbase 112 in. Overall length 168 in., width 77 in., height 81 in.
Ground clearance 9 in. Weight 4790 lb, gross 6100 lb.

AUTHOR'S OPINION:

I drove an ambulance version from Osnabrück to the island of Nordeney during late 1947. A comfortable and easy to drive vehicle with plenty of get up and go from the four litre engine.

Bedford MWD

Below: MWD GS (early).
Bottom left: Machinery 'K Light'.
Bottom right: MWC Water Tank.

Truck, 15-cwt, 4 x 2   Bedford MWD

GENERAL DATA:

From late 1939 until 1945 Vauxhall Motors supplied vast quantities of vehicles for the armed forces and nearly 66000 of these were based on the 15-cwt 4 x 2 MW chassis. In addition to the common GS truck (MWD) and its derivatives (FFW, Machinery, MWG Gun Portee, MWT Gun Tractor) there were other body types, e.g., water bowsers and radio vans. The Machinery 'K Light' carried a Murex electric welding set. Early MWs had an open cab as shown opposite.

TECHNICAL DETAILS:

Own 6-cyl. overhead-valve liquid-cooled petrol engine. Cubic capacity 3519 cc. Maximum output 72 bhp at 3000 rpm. Dry plate clutch. 4F1R gearbox. 6.2:1 axle gear ratio. Hydraulic brakes. Rigid axles with semi-elliptic leaf springs. 9.00-16 tyres on WD-pattern split-rim wheels. 12 volt electrics. 20-gallon fuel capacity.

DIMENSIONS AND WEIGHTS:

Wheelbase 99 in. Overall length 172 in., width 68 in., height 90 in. (minimum 63 in.). Ground clearance 9 in. Weight 4730 lb, gross 7730 lb.

AUTHOR'S OPINION:

Easy to drive, smooth gearbox, brakes adequate. Water Tank version, open cab with 'racing' windshields, a distinct disadvantage. Definitely not suitable for driving through blizzards, as experienced by the author.

Ford WOT2

Below: WOT2B GS Van.
Bottom left: WOT2A GS.
Bottom right: WOT2E Wireless Van.

Truck, 15 cwt, 4 x 2   Ford WOT2

GENERAL DATA:

This 15 cwt chassis was in production throughout WWII, with periodic improvements and changes. The majority were fitted with GS bodies and known as infantry trucks (Ford or Fordson WOT2A, C, E, F, H), others had a full length canvas tilt (WOT2B, D) and were known as GS vans. Some had special bodywork like house-type vans or fire service vans, the latter for the Home Front. Early models had an open cab with folding windscreens; from WOT2E a semi-enclosed cab was used. Total production, 1939-45, was nearly 60000.

TECHNICAL DETAILS:

Own 30 HP V-8 cyl. side-valve liquid-cooled petrol engine. Cubic capacity 3621 cc. Maximum output 60 bhp at governed 2840 rpm. Dry plate clutch. 4F1R gearbox. Rear-wheel drive. 6.8:1 axle gear ratio. Mechanical brakes. Rigid axles with semi-elliptic leaf springs (transversal at front). 9.00-16 tyres. 12-volt electrics (early production 6-volt). 23-gallon fuel capacity.

DIMENSIONS AND WEIGHTS:

Wheelbase 106 in. Overall length 177 in., width 79 in, height 90 in. (minimum 71 in.). Ground clearance 11 in. Weight 4520 lb, gross 7395 lb.

AUTHOR'S OPINION:

I don't remember driving this model but I do remember my ambulance being run into by one during my stay in Detmold in Germany.

Austin K2/Y

Below and bottom: Austin ambulance nicknamed 'Katy'

Truck, 2-ton, 4 x 2, Ambulance — Austin K2/Y

GENERAL DATA:

Most common British Heavy Ambulance, used by all services. Four stretchers or 10 sitting cases. Over 13000 were built, including some for other nations. Occasionally used as vans for other roles.

TECHNICAL DETAILS:

6-cyl. 63 bhp engine (own 3462-cc ohv) driving rear wheels via 4-speed gearbox. Hydraulic brakes. Leaf spring suspension. Tyre size 10.50-16.

DIMENSIONS AND WEIGHTS:

Wheelbase 134 in. Overall dimensions 216 x 87 x 110 in. Weight 6890 lb.

AUTHOR'S OPINION:

Good to drive with a fair turn of speed from an ungoverned engine, (probably 70 mph +). Light springing could be disconcerting to passengers as the vehicle did tend to 'lean over' somewhat when negotiating corners. Main disadvantage was in winter when canvas side pieces in lieu of doors were noticeably lacking in insulating the driver from inclement weather.

Bedford OYD

Below: OYD GS.
Bottom left: OYC Water.
Bottom right: OYC X-ray Laboratory.

Truck, 3 ton, 4 x 2   Bedford OYD

GENERAL DATA:

The OY was Britain's most numerous 3-tonner: 72385 were delivered during WWII. In addition to the OYD GS load carrier there were many other types, for example water and fuel bowsers (by Butterfield) on the OYC chassis/cab. There were also Battery Slave, Stores and Workshop modifications of the OYD, as well as Bread Carrying, Canteen, Disinfector, Horse Box, Office and other variants. Very early chassis had 32 x 6 tyres, dual rear, but by far the majority had 10.50-16s on split-rim wheels.

TECHNICAL DETAILS:

Own 6-cyl. overhead-valve liquid cooled petrol engine. Cubic capacity 3519 cc. Maximum output 72 bhp at 3000 rpm. Dry plate clutch. 4F1R gearbox. Rear wheel drive. 7.4:1 axle gear ratio (earliest production, with 32 x 6 tyres, 6.83:1). Hydraulic brakes with vacuum servo assistance. Rigid axles with semi-elliptic leaf springs. 10.50-16 tyres. 12-volt electrics. 32-gallon fuel capacity.

DIMENSIONS AND WEIGHTS:

Wheelbase 157 in. Overall length 245 in., width 86 in., height 122 in. Ground clearance 9 in. Weight 5940 lb, gross 14450 lb.

AUTHOR'S OPINION:

An excellent truck to drive, smooth gearbox and reliable engine. Closed cab made winter driving tolerable. I drove one of these from July 1943 to September 1944 whilst stationed in Aldershot. Top speed probably 40 mph - governed.

Bedford QLD

Below: QLD GS (RAF).
Bottom left: QLR Wireless.
Bottom right: QLT Troop Carrier.

Truck, 3-ton, 4 x 4   Bedford QLD

GENERAL DATA:

The Bedford QL was in production from 1941 until 1945; some 52250 were made. In addition to the most common GS cargo truck (QLD) there were several derivatives, e.g. the QLC chassis/cab (for bodywork by outside contractors, including refuellers and tractors for semi-trailers), the QLB Bofors gun tractor (qv), QLR signals vehicles, QLT troop carrier and QLW airportable tipper. QLB and QLW had a 5-ton winch. QL-series trucks were used by all the services for many years and a fair number have been preserved.

TECHNICAL DETAILS:

Own 6-cyl. overhead-valve liquid-cooled petrol engine. Cubic capacity 3519 cc. Maximum output 72 bhp at 3000 rpm. Dry plate clutch. 4F1R gear box. All-wheel drive. 2-speed transfer box with front axle disconnect. 6.16 axle gear ratio. Hydraulic brakes with vacuum servo assistance. Rigid axles with semi-elliptic leaf springs. 10.50-20 tyres. 12-volt electrics. 28-gallon fuel capacity.

DIMENSIONS AND WEIGHTS:

Wheelbase 143 in. Overall length 236 in., width 89 in., height 120 in. (min. 102 in.). Ground clearance 12 in. Weight 7225 lb, gross 15400 lb.

AUTHOR'S OPINION:

I had no driving experience on this truck and only got to ride in the back of a Troop Carrying version when I was demobbed at York in 1948.

Foden DG6/12

Logo

Truck, 10-ton, 6 x 4, GS — Foden DG6/12

GENERAL DATA:

Produced from 1941, with large tyres, for platform and house-type vans (Camera, Photo Mechanical and Printing) as well as Railway Breakdown vehicles.

TECHNICAL DETAILS:

6-cyl. 102 bhp engine (Gardner 6LW 8369 cc diesel) driving rear wheels via 4-speed gearbox and 2-speed auxiliary box (for first and reverse gears). Hydraulic brakes. Leaf spring suspension, inverted at rear. Tyres 13.50-20.

DIMENSIONS AND WEIGHTS:

Wheelbase 188 in. (BC 52 in). Overall dimensions 320 x 91 x 126 in. Weight 18590 lb.

AUTHOR'S OPINION:

A pig of a truck to drive. Very heavy steering coupled with brakes unsupported by either vacuum or compressed air. Gear change was marked by time it took for engine to lose revs, so long in fact that it was possible to come out of gear into neutral, take a cigarette out of the packet and light it before it was time to engage the next gear up! The presence of two air cleaners mounted on the in cab engine resulted in conversation killing noise. I had five and a half months on this truck between September 1944 and March 1945. It was, however, a powerful beast, but top speed only in the region of 32 mph.

Mack EH

Below: EH Cargo.
Bottom: EHT Tractors, commercial and military pattern types.

Truck, 5-ton, 4 x 2   Mack EH

GENERAL DATA:

Derived from commercial production the EH was extensively militarised and built in two wheelbase sizes: 170 in. Cargo and 146 in. Tractor. They had a soft-top cab and were sometimes designated 5-6 ton 4 x 2. During 1943-44 3450 cargo trucks were built and 2400 of these were shipped to Britain, under Lend-Lease. Tractor production was limited to 50 units. In 1942 100 37-passenger buses had been produced on a 230 in. wb version of this chassis. Of the commercial type a large number were supplied to Britain; a typical example is shown.

TECHNICAL DETAILS:

Own EN354 6-cyl. side-valve liquid-cooled petrol (gasoline) engine. Cubic capacity 353.8 cubic in. (5798 cc). Maximum output 110 bhp at 2620 rpm. Dry plate clutch. 5F1R gearbox. 8.59:1 axle gear ratio. Air-actuated brakes. Rigid axles with semi-elliptic leaf springs. 9.00-20 tyres. 6-volt electrics. 50-gallon fuel capacity.

DIMENSIONS AND WEIGHTS:

Wheelbase 170 in. Overall length 271 in., width 96 in., height 113 (94) in. Ground clearance 10 in. Weight 10500 lb, gross 20500 lb.

AUTHOR'S OPINION:

No experience driving this truck but aware that it developed problems of rear spring centre bolt failure which led to 'crabbing' as described in Chapter 3, 'Touring Holland'.

Mack NR

Below: NR9.
Bottom left: NR6.
Bottom right: NR14. (All shown in British Army service).

Truck, 10 ton, 6 x 4   Mack NR

GENERAL DATA:

The NR-Series General Service Load Carrier (GSLC) was in production throughout WWII, mainly for the long distance supply role. The British Army used large numbers of them (also as Tank Carriers, qv) and so did the Canadians. Altogether 16500 were built, with periodic detail changes (NR1 to 20). From NR8 (s/n NR4D-2871D) a soft-top cab was fitted and dual rear tyres (11.00-24 all round) appeared with the NR14 version. The NR proved an excellent truck, both for military and - when surplussed - civilian haulage work.

TECHNICAL DETAILS:

Own ED (Lanova) 6-cyl. overhead-valve liquid-cooled diesel engine. Cubic capacity 519 cubic in. (8505 cc). Maximum output 123 bhp at 2000 rpm. Dry plate clutch. 10F2R OD-top Mack TRD37 Duplex gearbox. Inter-axle power divider. Double-reduction axles with 9.02:1 gear ratio. Air brakes. Rigid axles with semi-elliptic leaf springs, inverted at rear. Tyres 11.00-24 front, 14.00-20 rear. 12-volt electrics (24-volt starting). 150-gallon fuel capacity.

DIMENSIONS AND WEIGHTS:

Wheelbase 200.5 (rear axles 55) in. Overall length 322, width 96, height 125 in. Ground clearance 13 in. Weight 21600 lb, gross 42750 lb.

AUTHOR'S OPINION:

Our platoon had the NR14 version. A superb truck to drive. Gearboxes and brakes a dream. Comfortable driver's seat and room for two front seat passengers. Disadvantage of lack of full cab doors and rather poor steering lock forgotten in face of other favourable features. Top speed 40+ mph.

Truck, 3-ton, 4 x 2, GS   Leyland Lynx WDZ1 (A-C)

GENERAL DATA:

During 1939-40 Leyland's Kingston (Surrey) factory produced 1497 of these trucks for the RASC and the Army. Some had a closed cab. A slightly different type was supplied to the Royal Navy.

TECHNICAL DETAILS:

6-cyl. 77 bhp petrol engine (own E117/K1 4730 cc ohv) driving rear wheels via 5-speed gearbox. Hydraulic brakes. Leaf spring suspension. Tyre size 8.25-20.

DIMENSIONS AND WEIGHTS:

Wheelbase 144 in. Overall dimensions 243 x 90 x 123 in. Weight 7300 lb.

AUTHOR'S OPINION:

I drove the closed cab version during driver training at Carlisle. Not an easy truck to manage as gear selection was difficult even with double de-clutching.

Truck, 10-ton, 6 x 4, GS — Albion CX23N

GENERAL DATA:

Superseded the CX6 type in production in 1941. Well over 400 built, under 5 contracts. Unlike its predecessor, the CX23N had articulating rear bogie suspension.

TECHNICAL DETAILS:

6-cyl. 100 bhp engine (own EN244 9080 cc diesel) driving rear wheels via 4-speed gearbox and 2-speed auxiliary box. Servo-assisted hydraulic brakes. Leaf spring suspension, inverted at rear. Tyres 13.50-20.

DIMENSIONS AND WEIGHTS:

Wheelbase 192 in. (BC 54 in.). Overall dimensions 316 x 98 x 132 in.
Weight 18420 lb.

AUTHOR'S OPINION:

I never got to drive this truck and the only contact I had with it was when I reversed into one during our evacuation from the Belgian Ardennes in Dec. 1944.

Truck, 10-ton, 6 x 4, Cargo   White 1064

GENERAL DATA:

2500 produced during 1942-45, the majority for Lend-Lease supplies. More than half of them went to the British who used them as GS Load Carriers (supplementing Mack NR).

TECHNICAL DETAILS:

6-cyl. 130 bhp (150 gross) engine (Cummins HB600 672 cid diesel) driving rear axles via 5-speed (OD top) gearbox. Double-reduction Timken driving axles. Air brakes. Leaf spring suspension, inverted at rear. Tyres 11.00-24 at front, 14.00-20 at rear.

DIMENSIONS AND WEIGHTS:

Wheelbase 200 (BC 52) in. Overall dimensions 327 x 96 x 122 in. Weight 20600lb

AUTHOR'S OPINION:

I only drove this truck for a few weeks in 1946 so I did not form any marked opinion.

APPENDIX H

GEORGE BALLS

On the following pages are two accounts of events that happened to George Balls.

Sadly George died suddenly during early March 2002. He was actually christened Russell Albert Balls but decided that this was not what he wished to be known as during his army service.

As I have recorded I first met George during May 1945 as we drove through the length and breadth of Holland and on into Germany. We enjoyed many happy times together until his demobilisation in late 1947. We subsequently kept in touch until his death. A good mate.

After we had retreated from the Belgian Ardennes, in the middle of December 1944, to the village of Bassily near Brussels, we were sent out on patrols in response to a report that German paratroops had been seen in the area. My part in this abortive exercise is described in the latter part of Chapter 3 - 'On The Road'. George Balls (right), who at that time was in B platoon, has described to me an event experienced by him whilst on a patrol.

This is his first story:

Memories of a winter's evening

On the night in question, there must have been something like fifteen or twenty of us out on this patrol. I remember it being cold with occasional clouds scudding across a bright moon. As this was the nearest we had potentially come to the dreaded foe, I suppose we were a bit twitchy to say the least, some more than others. It was fairly open country and we proceeded down a lane in a generally unmilitary manner. The lane led to an open field, and here we paused, starting at every untoward sound. Visibility, I recall was fairly good, when the moon was not obscured, and trees and hedgerows could be made out in the middle distance.

Unidentified sounds continued to undermine moral! Suddenly, one of our number could stand it no longer. "I'm going to let them have it" he said, or something very similar. And with a sweep of his body, he let go the full magazine of his Sten gun.

Now I was only a few feet from him, as were one or two others. One, a Scotsman, shouted: "Jock, Jock, they got me" as he fell to the ground. I immediately shouted: "Stop firing you've hit Jock." After much confusion, and some debate, I volunteered to go for help, and legged it back to the billet. After explaining things to our sergeant, who seemed reluctant to do anything, (I think he'd been drinking), I finally managed to persuade him to get the 15cwt truck, and together we retraced my path back to the scene of the incident - no one in sight, but after a short while somebody approached and said that they had carried the unfortunate fellow up to a farmhouse. When we loaded him into the truck however, it was a body and not a casualty.

Later when reminiscing, back at base, one or two chaps confessed that at the first sign of shooting they had dived into a ditch.

Thinking back, from the position we were in, I can only assume that in the arc of fire, the bullets must have passed both sides of me. As for the the guy who did the shooting, he was quickly transferred to another company and was not heard from again.

NOTE: I have intentionally missed out the name of the shooter, otherwise I have copied George's words, punctuation and all just as he wrote it down for me.

George's second story can be found on the next page.

This is George's second story:

A Narrow Escape

It was the middle of December 1944 or just after and I was in La Roche en Ardenne. Our platoon had been there about a couple of weeks mostly carting timber for 14 company - Canadian Forestry Corps.

Two days before, I'd taken my truck, a 5/6 ton Mack, into workshops at Salmchateau or nearby Vielsalm, either for inspection or for some fault to be put right. It had several bits and pieces of my personal stuff in it that I fully expected to see again, but alas, it was not to be, as that was the last I ever saw of that lorry.

On guard that night, I had taken the first shift; already there had been rumours of enemy activity, so much so that I had been ordered to check with the Yanks every hour to find out what sort of traffic was crossing the bridge they were guarding; the bridge being about half a mile from where we were at a hotel that had been commandeered.

So, having finished my second stint of guard (two hours on, four hours off), instead of kipping down in the guardroom, as I was supposed to do, I thought I'm not going to get much sleep here with the changing of the guards etc., and I slunk off to get a bit of peace and shuteye in one of the empty rooms in the hotel.

Sometime later, I was rudely awakened by the guard commander, who was having a quick look round before departing - most of the others had already done so - and it was grab your stuff and jump into one of the remaining vehicles and go - poste haste.

I've often wondered what would have happened to me if he hadn't been conscientious and had that last look around.

APPENDIX I

ALDERSHOT REVISITED

During the summer of 1999 returning northwards after a short holiday visiting my son on the Isle of Wight, my wife and I had made arrangements to stay for two nights in Farnborough, affording us the opportunity to drive into Aldershot and locate Clayton Barracks where I had spent some fourteen months during 1943 and 1944.

During the course of a prior telephone conversation with an office in the barracks I had been made aware that the landscape had changed considerably. I was, however, totally unprepared for the changes that had taken place since 1944. In place of the succession of numbers of barracks there were huge open grassed spaces. I was completely lost and only after a series of excursions round the area did we manage to find Clayton Barracks, or, what remained of them.

Half of the buildings had been demolished and replaced by car parking areas. Two of the remaining blocks have been newly painted in an 'off white' whilst the other two are coloured dull red. My memory is surprisingly faulty as to the colouring of 1943/4, but logic tells me that it must have been the dull red. Internally the buildings have been converted to offices or stores. The newer part of the barracks which were occupied by the ATS in 1943/4 are still intact and being used as accommodation for troops.

Where the mess hall and NAAFI canteen had been situated, across the road from the barrack blocks, there is now a landscaped area leading to the Officer's Mess. The most astounding sight there and elsewhere was the abundance of mature trees.

I sought and was given approval, by the Military Police, to take a few photographs and whilst doing so wandered around the area. At one point I identified the spot where I had stood half a century and more ago during morning roll call parade, and the memories of events and friends came flooding back across the years with the utmost of clarity. The moment could only have been improved had some of those long lost comrades been with me.

CLAYTON BARRACKS, ALDERSHOT

The older part of the barracks, shown in the accompanying diagram, consisted, (as far as I can remember), of eight two storey blocks with four barrack rooms in each The rooms were about forty five feet long by half that wide, capable of accommodating up to twenty four troops in 'bunk beds' arranged lengthwise down each side. The central core of each block contained washing and toilet facilities (ablutions) and between floor stairs. Heating in each room was provided by two centrally placed back to back coal fires.

The spaces to the rear of the blocks were used for morning roll call and other parades. Assembly prior to marching to the Motor Transport Yard was done on the road as traffic was minimal. Then, as now, the area was Military Police controlled and civilian presence at a minimum.

Only four of the blocks now remain, numbers three, four, seven and eight having been demolished and the areas are now used for vehicle parking. The remaining four blocks are now used as offices etc. and are not used to house troops.

Most of the original roofs have been replaced, without the chimneys, but examination of picture (Block 5) shows the original chimney still in place.

The front doors owe more to latter day practice than to 1943 styling and it is obvious that the 'window change brigade' have been on site.

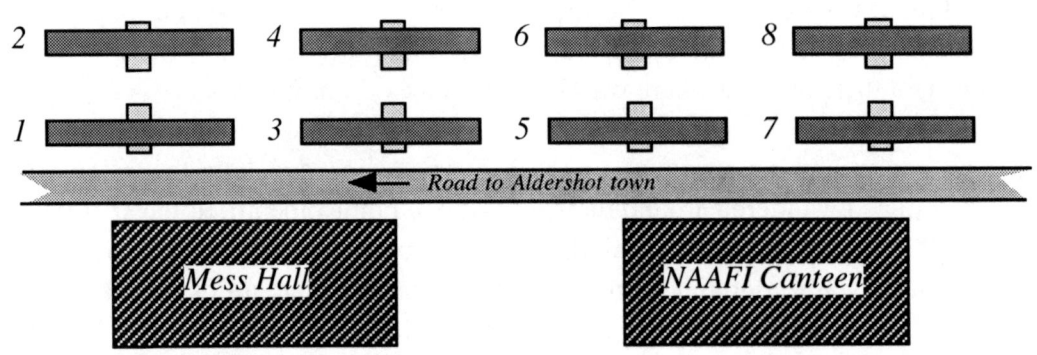

Clayton Barracks - showing block numbers for photographs.

The following two pages show the pictures taken in the summer of 1999 with reference to the diagram above.

CLAYTON BARRACKS 1

Left: Block 1.

Author's residence July 1943 to September 1944, top floor, left hand room.

Right: Block 1. View from the front.

Left: Block 1. Rear view - area for morning parade.

CLAYTON BARRACKS 2

*Left: Block 6.
Rear view with block 5 to left..*

*Right: Block 5.
End view with block 6 to left.*

*Left:
Area where Mess Hall and NAAFI Canteen used to be.*

APPENDIX J

GLOSSARY

a) Abbreviations

AFN	American Forces (radio) Network.
AFS	Auxiliary Fire Service.
AFV	Armoured Fighting Vehicle.
APC	Armoured Personnel Carrier.
ARV	Armoured Reconnaissance Vehicle.
ATS	Auxiliary Territorial Service. (Women's Army).
BAFVs	British Armed Forces Vouchers. Occupation Army money issued to stop use of German currency in canteens as more money was being spent in NAAFI canteens than the army was being paid! Note that the sale of six cigarettes in the 'grey market' would realise the sum of thirty shillings equal to one week's pay for a private soldier.
BAOR	British Army of the Rhine.
BFN	British Forces (radio) Network.
BLA	British Liberation Army.
CCG	Control Commission for Germany, - a civilian force replacing the Military Government put in place at the cessation of hostilities. Later became jocularly known as 'Charlie Chaplin's Grenadiers'.
CRS	Casualty Receiving Station.
D Day	June 6th 1944, the Allied Armies land in Normandy, France
ITC	Infantry Training Centre.
NAAFI	Navy, Army and Air Force Institute.
NCO(s)	Non Commissioned Officer(s).
MV	Motor Vehicle.
RAMC	Royal Army Medical Corps.
RAOC	Royal Army Ordnance Corps.
RASC	Royal Army Service Corps.
REME	Royal Electrical and Mechanical Engineers.
VE Day	Victory in Europe Day (May 8th 1945).

b) Words

Ablutions	Washrooms, showers and toilets.
Bevin Boy	Name given to men conscripted at the age of eighteen, who were directed to work in the coal mines as opposed to going into the Armed Forces. The idea and name was associated with Ernest Bevin, the Minister of Labour and National Service in the Wartime cabinet led by Winston Churchill.
Black Market	A source of supply for rationed or scarce food and /or materials usually at greatly enhanced prices. The word 'spiv' was coined to describe an individual who was involved in Black Market activities.
Browned off	Fed up.
Billet	Accommodation for troops, barracks, private homes etc.
Billeted	Accommodated in billet.
Blanco	A paste or powder, which mixed with water, was applied to webbing equipment. Colour was Khaki-green No. 3.
Cushy	Easy, comfortable.
Charge	Placed under open or close arrest for later disciplinary hearing by officer commanding unit. Army Form No.252 (charge sheet). Colloquial name 'fizzer'.
Chad	Cartoon character much in evidence in the winter of 1944.
Café	Continental name for pub or place of refreshment. Convenient front for more unorthodox activities.
Demob	Demobilisation, discharge from armed forces.
Doodlebug	Colloquial name for German V1 pilotless Flying Bomb.
Grey Market	A mild form of Black Market.
Jerrican	German designed fuel container, (capacity 20 litres).
Jankers	Punishment for action not in accordance with Army regulations. Usually a number of days CB (confined to barracks) in lieu of leisure time, more often than not performing menial labour in the cookhouse.
Mess Hall	Dining hall for troops other than officers.
Provost Sergeant	Usually in charge of a unit of Military Police. (Red Caps).
Wagon	Word used to describe a truck which in turn was used to describe a lorry.

APPENDIX K

LATE ARRIVALS

Shortly before the book was committed to print it was appreciated that the inclusion of three pictures within the main body of the text would cause movement of text and pictures to a degree that was felt undesirable. These have been inserted in this Appendix along with some additional material relating to the Mulberry Harbour at Arromanches.

Aldershot

Picture one is a photograph of B Platoon, 270 Company RASC stationed at Clayton Barracks, Aldershot, Hampshire during 1943 - 1944. The author is on the back row seventh from the left. Chapter 2 - page 47 onwards recalls the author's time at Aldershot.

Mulberry Harbour

Picture two is a schematic of Mulberry Harbour constructed at Arromanches in Normandy, northern France.

Picture three shows the location of what were known as 'Gooseberries'. These were old ships which were filled with concrete and then sunk off shore to form part of the Mulberry breakwater.

Two harbours were constructed, Mulberry 'A' for the American sector of the beaches and Mulberry 'B' for the British sector. Each harbour was large enough to enclose an area of water as big as Dover harbour. Together the various structures weighed about a million tons. The concrete caissons were code named 'Phoenix's', 212 of these were constructed in the UK at ports, slipways and basins excavated in open land on the banks of the river Thames.in sizes ranging from 1,672 and 6,044 tons. A number were built at the author's home port of Goole. Of the total number 147 were completed before D-day, the remaining 65 were used as additional breakwaters and replacements. The material used in their construction included 600,000 tons of concrete, 31,000 tons of steel girders, 1,500,000 yards of steel shuttering, 45,000,000 feet of timber and 100 miles of steel cable. Each caisson had accommodation for a crew and an artillery detachment to man the defensive armament necessary during transit to France. By June 18, 12 days after D-Day a large part of these structures were ready for use.

"B" Platoon, 270 Coy., R.A.S.C. (Command (Mixed) Transport)

Photograph by Mega, Aldershot.

Back row:- Drivers, Richard, Paling, Dickens, Thyer, Oxspring, Fox, **Houghton**, Corbett, Fullerton, Evans, Hollowood, MacDonald, Daniels, Gratton, Davies.
Third row:- Drivers, Simmons, Arnold, Jepson, Cummimgs, J S Green, McGeoch, Richardson, Hulme, Liddell, J Green, Tuck, Toombs, Harris, Carter, Ryan.
Second row:- Driver, Webb, L.Cpls. Thompson, Mellor, Cpls. Tinton, Hicks. Sgt. MacPherson. Lieut. Skellam, L/Sgt. Franks, Cpl. Dickens, L/Cpls. Whichello, Hasler, Fleming, Driver Laidlaw.
Front row:- Drivers, Twiner, Getgood, Pritchard, Tooley, Doxsey, Bowman, McLaughlin, Sullivan.

RASC   Page 244   Appendix K

Mulberry Harbour 'B'

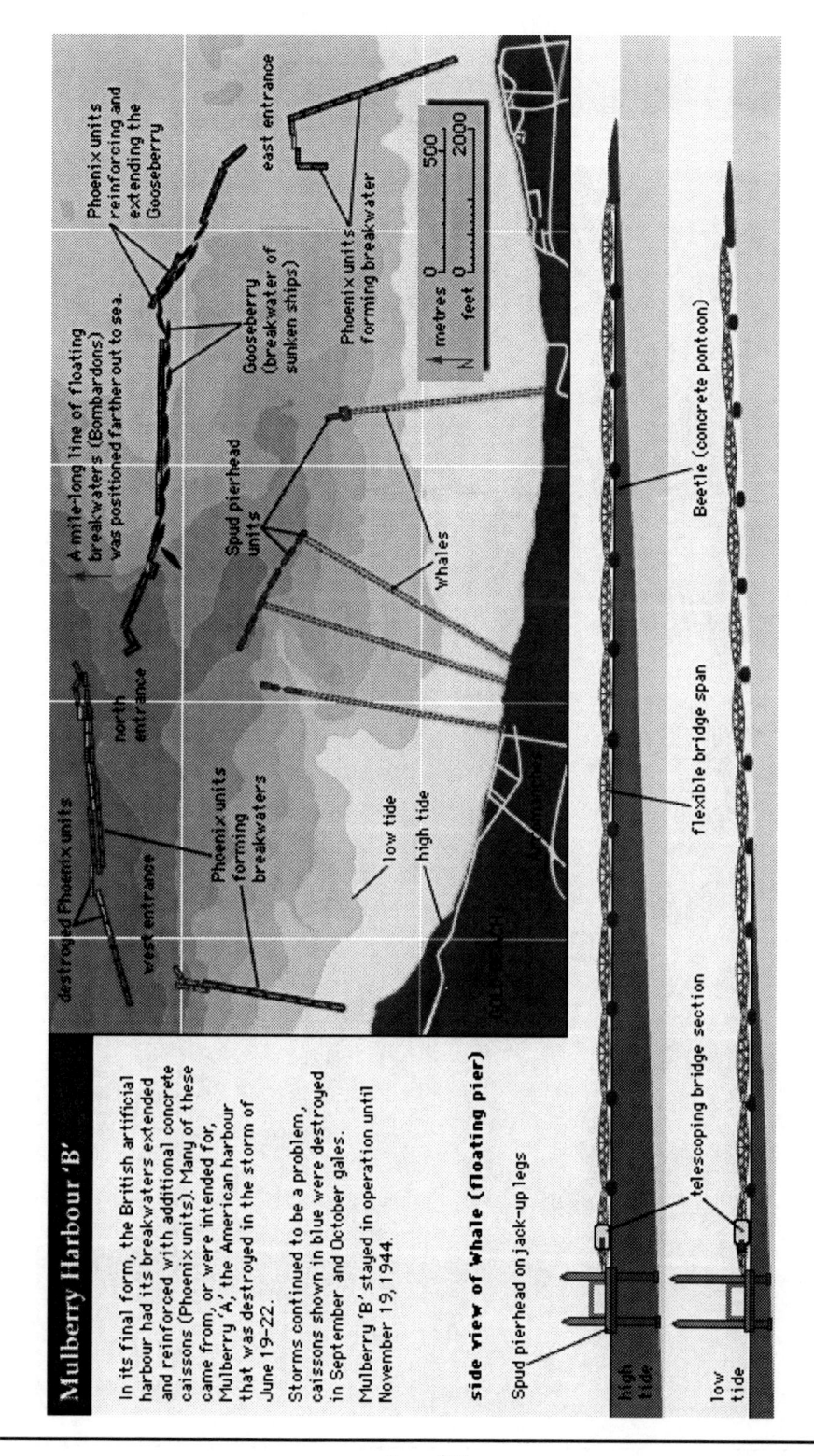

In its final form, the British artificial harbour had its breakwaters extended and reinforced with additional concrete caissons (Phoenix units). Many of these came from, or were intended for, Mulberry 'A,' the American harbour that was destroyed in the storm of June 19–22.

Storms continued to be a problem, caissons shown in blue were destroyed in September and October gales.

Mulberry 'B' stayed in operation until November 19, 1944.

Map labels:
- destroyed Phoenix units
- west entrance
- north entrance
- Phoenix units forming breakwaters
- low tide
- high tide
- A mile-long line of floating breakwaters (Bombardons) was positioned farther out to sea.
- Phoenix units reinforcing and extending the Gooseberry
- east entrance
- Gooseberry (breakwater of sunken ships)
- Phoenix units forming breakwater
- Spud pierhead units
- Whales
- metres 0 500
- feet 0 2000

side view of Whale (floating pier)

- Spud pierhead on jack-up legs
- telescoping bridge section
- flexible bridge span
- Beetle (concrete pontoon)
- high tide
- low tide

TYPICAL GOOSEBERRY

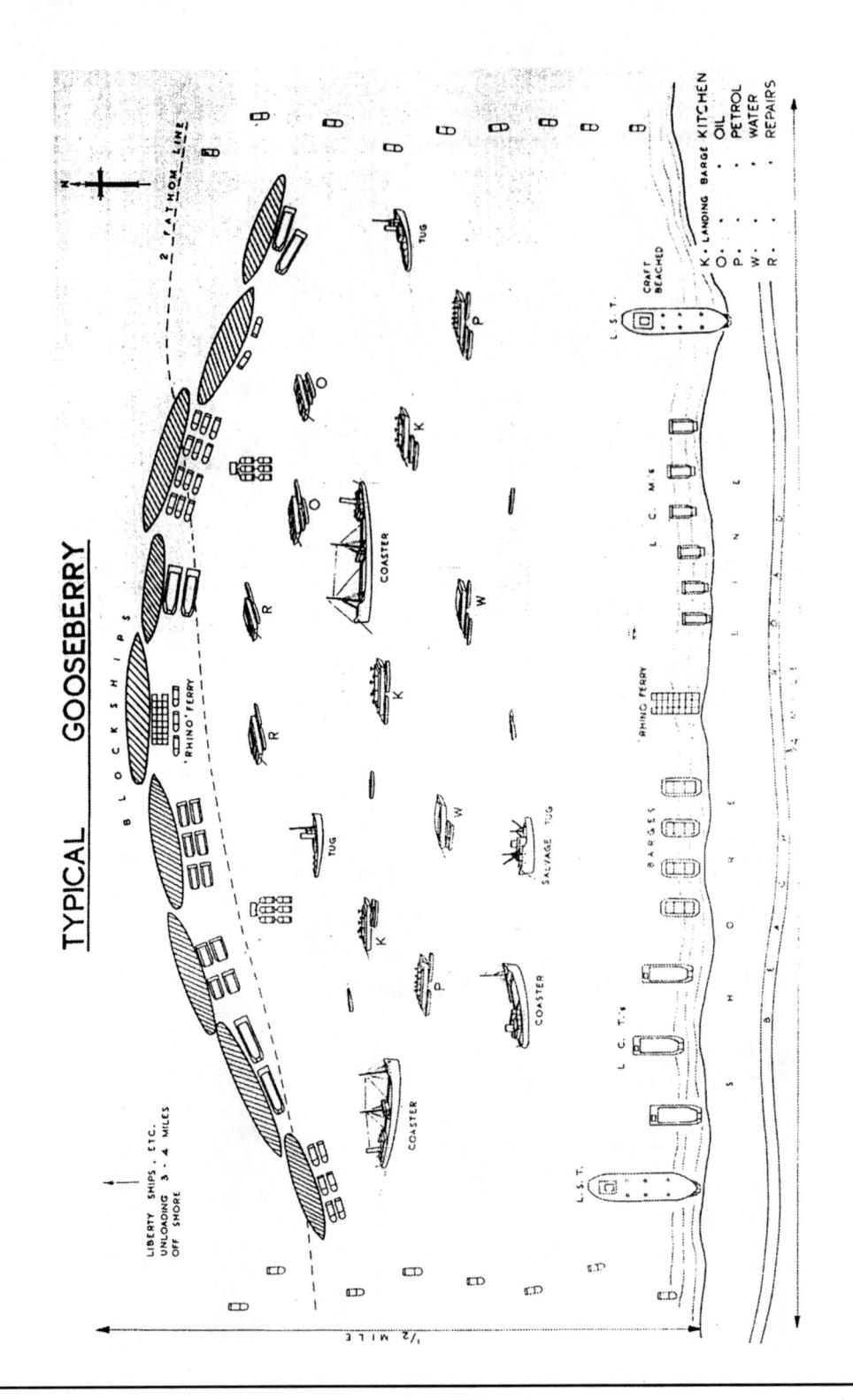